TEACH I

Cultivating Persona and Building Characters

Dr. BCMR

Dedication

To the students who taught me how to teach.

Contents

Preface

I began my journey as a reluctant teacher, held back by my introversion and low self-esteem. However, after 15 years of teaching Bachelor's and Master's students at the university level, I have evolved into an enthusiastic educator. Teaching has profoundly transformed my personality, a sentiment likely shared by many in the profession. While teachers are expected to influence their students, the impact of countless students on their teachers is equally significant. This reflects the profound power of the teaching profession.

In an age where education often feels mechanized and impersonal, *Teach I: Cultivating Persona and Building Characters* seeks to bridge the divide between human potential and educational practice. This book embarks on an exploration of the intricate relationship between humans, the brain, and the educational landscape. It delves into the cognitive complexities that underpin learning and teaching, revealing why intellectual engagement can be both challenging and rewarding.

The chapters provide a comprehensive framework for understanding the multifaceted nature of education. From examining the vision and mission of teaching to dissecting the dynamics of different learner types and classroom environments, this text encourages educators to adopt a holistic approach that integrates psychology, philosophy, and pedagogy. We consider teaching not merely as a profession but as an art form, wherein the teacher must adopt diverse roles, from mentor to performer, to inspire and engage students effectively.

Central to this book is the psychological concepts which serve as guiding principles to navigate the delicate balance between cerebral challenge and emotional support in the classroom. The discussion extends to the pivotal role of kindness in teaching, emphasizing that the cultivation of a supportive atmosphere is crucial for fostering student growth.

Ultimately, *Teach I* aims to empower educators to embrace their unique personas while developing their students' characters. By providing practical strategies and insights, this book encourages teachers to acknowledge their impact and potential as transformative figures in their students' lives. As we journey through these pages, we invite educators to reflect on their practices, embrace their challenges, and realize the profound significance of their role in shaping future generations.

This is neither a textbook nor a cookbook; rather, it is a reflective work infused with a sense of lightness. I invite you to engage deeply with the content, reflect on your own practices, and join in the collective effort to cultivate a generation of learners who are not only knowledgeable but also compassionate and equipped to thrive in an ever-changing world. In the second volume titled, *Teach II: Enhancing Thinking and Productivity*, is dedicated to reflections on imparting cognitive skills and motivation for productivity to students.

Disclaimer

In the creation of this book, I utilized artificial intelligence tools for proofreading, refining, and improving the clarity and flow of the content. The use of AI was intended to enhance readability and coherence, without altering the integrity of the work. All interpretations, perspectives, and reflections are grounded in my personal experience and understanding.

Author name: Dr. BCMR (Bhaskar Chandra Mohan Ramisetty)

Date October, 2024.

Chapter 1: Humans, brain and education

Humans are 'unnatural' animals

Most animals live in the moment. Animals respond instinctively to their immediate needs and surroundings. They eat when food is available, or hunger drives them, escape when threatened, hunt when prey is near, and rest or bask when conditions allow. Their behaviors are largely dictated by the immediate demands of survival, reflecting a natural, moment-to-moment existence. Some animals also exhibit behaviors that suggest a form of future-oriented thinking. Still, these actions are primarily driven by innate instincts rather than conscious, intellectual decision-making. For example, squirrels gather and store nuts to prepare for winter, demonstrating an instinctual understanding of future scarcity. Similarly, migratory birds, like the Arctic Tern, travel thousands of miles to exploit seasonal resources, guided by an intrinsic, biologically programmed knowledge of weather patterns and geography. Predatory evasion strategies in animals, such as the camouflage of a chameleon or the intricate burrowing systems of prairie dogs, further illustrate instinctive behaviors aimed at future survival. These actions, while indicative of a basic form of foresight, are largely automatic responses to environmental stimuli embedded in the animals' genetic makeup. Birds do not need schools for flying or building nests. They just do.

While animals exhibit future-oriented behaviors through instinctual actions, humans rely on conscious, intellectual decision-making processes that consider a broad spectrum of factors and implications. Our intellect is so developed that it can sometimes override our instincts. The distinctive capacity for foresight and strategic planning highlights the complex interplay between individual survival, kinship responsibilities, and long-term societal well-being, underscoring the unique nature of human cognition and behavior.

Humans are often described as 'unnatural' animals due to their unparalleled ability to manipulate and transcend their environment through culture, technology, and societal structures. Unlike other species, humans have developed complex languages, established intricate social systems, and created technologies that allow them to alter their habitats in ways that are fundamentally different from natural processes. The construction of cities, the development of agriculture, and the creation of global transportation networks have significantly reshaped the Earth's landscape. These advancements, driven by cognitive abilities and abstract thinking, highlight a divergence from typical behaviors observed in the animal kingdom, where species primarily adapt to their environment rather than reshape it. This capacity for transformation and innovation underscores the notion of humans as 'unnatural' in their impact and behavior.

The concept of morality and ethical reasoning further sets humans apart within the animal hierarchy. Humans possess a unique consciousness that allows for reflection on their actions and the establishment of moral frameworks that guide behavior beyond instinctual drives. This moral dimension influences decisions on issues ranging from environmental conservation to social justice, reflecting a capacity for altruism, empathy, and long-term planning that is rare in other species. Additionally, humans engage in activities such as art, philosophy, and science, which are not directly linked to survival but rather to exploring and expressing abstract ideas and intrinsic curiosity. These intellectual pursuits further illustrate the divergence of human beings from what is typically considered 'natural' animal behavior, emphasizing their distinct place within the broader context of life on Earth.

A human's "present moment" extends far beyond the immediate "here" and "now," encompassing potential influences across time and space. This unique temporal and spatial awareness compels humans to think not only about their survival in the present but also about their future well-being and the challenges posed by different environments. For instance, when parents invest in a child's education, they are not simply addressing current needs but considering long-term benefits, aiming to equip the child with knowledge and skills crucial for future success. This decision reflects an understanding of its lasting impact on future generations, ensuring that the child can thrive in a complex, evolving world.

Similarly, many human decisions consider survival and prosperity across different spaces. In agriculture, farmers do not focus solely on the immediate crop yield; they also account for factors like soil health, water resources, and climate change to ensure sustainable farming for the future. By implementing sustainable practices, they secure the land's productivity for their descendants. Community initiatives and social programs also embody this foresight, aiming to improve healthcare, education, and social welfare for current and future generations alike.

Human awareness of time and space integrates past experiences, present realities, and future possibilities. This expanded consciousness highlights a profound responsibility and the extraordinary capacity to influence both individual lives and the broader trajectory of human civilization.

Human civilization is built upon a vast accumulation of knowledge and information, developed over thousands of generations by various lineages from different lands. Each generation, across distinct geographical and cultural contexts, has contributed to the reservoir of human understanding, ranging from survival techniques to complex intellectual and technological advancements. Unlike in ancient times, when people primarily focused on learning basic survival skills like hunting, gathering food, and evading predators, modern humans are faced with an overwhelming amount of knowledge that extends far beyond immediate survival.

Today's individual must acquire not only practical skills but also abstract concepts in science, technology, philosophy, and the arts, all of which require intellectual engagement on a much broader scale. This creates a situation where learning is no longer confined to what is immediately necessary for day-to-day survival but encompasses vast realms of information that may not have direct or immediate utility in daily life.

For children, this burden is even more pronounced. A child must absorb a wide range of subjects and skills that are not instantly rewarding or beneficial. Learning mathematics, science, history, and other subjects often requires effort and patience, with rewards appearing only much later in life, creating a challenging but necessary process for future success and growth.

Our entire way of living has undergone a profound transformation, shifting from predominantly physical labor to increasingly mental work, driven by the development of language, tools and technology. In earlier times, human survival depended largely on physical exertion—hunting, farming, building shelter, and other forms of manual labor. These activities shaped not only our bodies but also our relationship with the environment. However, the advent of technology has gradually lessened the need for direct physical effort in daily tasks, replacing it with machines and automated systems that perform much of the work humans once did. As a result, we are no longer the same animals we once speciated as. Our evolution has taken a sharp turn from our original state as creatures of the natural world to something entirely new—beings increasingly defined by our cognitive capacities and technological reliance. With the rise of artificial intelligence, automation, and digital systems, we are evolving towards a more humanoid existence, where mental exertion and intellectual capabilities dominate our daily lives. This shift has not only altered the way we work but also redefined our social structures, interactions, and sense of identity, making us less bound by the biological constraints of our original species.

Why Focusing and Intense Thinking Are Difficult

People often speak of concentration and focus as if they are inherent qualities. They tend to view students who struggle with these skills as anomalies. The notion that humans are naturally inclined towards intense focus and prolonged higher-order thinking is a modern construct largely driven by the demands of contemporary society. Evolutionarily, early humans did not have the same need for sustained cognitive engagement as we do today. Their primary concerns revolved around survival—finding food, seeking shelter, and avoiding predators. These tasks required alertness and quick decision-making rather than prolonged periods of deep thought or intense focus.

In the early stages of human evolution, the cognitive demands placed on individuals were more immediate and situational. For example, hunting, gathering, and other survival activities required acute attention but in short bursts, often dictated by external stimuli rather than internal reflection or abstract reasoning. The ability to switch focus quickly, respond to threats, and process sensory information efficiently was more critical than the kind of sustained, concentrated thinking that is often emphasized in modern education and work environments.

This evolutionary background suggests that the human brain is naturally wired for adaptability and responsiveness to changing environments rather than for prolonged focus on a single task. As society evolved and became more complex, so too did the demands on human cognition. The development of agriculture, the rise of civilizations, and the advent of formal education introduced new challenges that required sustained intellectual effort. However, the need for intense, continuous focus is a relatively recent development in human history, and it is not an innate trait. It is a skill that must be cultivated and nurtured, often in environments that are conducive to learning and concentration.

The need for thinking arises predominantly in situations characterized by uncertainty and complexity. Whether it is attempting a novel task, solving an unfamiliar problem, making decisions with limited information, adapting to new conditions, or creating innovative solutions, these instances all require engaging in higher-order cognitive processes. Such activities demand more than routine responses; they necessitate critical thinking, problem-solving, and strategic planning. When confronted with these scenarios, individuals must employ cognitive resources to process new information, weigh various options, and navigate through ambiguous or challenging circumstances.

A human is born with a blank slate in terms of cognitive development, entering a world increasingly characterized by complexities and novelties that evolve rapidly with the progression of human society. The biggest asset the child has is the potential of the brain to absorb enormous amounts of information and make sense of what could be perceived and learning through testing, trials and errors. From infancy, individuals encounter a myriad of new experiences, challenges, and information that demand constant adaptation and learning. As the human species advances, the environment becomes more intricate, with technological, social, and cultural innovations introducing new layers of complexity. This ever-expanding landscape requires the developing brain to continuously process and integrate novel information, adapt to changing circumstances, and navigate increasingly sophisticated challenges, reflecting the dynamic interplay between innate cognitive potential and an ever-evolving external world.

Prolonged attention is often hindered by several interconnected factors that complicate focus and impede cognitive processes. One primary reason is cognitive load, which refers to the brain's limited capacity for processing information. When confronted with excessive or complex information, cognitive load increases making it challenging to concentrate and think deeply. Overloading working memory can impair the ability to analyze details effectively, leading to diminished cognitive performance.

Environmental distractions also play a significant role in reducing attention spans. Noise, interruptions, and digital notifications can disrupt concentration and prevent engagement in cognitive tasks. A cluttered or noisy environment complicates the ability to maintain focus while multitasking further diminishes efficiency. The brain struggles to switch between tasks effectively, reducing overall performance and productivity.

Mental fatigue is another critical factor. Sustained mental effort demands significant energy, and without adequate breaks, this cognitive strain can lead to exhaustion, diminishing one's capacity to focus. High levels of stress and anxiety exacerbate these challenges, impairing concentration, memory, and the ability to think deeply.

Furthermore, motivation—or lack thereof—greatly influences attention. While we are naturally inclined to pursue activities that offer immediate gratification, academic tasks often lack such immediate rewards. This absence of instant gratification can make it difficult for students to sustain motivation. Academic success requires cultivating delayed gratification, as rewards often manifest later in the form of recognition or improved performance.

In addition to motivation, cognitive and developmental factors can impact attention spans. Attention deficits, such as those seen in ADHD, can severely affect the ability to maintain focus. Similarly, younger individuals may face challenges in sustaining attention due to their developmental stage. Tailored strategies are necessary to accommodate varying attention capacities and developmental needs.

Emotional and psychological states also significantly affect cognitive processes. Mood disorders, including depression and anxiety, can impair concentration and motivation, creating distractions that divert cognitive resources from the task at hand. These emotional challenges require effective management and strategies to mitigate their impact on cognitive performance.

The lack of practice and skill development further complicates the ability to engage in intense thinking. Cognitive skills, like physical skills, improve with practice. Without regular, deliberate practice, individuals may struggle to develop the necessary concentration and sustained mental effort required for complex cognitive tasks.

Variations in brain function, whether due to neurological conditions or differences in brain chemistry, can significantly impact cognitive tasks. Fatigue and sleep deprivation also profoundly affect cognitive functioning; insufficient sleep impairs attention, memory, and problem-solving abilities. This underscores the necessity of adequate rest for optimal cognitive performance and sustained focus in complex tasks. By understanding these factors, educators and students can work collaboratively to create environments and practices that enhance attention and facilitate deeper cognitive engagement, ultimately leading to greater academic success and personal development.

Effortful parenting and efficient schooling play crucial roles in cultivating the ability to focus and engage in prolonged thinking. These capacities are not innate but are developed through consistent practice and guidance from a young age. Parenting that emphasizes patience, curiosity, and intellectual engagement can set a strong foundation for children, encouraging them to explore ideas, ask questions, and persist in problem-solving. By modeling focused behavior and creating environments that limit distractions, parents can help children gradually build their capacity for sustained attention.

In parallel, efficient schooling systems are designed to reinforce and expand upon these skills. Schools that prioritize not just rote memorization but critical thinking, creativity, and deep engagement with material foster an environment where students learn to focus and think critically over extended periods. Effective teachers use strategies that challenge students to think more deeply, encouraging them to go beyond surface-level understanding. Through a curriculum that balances stimulation and discipline, schools can help students develop the mental stamina needed for higher-order thinking and concentrated effort.

Together, effortful parenting and efficient schooling create a synergistic effect. They provide children with the tools, environments, and experiences necessary to cultivate focus and prolonged thinking, laying the groundwork for success in both academic pursuits and life beyond the classroom. These skills, once ingrained, serve as the foundation for lifelong learning, problem-solving, and innovation. However tough, humans are the biological entities where both teaching and learning have reached their epitome.

Why Using the Body Is Easier Than Using the Brain

The ease of using our bodies compared to our brains can be attributed to several fundamental differences between physical and cognitive tasks. Physical actions—such as walking, lifting, or reaching—are generally governed by established neural pathways and motor functions, making them relatively straightforward and automatic. With practice, these movements become second nature, requiring minimal conscious effort. In contrast, cognitive tasks like problem-solving and abstract reasoning involve far more complex mental processes. These activities necessitate the coordination of multiple brain regions, each contributing to various aspects of cognition, thus highlighting the considerable effort and complexity required for cognitive functions compared to the relative simplicity of physical actions.

Another critical distinction lies in the nature of automaticity versus deliberation. Automaticity refers to the process by which physical tasks become reflexive through repetition and practice, enabling individuals to perform them efficiently with little conscious thought. Activities like typing or driving exemplify this phenomenon, allowing mental resources to be freed for other tasks. Conversely, cognitive tasks demand sustained mental effort, requiring conscious control and strategic planning, which can be mentally taxing and resource-intensive. The demands of automatic versus deliberate activities illustrate the significant differences in cognitive load associated with physical and mental tasks, revealing why engaging the brain often feels more arduous.

Moreover, physical tasks typically yield immediate sensory feedback, enabling quick adjustments and refinements, while cognitive tasks often involve abstract processing with less direct feedback. This lack of concrete feedback complicates the assessment of progress in cognitive tasks, increasing their difficulty. Additionally, physical fatigue—resulting from exertion—is more tangible and easier to recover from than cognitive fatigue, which can manifest as diminished attention and memory, requiring mental relaxation for restoration. Emotional and psychological states also play a role, as mood disorders and anxiety can impair cognitive performance but generally have a lesser impact on physical tasks. Thus, understanding these distinctions—ranging from the simplicity of physical actions to the complexity of cognitive processes—can help develop strategies to enhance mental performance and manage cognitive workload more effectively.

Humans are inherently designed for physical activity, with our evolutionary history favoring movement and engagement with the environment. However, in typical educational institutions, there is often a disproportionate emphasis on prolonged mental activity at the expense of physical engagement. This imbalance stifles natural tendencies towards physical exploration and movement, demanding that students remain sedentary for extended periods. Such an approach is both difficult and unnatural for children, as it contradicts their innate need for physical expression and activity.

The Evolutionary Paradox of Cognitive Skills

Human cognition has reached extraordinary heights, allowing for complex thinking, problem-solving, and abstract reasoning. This cognitive prowess is distinct from the physical activities that both humans and animals share. The contrast between the naturalness of physical activities and the evolutionary novelty of intense cognitive tasks highlights a fascinating paradox in human development.

The Evolutionary Novelty of Intense Thinking

Intense and complex thinking is a relatively recent development in the evolutionary timeline. While other animals exhibit forms of problem-solving and communication, the depth and complexity of human cognitive skills are unparalleled. Evolution has not specifically tailored the human brain for the advanced cognitive tasks seen in modern civilization. Instead, the human brain, with its remarkable capacity for learning and adaptation, has developed these skills through cultural and intellectual evolution over thousands of generations.

The Potency of the Human Brain

Humans are born with a potent brain capable of extraordinary cognitive functions. This potential is evident in the ability to engage in abstract reasoning, strategic planning, and sophisticated problem-solving. However, the extent to which these cognitive abilities are realized depends on individual learning, skill development, exposure and experience. Unlike physical activities, which are more universally practiced and refined, cognitive skills require intentional nurturing and practice.

The Impact of Nurture on Cognitive Development

Two individuals born with the same cognitive potential can develop vastly different skills depending on their environment and experiences. The conditions in which a person is nurtured—such as educational opportunities, social interactions, and cultural influences—play a significant role in shaping cognitive abilities. While one person may be exposed to stimulating intellectual environments that foster complex thinking, another may experience less emphasis on cognitive development, leading to diverse skill sets and levels of cognitive capacity.

Surpassing the Evolutionary Timeline

Human civilization has indeed surpassed the evolutionary timeline with regard to cognitive skills. The demands of modern life, including technology, complex social structures, and advanced problem-solving needs, have driven the development of cognitive abilities beyond what was required for survival in earlier stages of human evolution. This advancement has led to the cultivation of skills and capacities that were not explicitly selected for during the evolutionary process but have emerged as a result of cultural and intellectual progression.

The distinction between the naturalness of physical activities and the novelty of intense cognitive tasks underscores a profound aspect of human development. While physical actions are deeply rooted in evolutionary history and are shared with other animals, intense thinking represents a unique and recent evolution in human cognitive abilities. The remarkable potential of the human brain, combined with diverse nurturing environments, results in a wide range of cognitive skills and capacities. As human civilization continues to advance, the relationship between our evolutionary heritage and our cognitive achievements remains a dynamic and intriguing aspect of our existence.

The Complexity of the Human Mind

William James's assertion that "The human mind is the most complex system in the universe" captures the profound intricacy of human cognition. This statement underscores the remarkable complexity and multifaceted nature of human thought processes, knowledge acquisition, and consciousness, distinguishing the human mind from any other known system. To appreciate this complexity, it is crucial to explore various dimensions of the human mind, including its structure, functionality, and the profound implications for understanding human nature and intelligence.

Structural Complexity

The human brain, with its approximately 86 billion neurons interconnected by around 100 trillion synapses, represents one of the most intricate biological networks known. Each neuron communicates with thousands of others through these synapses, facilitating a vast array of cognitive processes from sensory perception to complex decision-making. The brain's division into specialized regions underscores its complexity; for example, the prefrontal cortex is pivotal for executive functions such as planning and judgment, while the hippocampus is essential for memory formation. This regional specialization and the dynamic interactions among various brain areas contribute significantly to the brain's overall complexity, enabling it to handle a wide range of cognitive tasks.

Neuroplasticity, or the brain's ability to reorganize and form new neural connections, is a fundamental aspect of its functionality. This remarkable adaptability allows the brain to learn new skills, retain information, and recover from injuries by continually reshaping its neural networks. Neuroplasticity underlies the capacity for cognitive development and rehabilitation, highlighting the brain's dynamic nature. As individuals engage in learning and experience new stimuli, the brain's structural and functional connectivity evolves, demonstrating its capacity to adapt and respond to both environmental demands and internal changes. This plasticity adds a further layer of complexity to the brain's operational framework, reflecting its continuous evolution throughout life.

Functional Complexity

Human cognitive processes exhibit remarkable complexity, characterized by advanced consciousness and self-awareness. Unlike other species, humans possess a heightened ability for introspection and self-reflection, enabling them to contemplate abstract concepts such as morality and existence. This profound self-awareness underpins a range of higher cognitive functions, including abstract thinking, complex problem-solving, and creativity. These capabilities allow humans to engage in artistic endeavors, formulate scientific theories, and participate in philosophical discourse, reflecting the depth and sophistication of human cognitive processes.

In addition to cognitive prowess, humans also demonstrate a high degree of emotional and social intelligence. Emotional processing involves the capacity to experience, understand, and regulate emotions, which is essential for empathy and effective interpersonal relationships. This emotional intelligence enhances social interactions and contributes to personal well-being. Furthermore, social cognition enables individuals to navigate complex social dynamics, including understanding social norms, group behavior, and interpersonal relationships. This ability to comprehend and respond to social cues is fundamental to forming cohesive societies and managing social interactions, adding another dimension to the overall complexity of human intelligence.

Knowledge Acquisition and Learning

Language is a defining characteristic of human cognition, enabling intricate communication and the transfer of knowledge across generations. If it weren't for language, we would never have grasped the concepts of time and space in the way we do today. How else would we explain what has already happened, what is yet to come, or what is occurring in a place far beyond our immediate senses? Without language, there would be no way to describe events that are not directly in front of us or to share stories of the past with a friend who wasn't there. Language allows us to communicate experiences and events that transcend the present moment and immediate surroundings. It enables us to share not just what we see and feel but what has been, what might be, and what exists beyond the boundaries of our perception.

Animals, on the other hand, lack this complexity in communication. Their interactions are bound to the here and now, relying solely on their senses and memories of sensory experiences. While they may communicate danger, territory, or needs, they cannot relay the detailed stories of the past or the intricacies of future plans. They live in the present, guided by instincts, whereas humans, through language, bridge the gap between what is known and what can be imagined, what has been experienced and what is yet to come. Language gives us the power to stretch beyond our immediate reality, exploring time and space in ways no other species can. Think of the effects of poems and expletives!

The development of complex language systems facilitates nuanced expression, allowing individuals to convey abstract concepts, emotions, and cultural values. This capacity for sophisticated language not only supports interpersonal communication but also plays a critical role in the transmission of cultural knowledge and the preservation of societal norms. Additionally, humans employ a variety of learning mechanisms, such as formal education, experiential learning, and cultural transmission, which reflect the mind's versatility in acquiring and applying knowledge across diverse contexts.

Memory and Learning Systems

One of the most remarkable inventions of evolution is the nervous system, and within that, perhaps one of the most profound innovations is memory. Memory forms the very foundation upon which both the human brain and computers are built. Without memory, we would be perpetually trapped, reliving the same events and making the same mistakes, possibly every single day or even every moment. It is the memory that allows us to transcend the immediate present, to reflect on past experiences, learn from them, and adjust our actions accordingly. This ability to store information in our brains enables us to assess outcomes, refine our behavior through trial and error, and evolve in the way we approach our daily lives.

Imagine a life without memory. Consider the devastating effects of Alzheimer's disease, where a person progressively loses the ability to recall people, events, and experiences from their past. In such cases, it can feel as though a lifetime has been erased—like living without the essence of what has been learned or experienced. Without memory, it is as if existence itself is fragmented, with each moment disconnected from the next, devoid of continuity or meaning. Memory anchors us, allowing us to live not just in the present but to carry with us the wisdom, joy, and even pain of the past, shaping who we are and how we navigate the world. Without it, life would feel like a series of disconnected moments without progression or purpose.

Human cognition is supported by a multifaceted memory system encompassing sensory memory, short-term memory, and long-term memory. These distinct but interrelated systems are essential for encoding, storing, and retrieving information, illustrating the complexity of cognitive functions. Sensory memory captures immediate sensory impressions, while short-term memory holds information temporarily for active processing, and long-term memory consolidates knowledge for extended recall. Furthermore, the adaptability of learning strategies based on experience and feedback highlights the flexibility and sophistication inherent in human cognition. This capacity for dynamic learning enables individuals to adjust their approaches and integrate new information effectively, demonstrating the mind's ability to evolve and refine its cognitive processes.

The Nature of Consciousness

Consciousness is one of those enigmatic concepts that eludes easy definition. It is not just about being awake or aware; rather, it seems to involve a profound understanding of the self in relation to the wider context of existence. What is this "self"? The self is not a static entity; it is a dynamic amalgamation of past experiences, current needs and desires, and future aspirations or visions. Consciousness, then, can be thought of as the ability to recognize and navigate this complex web of internal and external realities. It is the awareness of one's place in time—how the past informs the present and how the present shapes the future. The time, energy, and cognitive ability to reflect on these dimensions reinforce and deepen our consciousness.

But what about animals—do they possess consciousness? This is a challenging question, as consciousness in humans is layered and deeply entwined with language, memory, and abstract thinking. However, as we move along the evolutionary spectrum, the notion of consciousness seems to become more pronounced. In lower animals, much of existence is consumed by the struggle for survival—finding food, evading predators, and reproducing. Their world is largely immediate, driven by instinct and reflex. Yet, as we ascend the evolutionary ladder, certain animals—especially those closer to humans—appear to display behaviors that suggest something more than mere survival.

Higher animals, while still engaged in the daily fight for existence, also exhibit moments of what could be interpreted as reflection or contemplation. Elephants, for instance, have been observed mourning their dead, dolphins exhibit playful curiosity, and primates display complex social behaviors that imply an understanding of relationships, fairness, and even empathy. These moments hint at an emerging consciousness, one that, while not as developed or articulated as in humans, suggests that animals may possess a rudimentary form of self-awareness, one that evolves alongside their cognitive capacities.

In my view, consciousness serves as a reflective lens through which individuals perceive themselves in relation to their environment and others. This self-awareness encompasses an understanding of one's identity and actions across varying temporal and spatial contexts, highlighting the interconnectedness of personal experience with the broader world. It evolves gradually, becoming more complex with time and cognitive development, allowing beings to not just react to the world but also to reflect on it, positioning themselves within the broader context of existence.

Ethical Considerations

The advanced cognitive abilities of the human mind enable sophisticated moral and ethical reasoning, which significantly impacts individual and societal decision-making processes regarding right and wrong. This capacity for ethical reflection allows individuals to assess actions and choices through the lenses of justice, fairness, and moral principles. It shapes how societies develop laws, norms, and values that govern behavior and interactions. The complexity of moral reasoning is a defining feature of human cognition, highlighting our ability to engage in nuanced ethical deliberation and make decisions that align with collective values and personal principles.

William James's characterization of the human mind as "the most complex system in the universe" reflects the profound intricacy of human cognitive and emotional processes. From the intricate neural architecture and functional capabilities to the sophisticated mechanisms of learning and memory, the human mind exhibits unparalleled complexity. This complexity not only defines our intellectual and emotional experiences but also shapes our understanding of ourselves and our place in the universe. The ongoing exploration of the human mind continues to reveal new dimensions of its complexity, underscoring its unique and unparalleled nature in the realm of known systems.

Cerebral work is a stress.

We humans possess two invaluable commodities: time and focus. These are expended daily, shaped by our needs for survival, relationships, and progress. In ancient times, the pursuit of food and basic survival consumed both time and attention. But in the modern era, survival is largely secured, and our focus shifts towards securing not just the present but also the future. Humans, unique in their foresight, spend each day honing skills and crafting solutions for the days, months, and generations ahead. This ability to think long-term defines our species. However, the skills required for the future—especially those demanding deep cognitive engagement—are complex. While we are not innately prepared for such mental tasks, we possess the potential to develop them. Training the mind to focus on intricate problems, like mathematical calculations, requires disconnecting from distractions and sharpening cognitive faculties. This is the essence of education: guiding students to harness their time and focus, not just for today's tasks but for mastering the intellectual challenges of tomorrow. Each of us is expected to learn the refined knowledge and intelligence accumulated by our species from its origin to the present day. That requires significant cerebral engagement, and it is undeniably challenging. As children, many of us likely hated the process of learning. Over time, we fall in line with it, and eventually, we become desperate to learn in order to make a living. After that, we focus on making a living. This is the rhythm of modern life. Recollect the difficulty of focusing and learning—it is often a traumatic experience for a child who would much rather munch on chocolate or play with friends and toys. Now, imagine the child of the modern era, with even more to learn and an increasing mental burden. Should we abandon learning altogether to reduce stress? That is not a viable solution. Instead, we must focus on improving and smoothing the process by which a child learns and is trained with minimal stress. To minimize the burden of mental stress, we need to dissect the stress arising from cerebral work.

Cerebral work induces stress due to high cognitive demands, uncertainty, and time constraints. The complexity of tasks can overwhelm working memory, leading to mental fatigue. Pressure from tight deadlines and high stakes amplifies stress, while self-doubt and perfectionism further exacerbate anxiety. Supportive strategies are essential to mitigate these challenges and enhance performance.

The school system

The evolution of teaching and learning skills has significantly shaped human civilization, driven by the necessity for knowledge transmission and cultural continuity. In prehistoric times, learning was primarily experiential and informal, occurring through observation and imitation within familial and community structures. As societies advanced, formalized teaching emerged, particularly in ancient civilizations like Mesopotamia, Egypt, and Greece, where structured education began to take shape through written language, philosophical inquiry, and dedicated educators.

The coevolution of teaching and learning skills is evident in the dynamic relationship between pedagogical methods and cognitive development. As learners' needs evolved, so did the approaches of educators, who adapted their techniques to foster critical thinking and problem-solving skills. This reciprocal process laid the foundation for more sophisticated educational systems and methodologies, such as the Socratic method, which emphasized dialogue and inquiry.

The impact of this evolution on modern civilization is profound. The development of literacy, scientific inquiry, and critical reasoning has propelled advancements in technology, governance, and social organization. Today, the ongoing evolution of teaching and learning, influenced by technological advancements and cognitive research, continues to redefine educational paradigms, fostering adaptability and innovation essential for addressing contemporary global challenges. This transformative journey underscores the crucial role of education in shaping society and empowering individuals to contribute meaningfully to civilization.

The evolution of dedicated teaching-learning systems has been marked by a gradual shift from informal education to structured frameworks designed to enhance knowledge acquisition. In ancient times, apprenticeships and mentorships provided foundational skills in trades and crafts. The establishment of formal institutions, such as the Academy in Athens and medieval universities, marked significant milestones, emphasizing curricula and credentialing. The Renaissance further catalyzed educational reform, introducing humanistic principles that prioritized critical thinking. In the modern era, dedicated systems have expanded to include diverse methodologies, such as Montessori and online learning platforms, reflecting an increasing understanding of different learning styles and the need for personalized education.

I tried homeschooling my child during the COVID-19 pandemic because it was immensely stressful to learn online. I had the time, and I am a teacher, so I tried to homeschool my elder child, who is much more complying compared to my younger one. Homeschooling was hard on both the child and the parent. Because of my child's compliance, we could get a lot of study done, which is a lot more than what a school typically covers. I still like homeschooling, but I do not have the time and patience to do so. Moreover, the school system gives the advantage of social stimuli.

Teaching a student in isolation, especially for extended hours at home, is an exceptionally challenging task for students and teachers, as I experienced during the homeschooling experiment. The absence of a structured environment like a classroom, where students are naturally engaged through peer interaction, limits the overall learning experience. In a classroom setting, students thrive on the dynamic energy, shared focus, and motivation that comes from collective study. At home, this environment is harder to replicate.

The lack of social stimuli and external competition can lead to diminished focus and motivation. In isolation, students often face distractions that are difficult to avoid, whether it be the comfort of home or digital entertainment. Moreover, long hours of solitary learning can be mentally exhausting without the breaks and transitions typically provided in a school day. This isolation can also hinder emotional and social development, as students miss opportunities to collaborate, discuss, and challenge ideas with their peers.

On a psychological level, sustained attention and cognitive engagement are harder to maintain without external guidance and stimulation. Teaching, especially when confined to the home for long durations, risks becoming monotonous, making it harder to retain the student's interest. Over time, this can lead to disengagement and resentment towards learning, making it even more difficult to foster academic growth.

The school system is inherently designed to balance various psychological forces that influence student development, motivation, and learning. Understanding the psychological underpinnings of how the system shares the stress of learning, fosters competition, and incorporates entertainment is crucial in appreciating how students navigate their academic experiences.

Norms shape our lives, and study is one of those norms. Everyone ought to study, and therefore, we all do. Progress in study is inevitable, even though it often brings stress. Who doesn't prefer fun over work? Especially as children, we instinctively seek pleasure and ease. The thought of structured learning, filled with assignments and deadlines, does not naturally appeal. Yet, schooling guides us to fall in line with the expectations of academic growth and discipline.

Through the years, we are conditioned to transition from the playful freedom of childhood to the rigors of intellectual labor. Schooling prepares us for this shift by encouraging higher-order thinking, problem-solving, and focused study—an intense cognitive effort that becomes essential in adulthood. Though work and study may feel burdensome, they are integral to personal and societal progress. We might resist it initially, but slowly, we adapt, learning to navigate the demands of education and later in professional life. The norm of study, ingrained from a young age, helps shape our ability to thrive in a world that demands cognitive engagement. It is through this framework that we learn to balance the stress of work with the need for progress, ultimately enabling us to contribute to society effectively.

Sharing the stress makes learning bearable.

Learning, by its very nature, involves cognitive effort, and often, this effort is accompanied by stress. The stress of learning can arise from various factors, such as the pressure to perform well, deadlines, and the complexity of the subject matter. Schools, through their structures of group learning, classroom interactions, and collaborative activities, distribute this stress among students. Sharing stress can significantly alleviate its burden and make the learning process more bearable. When individuals feel connected to others who are experiencing similar challenges, they are less likely to feel isolated or overwhelmed. This sense of camaraderie can foster a supportive and encouraging environment where learners can openly discuss their struggles, seek advice, and offer encouragement to one another.

From a psychological perspective, social learning theory suggests that students observe and learn from each other, not only academically but also in how they manage stress. By engaging in group work or classroom discussions, students see their peers facing similar challenges, which normalizes the experience of stress. This collective experience alleviates feelings of isolation and helps students manage anxiety more effectively. Emotional contagion also plays a role here, where positive attitudes and stress-management strategies can be shared among peers, lightening the load for everyone.

Competition as motivation

Competition within the school system is a significant driver of motivation. While excessive competition can lead to negative outcomes, such as anxiety or unhealthy rivalries, moderate and well-structured competition taps into the psychological principle of achievement motivation. Atkinson's expectancy-value theory explains that students are motivated to achieve success when they value the outcome and believe they have a reasonable chance of succeeding. In this context, the competition provides students with a clear, measurable goal: outperforming their peers or achieving high grades.

Healthy competition fosters an environment where students strive for self-improvement. It triggers the fight-or-flight response in a controlled, constructive manner, pushing students to challenge themselves and their capabilities. As they compete academically, students develop resilience and a growth mindset, where effort and persistence become valued as much as natural ability.

Entertainment as a Stress Reliever

Integrating occasional entertainment into the learning process helps balance the stress of academic demands. The use of fun activities, games, or creative breaks plays into the psychological need for rewards and reinforcement. Cognitive load theory posits that when students are overburdened with excessive information or tasks, their learning efficiency decreases. By incorporating entertainment or light-hearted moments, schools provide mental breaks that allow students to recover and return to tasks with renewed focus and energy.

Additionally, entertainment and relaxation are essential in fostering intrinsic motivation. According to self-determination theory, students are more engaged and motivated when they find personal enjoyment and relevance in their activities. Occasional fun activities or learning through gamification helps students associate learning with positive emotions, making them more likely to be engaged in their academic endeavors long-term.

A balanced system

The school system's structure, which mixes learning stress, competition, and entertainment, strikes a delicate balance between maintaining discipline and encouraging motivation. This balance reflects Maslow's hierarchy of needs, where both the basic need for security (in terms of consistent learning outcomes and shared stress) and higher-order needs like esteem and self-actualization (through competition and motivation) are met.

In essence, the school system orchestrates a delicate interplay of psychological forces. Sharing the stress of learning ensures emotional and mental support, competition taps into motivational drives for achievement, and occasional entertainment provides relief, enhancing students' cognitive and emotional well-being. Together, these elements foster a holistic environment where students are challenged but supported, competitive but collaborative, and focused yet relaxed enough to enjoy the process of learning.

The quote, "Everybody is a genius. But if you judge a fish by its ability to climb a tree, it will live its whole life believing that it is stupid," is often attributed to Albert Einstein. It highlights the notion that individuals possess unique talents and capabilities, but when they are evaluated based on inappropriate criteria or standards, they may feel inadequate. The metaphor of the fish and the tree suggests that applying the wrong measure of intelligence or success can lead to frustration, self-doubt, and a sense of failure, even though the individual may excel in other areas. This quote emphasizes the importance of recognizing and valuing diverse abilities rather than imposing a one-size-fits-all standard of competence or success.

However, when viewed in the context of modern society, the quote overlooks a crucial aspect of social integration and the demands of contemporary life. Human society today is based on information, skills, and shared standards that allow individuals to contribute meaningfully to collective progress. In order to thrive, citizens must acquire a range of skills that are often standardized, such as literacy, counting, communication, and problem-solving. These are not arbitrary measures but necessary tools for participation in the "grid" of modern civilization, which relies on interdependence and collaboration.

In this context, dismissing standard metrics as irrelevant, as the quote suggests, may undermine the need for individuals to meet certain societal expectations to survive and be respected. While it is essential to recognize individual strengths, it is equally important to acknowledge that society depends on collective competence. People need to develop skills that may not come naturally but are crucial for integration into modern structures. For instance, learning to adapt to technology, critical thinking, and effective communication are foundational for success in most professions and social roles today. Focusing exclusively on personal strengths without addressing societal requirements risks alienation or marginalization in a world increasingly driven by shared knowledge and expectations.

There is only one path into modern civilization, and that is through learning—whether it happens at home, in school, or through self-education. Knowledge equips individuals with the skills necessary to navigate the complexities of contemporary life. From technological literacy to social awareness, learning provides the tools to engage with and contribute to society. As a matter of fact, we have a whole intellectual legacy of the human species that we ought to learn, including cultural and technological advancements. Animals do not have any technological advancements, only cultural learning, maybe. In today's world, where information drives progress, the pursuit of learning is not optional but essential for survival and success. There is no alternative to the training of the mind. "Education is not the learning of facts, but the training of the mind to think." Einstein

Chapter 2: The vision and mission of teaching

Over the years, my perspective on the purpose of education has evolved significantly. Initially, my vision was closely aligned with the objectives of many research institutions, focusing on concepts such as knowledge, intelligence, and research. However, as I reflect on the role of education within modern human society, I am reminded that it is fundamentally about teaching and learning. But, education should foster individuals who contribute to the betterment of society and help shape a world where citizens are not only knowledgeable but also engaged in socially beneficial activities.

This shift in perspective brings me back to a course I took in the 10th grade called Socially Useful Productive Work (SUPW). In this course, we learned practical skills like making soaps, shampoos, and candles, as well as gardening. The name of the course, "Socially Useful Productive Work," left a lasting impression on me. Now, as an educator, I envision my role as one that develops students into socially useful and productive citizens. This vision encompasses a holistic approach to education, aiming to cultivate individuals who are not only competent and ethical but also motivated and well-rounded. I envision an educational paradigm where these attributes are thoughtfully nurtured, acknowledging their profound impact on both personal growth and societal advancement.

The vision

"To create Socially Useful, Productive Citizens through education that fosters knowledge, skills, and responsibility for the betterment of society."

The goal of education is to make a Socially Useful Productive Citizen (SUPC). Social is about transgressing the lines of self-interest into the contribution of society. In fact, our contribution to society is in our own self-interest. We live in groups, and maintaining the group is essential for the survival of the individual. Therefore, some form of contribution from each individual is important. The contribution should be useful to the survival or upliftment of society, which is made up of individuals, including ourselves. The product that we could contribute should be useful to at least a small section of society other than our own family. By providing our unique service, we receive other services through the contributions made by other members of the society. As a child, we are born with no skill but with self-interest. Moreover, we have to live a life of plans for the future, not just for the moment. Therefore, we need to learn some skills and be able to contribute to society so that we are not deadweight but respected citizens of society. It takes effort to learn skills, especially cognitive skills. We can develop physical skills through repeated practice of specific movements. The learning of physical skills is built in us. All we had to do was experience the movements, variations of movements and refine our responses. But cognitive skills are much more demanding. We should learn to absorb the information even without experience. We have to understand language, logic and reading, all of which demands immense focus and brain time.

The vision statement "to make socially useful productive citizens" represents a holistic approach to education that integrates academic excellence with a strong commitment to societal and environmental responsibility. By emphasizing "socially useful," this vision underscores the importance of developing students who are not only knowledgeable and capable but also environmentally conscious, beneficial to society, and relevant in their actions. Educators who align with this vision aim to instill in students a sense of responsibility towards societal and environmental issues, fostering a deep understanding of how their actions can contribute to the collective well-being and sustainability of their communities.

In this framework, "socially useful" implies that students should be equipped with the skills and values needed to make positive contributions to society while being mindful of their impact on the environment. Educators work to ensure that students acquire both the practical skills and ethical awareness necessary to address global and local challenges. This approach emphasizes the importance of acting in ways that are not only effective but also considerate of societal needs and environmental sustainability, promoting a sense of relevance and responsibility in their actions.

Productivity is dependent on a variety of factors, including cognitive skills, physical skills, psychological skills, and philosophical skills. The term "productive" is enriched by including attributes such as being knowledgeable, intelligent, motivated, competent, resourceful, happy and healthy. A productive citizen is one who excels academically and professionally while maintaining overall well-being and happiness. This aspect of the vision focuses on preparing students to be effective and impactful in their endeavors, ensuring they possess the drive and capability to make significant contributions to their fields and society. By fostering a balanced approach to success, educators help students achieve not only professional excellence but also personal satisfaction and health.

Lastly, the concept of "citizen" highlights the ethical and moral dimensions of students' roles as members of both local and global communities. It reflects the vision of developing individuals who are not only engaged and responsible but also guided by strong ethical principles. Teachers who aim to cultivate such citizens prepare students to act with integrity and compassion, contributing positively to their immediate communities while also considering their broader global impact. This approach promotes a sense of ethical responsibility and moral commitment, encouraging students to participate in and contribute to societal and global initiatives with a clear sense of purpose and fairness.

Within the limitations of an academic setting, each of these characteristics has multiple components. Motivation is a product of the drive for work/learning with enthusiasm. In my view, motivation is by far the most important characteristic in the list. Motivation falls in the purview of humanities, and that is why this whole book is inclined towards the humanities of teaching. Motivation is deeply rooted in the human experience, shaped by emotions, values, and social interactions, which places it firmly within the domain of the humanities. Teaching, as an act of fostering motivation, goes beyond the mere transfer of knowledge—it requires understanding the psychological and emotional landscapes of students. This is why the entire book leans towards the humanities of teaching, recognizing that true education engages both the mind and the human spirit. Competence is a major part of what teaching means in modern civilization. Competence encompasses the full spectrum of knowledge, intelligence, skills, and productivity, serving as the foundation of one's ability to perform effectively in any field. It is not limited to mastering a specific set of tasks but extends to the capacity for continuous learning and adaptation. Whether as a specialist with deep expertise in one area or as a generalist with a broad range of abilities, competence includes the drive to acquire more knowledge, hone skills, and refine one's approach to evolving challenges, ensuring sustained personal and professional growth.

Mission

"To empower individuals with the knowledge, skills, and values needed to contribute to society and lead fulfilling, productive lives."

My mission as an educator is to cultivate individuals who are not only knowledgeable and competent but also socially useful and productive. This involves instilling in students a strong ethical foundation, a deep sense of environmental responsibility, and the ability to work cooperatively with empathy and positivity. I am committed to fostering a learning environment that promotes health, happiness, and motivation, ensuring that students develop the skills and intelligence necessary to thrive in their personal and professional lives. By nurturing responsible and integrative citizenship, I aim to prepare students to contribute meaningfully to society and enhance their overall well-being.

Socially Useful Traits

Socially useful traits define the direction and purpose of education. Education must extend beyond the acquisition of knowledge to include the development of socially useful traits such as ethics, environmental consciousness, cooperation, positivity, and empathy. Ethics provide the moral compass necessary for making sound decisions and fostering trust within communities. An environmental consciousness ensures that students understand their role in preserving and protecting the planet, contributing to sustainable practices. Cooperation and positivity are essential for working effectively with others and creating a supportive learning environment. Empathy allows students to connect with diverse perspectives and contribute to a more compassionate society. By integrating these traits into the educational process, we prepare students to become conscientious individuals who contribute positively to society.

Productive Traits

Productivity is a citizen's true contribution to society, reflecting both the quality and magnitude of their impact. Productivity in education encompasses traits such as health, happiness, competence, motivation, knowledge, intelligence, and efficiency. Health and happiness are foundational for effective learning and personal growth; a well-balanced and fulfilled individual is more likely to engage actively and perform well as a student and later as a citizen. Competence and motivation drive students to pursue excellence and achieve their goals, while knowledge and intelligence form the core of their intellectual development. Efficiency in applying skills and knowledge ensures that students can achieve their objectives with minimal wasted effort. By emphasizing these traits, education equips students with the tools needed to be successful and productive members of society.

Citizenship Traits

Being a citizen means recognizing that individuals collectively form society, and each is responsible for making it better, safer, and brighter for both the present and future generations. To foster responsible and integrative citizenship, one must instill a sense of responsibility and the ability to integrate diverse aspects of one's identity and community. Responsible citizenship involves understanding and fulfilling one's duties towards society, contributing to civic engagement and ethical behavior. Integration refers to the ability to harmonize various facets of one's life—personal, professional, and social—into a cohesive and balanced approach. Educating students to be responsible and integrative citizens ensures that they can navigate complex societal structures and contribute meaningfully to the common good.

Holistic Educational Approach

A holistic approach to education integrates the development of socially useful and productive traits with the cultivation of responsible citizenship. This approach not only emphasizes academic achievement but also considers the emotional, ethical, and social dimensions of student development. By creating a learning environment that supports health, happiness, and motivation while fostering ethical behavior and environmental awareness, educators prepare students to excel both personally and professionally. This comprehensive educational paradigm recognizes the interconnected nature of individual development and societal contribution, aiming to produce well-rounded individuals who are equipped to tackle the challenges of the modern world and contribute positively to their communities.

Navigating through enormous spaces and into a distant future requires education. To train the child, before he/she has the influence on himself and others, to get ready to deliver from the prime time on. Education requires not only navigating through space and time as an individual but also communicating and understanding the ideas of others, without which the concept of human society would collapse. The mission is to increase knowledge, improve intelligence, and build personalities beaming with motivation, confidence, productivity and positivity.

The fundamental aim of academics is to acquire knowledge from past or concurrent events, even without firsthand experience, while training the mind to analyze, manage data, and predict both future and historical outcomes.

Focused Study and Attention

The single most determining factor in academic success is the ability to engage in focused and productive study. This skill forms the foundation of effective learning, as it directly influences how students absorb, process, and retain information. Productive study involves not merely sitting with textbooks or attending classes but approaching learning with intent, structure, and a clear goal while maintaining focus for sustained periods.

Focused study refers to the ability to concentrate on a single task without being easily distracted. This requires attentional control, a key component of cognitive function, which allows students to block out distractions and maintain attention to the subject matter. Executive functioning, which is responsible for planning, prioritizing, and organizing thoughts, plays a significant role here. The ability to filter out irrelevant stimuli and focus on the task at hand ensures that learning is deep rather than superficial.

In a world increasingly filled with distractions—social media, noise, and endless streams of information—the capacity to maintain focus is a crucial skill. Selective attention, the process of focusing on relevant information while disregarding the irrelevant, allows students to maximize the efficiency of their study sessions. Psychologically, focused study activates the prefrontal cortex, the area of the brain responsible for complex cognitive behavior and decision-making, ensuring that the effort expended in study is directed towards meaningful academic progress.

Productive Study and Efficiency

Productivity in study, on the other hand, emphasizes not just effort but the quality of effort. Productive study habits involve breaking down large tasks into manageable chunks, prioritizing important topics, and using evidence-based techniques such as spaced repetition, active recall, and self-testing. These strategies leverage memory consolidation processes in the brain, helping students to move information from short-term memory into long-term storage more effectively.

Productive study is also tied to time management skills. Students who excel academically often display an understanding of how to allocate their time effectively, balancing study with rest, social interaction, and other responsibilities. This balance is crucial because prolonged periods of study without breaks can lead to cognitive fatigue, diminishing the overall quality of learning. By incorporating structured breaks (as seen in techniques like the Pomodoro method), students maintain higher levels of mental energy, allowing for sustained productivity.

Focussed and Productive Study as an Academic Differentiator

What sets successful students apart is not necessarily higher intelligence but the ability to combine focus with productivity. Grit and self-discipline, as noted by psychologist Angela Duckworth, often outweigh raw talent in determining academic success. Students who can focus deeply, engage in deliberate practice, and consistently apply themselves to productive study routines are more likely to retain information, perform well in assessments, and master complex concepts.

The ability to study in a focused and productive manner equips students with the tools necessary for lifelong learning. It fosters metacognitive skills—awareness and understanding of one's own learning processes—which are crucial not only for academic achievement but also for personal and professional growth beyond the classroom.

The skills that need to be imparted and inculcated in the students can be categorized into three categories: skills of input, skills of processing and skills of output.

Effective learning and impactful productivity

To achieve overall growth and become an impactful and successful professional, students must cultivate a variety of essential skills. The following list presents these skills in a logical order, with elaboration on how each contributes to a student's holistic development:

1. Curiosity

Curiosity is the foundation of learning, driving students to explore and seek out new knowledge. It fosters a deep engagement with the world and encourages the desire to ask questions, delve into unfamiliar subjects, and broaden one's intellectual horizons. Without curiosity, the motivation to learn fades, limiting both personal and professional growth.

2. Enthusiasm

Enthusiasm ignites passion and energy in pursuing goals and projects. It helps students approach challenges with a positive mindset and fuels creativity and active participation. When enthusiasm is paired with curiosity, it creates an unstoppable drive for continuous learning and achievement. Enthusiasm for learning and problem-solving earns professional respect and laurels.

3. Imagination

Imagination allows students to think beyond existing boundaries and envision possibilities that may not yet exist. It is crucial for problem-solving and innovation, enabling students to approach challenges from novel perspectives. A vivid imagination lays the groundwork for creativity, which is essential in any profession.

4. Creativity

Creativity is the ability to transform imagination into tangible outcomes. It involves thinking outside the box, developing new solutions, and expressing unique ideas. In a competitive professional world, creativity distinguishes an individual and contributes to innovation, enhancing overall impact and success.

5. Motivation

Motivation is the inner drive that pushes students to take action and pursue their goals. It serves as the engine for persistence, even in the face of challenges. A motivated student continuously seeks improvement and strives to reach new heights, both academically and professionally.

6. Critical thinking

Critical thinking is the ability to observe the available data and provide an interpretation of analysis based on contextual constraints or objectives. This is a skill that a student is obliged to learn by practicing over and over. The thinking dimensions are diverse, as well as needs/constraints. The degree and type of critical thinking sets individuals apart in personal, professional and social spheres of life.

7. Perseverance

Perseverance complements patience by fostering a determination to keep going, even when progress is slow. It instills resilience that helps students overcome repeated failures and challenges. Perseverance is critical for mastering complex skills and achieving lasting success.

8. Grit

Grit represents a combination of passion and perseverance. It is the ability to maintain focus and drive over extended periods, especially when working towards challenging goals. Grit is vital for long-term success, as it helps students push through difficulties and remain committed to their objectives.

9. Delayed Gratification

The ability to delay gratification reflects a student's maturity and capacity to prioritize long-term rewards over immediate pleasures. It teaches students to focus on enduring efforts that lead to meaningful outcomes, a skill that is indispensable in both personal and professional growth.

10. Mental Endurance

Mental endurance equips students with the strength to persist in demanding intellectual tasks. It allows them to maintain focus during long hours of study or complex projects. Mental endurance ensures sustained productivity and prevents burnout, which is critical for success in high-stress environments.

11. Confidence

Confidence enables students to trust their abilities and take calculated risks. It helps them present ideas clearly, make decisions decisively, and engage with peers and professionals without hesitation. Confidence is essential for leadership and is a key factor in achieving career success.

12. Emotional Stability

Emotional stability refers to the ability to remain calm and composed in stressful or unpredictable situations. It ensures that students can manage their emotions effectively, preventing impulsive reactions that could undermine their efforts. In the professional world, emotional stability enhances decision-making and interpersonal relationships.

13. Composure

Composure builds on emotional stability by enabling students to stay cool under pressure. It helps maintain focus and clear thinking in high-stress situations, which is vital in crisis management or challenging professional scenarios. Composure allows students to project confidence and reliability.

14. Integrity

Integrity is the foundation of trustworthiness. Students who act with integrity are consistent in their principles and honesty, ensuring that they are reliable and credible in both academic and professional settings. Integrity fosters a reputation of authenticity, which is invaluable in leadership roles.

15. Ethics

Ethics is the guiding principle for moral decision-making. Students who adhere to ethical standards are better equipped to make fair and responsible choices, especially when faced with dilemmas. Ethical behavior builds trust and respect within teams, making it crucial for long-term professional success.

16. Compassion

Compassion involves empathy and understanding toward others' feelings and experiences. It helps students build strong, supportive relationships and fosters a collaborative environment. Compassionate professionals are more effective leaders and team members as they are attuned to the needs of those around them.

17. Cooperation

Cooperation is the ability to work well with others toward a shared goal. It fosters teamwork and collective problem-solving, both of which are essential in any professional environment. Students who are skilled in cooperation are better able to collaborate and achieve results that surpass individual efforts.

18. Inclusivity

Inclusivity ensures that students recognize and value diverse perspectives, backgrounds, and experiences. It helps create environments where everyone feels respected and valued, which is key for both personal growth and fostering innovation in professional settings.

19. Productivity

Productivity is the culmination of focus, time management, and efficiency. It ensures that students can complete tasks effectively while balancing multiple responsibilities. High productivity is crucial for achieving success, as it demonstrates the ability to consistently meet or exceed expectations.

20. Patience

Patience is the ability to stay calm and composed when facing obstacles or delays. It ensures that students do not become discouraged by temporary setbacks. In professional life, patience helps develop long-term strategies and endure difficult periods without losing sight of ultimate goals.

These interconnected skills provide a solid foundation for students to grow into impactful and successful professionals. Education is meant to provide the foundation for manners, morality, and integrity, but it does not inherently guarantee them. These qualities require more than academic instruction; they demand self-awareness and intentional training. While education exposes individuals to ethical principles and societal norms, truly embodying these virtues requires conscious effort, reflection, and practice. Without an intentional focus on personal growth, students may gain knowledge without developing the character necessary to apply it responsibly. Therefore, cultivating manners, morality, and integrity involves both formal education and the deliberate pursuit of self-improvement and ethical behavior in everyday life. Each skill builds on the others, creating a well-rounded individual capable of thriving in diverse and challenging environments.

Integrating Psychology, Philosophy, and Pedagogy

The confluence of psychology, philosophy, and pedagogy forms the bedrock of a comprehensive educational framework. Grounded in the idea that education extends beyond the mere transmission of facts, this essay explores the intricate interplay of these disciplines in crafting teaching objectives.

The following objectives serve as a guiding beacon in shaping a holistic and transformative educational experience.

1. Psychology in Education:

Psychology, the study of the mind and behavior, offers profound insights into the learning process. The statement's initial clause, "The learner should learn upon instruction," aligns with the principles of cognitive psychology. Understanding how individuals acquire, process, and retain information is fundamental to effective teaching. Educational psychologists emphasize the importance of diverse instructional methods catering to different learning styles. Incorporating visual aids, hands-on activities, and interactive learning experiences taps into the cognitive diversity of students, ensuring optimal knowledge absorption.

2. Communication of Learned Knowledge:

The second clause, "The learner should communicate the learned knowledge," draws on both psychology and philosophy. From a psychological standpoint, effective communication is a multifaceted skill encompassing verbal, nonverbal, and interpersonal aspects. Teaching strategies rooted in social psychology, such as collaborative learning and peer-to-peer interactions, enhance communication skills. From a philosophical perspective, communication is intrinsic to the dialogical nature of education. Philosopher Paulo Freire's dialogical pedagogy underscores the importance of reciprocal communication, fostering a dynamic exchange between teachers and learners.

3. Philosophy in Education:

Philosophy serves as the philosophical underpinning of education, shaping its purpose and guiding principles. The clause, "The learner should learn how to learn," resonates deeply with the philosophy of education. The ability to learn how to learn aligns with a Socratic approach that values critical thinking and self-discovery. Philosophers such as John Dewey emphasize experiential learning, promoting an educational philosophy that transcends rote memorization encouraging learners to actively engage with the learning process.

4. Synthesizing Knowledge:

Synthesizing knowledge, as stated in the next clause, aligns with philosophical notions of epistemology—the study of knowledge. Philosophers like Aristotle and Immanuel Kant have explored how knowledge is constructed and understood. Synthesis requires learners to go beyond surface-level understanding, engaging in higher-order thinking processes. This objective converges with educational psychology, which advocates for activities that foster critical thinking and the integration of information from various sources.

5. Ethics and Morality in Education:

The clause "The learner should manifest ethics and morality" extends into philosophical and psychological realms. From a philosophical perspective, ethics and morality are integral components of character education. Philosophers such as Confucius and Aristotle emphasized the cultivation of virtues as central to education. Psychology contributes by exploring moral development theories, such as Lawrence Kohlberg's stages of moral reasoning. The integration of ethical discussions in the classroom creates a moral compass, fostering responsible and empathetic citizens.

6. Identifying Mistakes and Misinformation:

The psychological aspect of metacognition intersects with the philosophical pursuit of intellectual integrity in the clause, "The learner should identify mistakes and misinformation." Metacognition involves thinking about one's thinking, a process essential to recognizing errors and misinformation. Philosophically, Socratic questioning encourages learners to critically evaluate information, fostering intellectual autonomy and a discerning attitude towards knowledge.

7. Solving Real-Time Problems:

Solving real-time problems integrates principles from both psychology and philosophy. From a psychological perspective, problem-solving is a cognitive skill linked to creativity, critical thinking, and adaptability. Philosophically, pragmatism, as advocated by William James and John Dewey, emphasizes the practical application of knowledge. Combining these perspectives promotes an education that equips learners with the ability to navigate real-time challenges effectively.

8. Solving Real-Life Problems:

Expanding on real-time problem-solving, the clause "The learner should solve real-life problems" aligns with pragmatism and existentialist philosophy. Existentialists like Jean-Paul Sartre emphasized the significance of applying knowledge to real-world situations. From a psychological standpoint, this objective underscores the importance of cultivating transferable skills and preparing learners for the complexities of life beyond the classroom.

9. Becoming a Lifelong Learner:

Transitioning to the philosophical dimension, "The learner should become a lifelong learner" encapsulates the essence of existentialist and humanistic philosophies. Existentialists, including Albert Camus and Jean-Paul Sartre, championed the idea of continuous self-development. Humanistic psychology, represented by Abraham Maslow and Carl Rogers, emphasizes self-actualization—the ongoing process of realizing one's potential. Encouraging a love for learning aligns with the existentialist belief in individual agency and the humanistic focus on personal growth.

10. Facilitating, Evaluating, and Celebrating Learning:

The final clause, "The learner should facilitate, evaluate, and celebrate learning," bridges psychology and pedagogy. Educational psychology informs effective facilitation methods, emphasizing the role of teachers as facilitators who create an inclusive and engaging learning environment. Evaluation techniques rooted in psychology, such as formative assessments and feedback, contribute to a growth-oriented mindset. Celebrating learning aligns with positive psychology, fostering a culture of appreciation and motivation within the educational community.

In weaving together psychology, philosophy, and pedagogy, the provided teaching objectives transcend the boundaries of traditional education. Grounded in psychological principles, these objectives emphasize cognitive processes, metacognition, and socio-emotional development. Philosophically, the objectives align with diverse educational philosophies, from Socratic methods to existentialism, shaping the purpose and nature of learning. Pedagogy acts as the practical bridge, translating these principles into actionable teaching strategies creating an environment where learners flourish intellectually, emotionally, and ethically.

Teachers have a profound role in shaping the mindset of students, especially in fostering a love for knowledge rather than just a fixation on grades. In the modern educational environment, the pressure to excel in terms of scores often overshadows the true purpose of learning. However, teachers should instill in students the habit of seeking knowledge as a lifelong pursuit. When students focus solely on achieving high grades, their relationship with education becomes transactional—learning is seen merely as a means to an end. This limits their ability to develop critical thinking, creativity, and problem-solving skills. Therefore, teachers must encourage students to find intrinsic value in the process of learning itself.

At the same time, it is essential for teachers to guide students in understanding the concept of timing and pacing between the learning mode and the winning mode. Learning mode involves curiosity, exploration, and the absorption of knowledge without the immediate pressure to succeed. It is a state where mistakes are seen as part of growth, and failure is an opportunity to deepen understanding. Winning mode, on the other hand, involves applying what has been learned to achieve specific goals—be it exams, projects, or other forms of assessment. Would you want a player in the Olympic final experiment too much or play the standard game? Learning requires experimentation, and experimentation increases the probability of loss. Therefore, in sports, the learning mode is in the training or practice period. One refines their skill to the best of possibilities. During the tournaments, the player has to harvest all their practice by executing the training to win laurels. While the general tendency is to be in learning or explorative mode, there are times and situations where one has to prove one's mettle by winning against others; that is the winning mode.

Psychologically, this balance between learning and winning is key to cultivating a growth mindset, where students see their abilities as malleable and capable of development. Students must understand that winning—achieving excellence or success—should not become the goal at the cost of learning. Winning should be seen as an outcome of a learning process. By teaching students this balance, teachers can help reduce the anxiety associated with performance, allowing them to see assessments as part of their growth rather than a final judgment of their abilities.

Pedagogically, this requires designing teaching methods and assessments that reward both the process of learning and the outcome of success. For example, assessments can be structured to value critical thinking, creativity, and problem-solving rather than rote memorization. Teachers can incorporate projects, discussions, and real-world problem-solving exercises that emphasize the application of knowledge, giving students a chance to focus on learning while also recognizing their progress.

Moreover, emphasizing formative assessments over purely summative ones can also cultivate this balance. Formative assessments allow students to reflect on their learning, receive feedback, and make improvements without the high stakes of a final grade. This reinforces the idea that learning is continuous and that excellence comes from constant growth, not the accumulation of awards or grades.

The approach should be learning, and the objective should be winning. Through learning, students are on the path to winning but winning should not be mistaken for the path itself. Teachers must cultivate an environment where excellence is defined not by medals but by the knowledge gained on a daily basis, ensuring that students are motivated by curiosity and a genuine passion for learning.

The objectives of teaching

Over the years of teaching, my teaching or educational philosophy has evolved into "Knowledge and skill are the goals, not grades and degrees. Grades and degrees are only benchmarks of one's pursuit of excellence. Pursue excellence, and success will chase the learner" encapsulates a profound philosophy that urges both educators and learners to shift their focus from the traditional emphasis on grades and degrees to a more holistic pursuit of knowledge, skill development, and excellence.

The distinction between goals and benchmarks is crucial in understanding the essence of this teaching tip. Knowledge and skill represent the intrinsic goals of education—the acquisition of understanding, competencies, and capabilities that enable individuals to navigate the complexities of their chosen fields. In contrast, grades and degrees serve as external benchmarks, measuring performance and achievement within a specific educational framework.

The advice to prioritize knowledge and skill underscores the idea that true education goes beyond the accumulation of grades or the attainment of degrees. It encourages learners to engage deeply with the subject matter, fostering a genuine passion for learning and a commitment to mastering essential concepts and skills. In doing so, the emphasis shifts from merely seeking external validation (grades and degrees) to an internal pursuit of personal and professional development.

Viewing grades and degrees as benchmarks aligns with the understanding that they are indicators of progress rather than the ultimate objectives. They provide valuable feedback on a learner's journey, reflecting achievements and areas for improvement. Embracing this perspective can alleviate the undue stress associated with a singular focus on grades, allowing learners to appreciate the learning process itself.

The notion of pursuing excellence emphasizes a commitment to continuous improvement and the highest standards of performance. By fostering a mindset of excellence, learners are encouraged to set high standards for themselves, persist in the face of challenges, and approach their studies with a sense of purpose and dedication. This commitment to excellence becomes a driving force, propelling learners toward success in their academic and professional endeavors.

The increase in knowledge and the increase in the abilities of the learner in acquiring knowledge and solving problems. These are two different but entangled issues. Acquiring knowledge is about the input of new information. On the other hand, abilities are traits of personalities, such as the ability to acquire, think, communicate, analyze, etc. The distinction between the increase in knowledge and the increase in the abilities of the learner is a critical but often overlooked aspect of education. While these two elements are deeply intertwined, they represent different facets of the learning process.

While knowledge and abilities are distinct, they are deeply connected. Knowledge provides the content that abilities act upon, while abilities determine how effectively knowledge can be utilized and expanded. A student with strong analytical skills will not only retain more information but will also be able to apply that knowledge in novel ways, leading to a deeper and more robust understanding. Conversely, a well-rounded base of knowledge enhances the development of intellectual abilities, as it provides the necessary context and examples that make higher-order thinking possible.

In the mission to teach and learn, a teacher's proficiency with language is vital. Words possess significant psychological power, shaping students' perceptions, emotions, and motivation. Teachers' speech provides cues to students about how and what they ought to do, making verbalization an essential component of effective teaching. By consciously employing language that encourages and uplifts, educators can cultivate a positive and nurturing environment conducive to learning. For instance, phrases such as "You're making great progress" or "I believe in your abilities" enhance self-esteem and bolster students' confidence. Motivational statements like "Keep going, you're almost there" stimulate persistence, fostering resilience and a growth mindset even when faced with challenging tasks.

Effective classroom management relies on clear and respectful communication, exemplified by phrases like "Let's stay focused together," which guide behavior without alienating students. When teachers utilize psychologically uplifting language, they help students feel valued, understood, and supported, ultimately leading to heightened engagement and academic success.

Moreover, the intentional use of language not only enhances classroom dynamics but also significantly contributes to the emotional and intellectual development of students. By recognizing the impact of their words, educators can inspire actions, generate momentum, and cultivate a productive learning atmosphere. This emphasis on language underscores the teacher's role as a facilitator of growth, promoting not just academic achievement but also the overall well-being of students in their educational journey. In the following chapters, wherever necessary with minimal redundancy, I have included some psychologically driven sentences that a teacher could utter to the class for better outcomes in mood, motivation and educational outcomes. One can try!

Descriptive language: the greatest teaching tool

Descriptive language wields significant psychological power in educational contexts, engaging multiple cognitive processes that enhance comprehension and emotional resonance. When teachers incorporate vivid imagery and detailed descriptions into their lessons, they stimulate students' imaginations, enabling them to visualize concepts and experiences concretely. This visualization not only makes the material more relatable but also enhances memory retention, as students are more likely to remember information presented in an engaging manner.

Furthermore, descriptive language evokes emotions, tapping into students' feelings and motivations. Emotional engagement fosters deeper connections to the material, creating a sense of relevance and personal investment in learning. Positive and encouraging language can also bolster self-efficacy, leading students to perceive their capabilities more favorably.

Additionally, the use of descriptive language fosters a supportive classroom atmosphere, promoting a sense of belonging and safety. When students feel respected and valued through thoughtful communication, their motivation and willingness to participate increase, ultimately leading to enhanced learning outcomes.

By appealing to students' senses and emotions, descriptive language serves as a powerful tool for capturing and maintaining attention. When teachers employ rich metaphors and vivid details, they anchor students' focus and invite them into the narrative of the lesson. This incremental engagement not only captures attention but also fosters curiosity and anticipation, encouraging students to remain invested in the unfolding discussion.

Incorporating descriptive language into teaching establishes a connection between educators and students, reinforcing the teacher's credibility while enhancing the overall impact of the message. This strategy transforms passive listeners into active participants, deepening their understanding and retention of the material, thereby fostering a more effective learning environment.

Descriptive language can serve as a powerful tool for teachers to convey kindness, motivation, respect, friendliness, and well-wishing, all of which contribute to a positive learning environment. By carefully choosing words and crafting vivid descriptions, teachers can create a classroom atmosphere that encourages emotional connection, fosters motivation and promotes respect among students. This book, along with the other title in this series, features numerous sentences that teachers can utilize in the classroom. These sentences are crafted to convey important messages, exert psychological influence, and foster the desired traits in students while eliciting specific outputs.

Below are several strategies teachers can use to effectively employ descriptive language in these contexts:

1. Conveying Kindness

Using Warm and Inviting Language:

Descriptive language can establish an atmosphere of kindness and support. By using gentle and inviting phrases, teachers can help students feel valued and welcomed.

- Example: "As you step into our classroom today, take a moment to breathe in the warm, friendly energy that surrounds you. Here, you are safe to share your thoughts and ideas, and every contribution is cherished."

Such phrases not only make students feel at ease but also signal that the teacher cares about their emotional well-being.

2. Inspiring Motivation

Creating Enthusiastic Imagery:

Teachers can use descriptive language to create excitement around learning. By painting vivid pictures of what students can achieve, they can ignite their passion for knowledge.

- Example: "Imagine standing at the edge of a vast ocean of knowledge, where every wave brings new discoveries and each drop of water represents a skill waiting to be mastered. Your journey in this class is just beginning, and the possibilities are endless!"

This kind of imagery encourages students to see their education as a thrilling adventure rather than a chore.

Encouraging Perseverance:

When students face challenges, descriptive language can provide motivation and encouragement, helping them to visualize their potential success.

- Example: "Think of the challenges in this assignment as stepping stones across a beautiful river. With each step you take, you build strength and resilience, bringing you closer to the other side, where achievement awaits."

3. Demonstrating Respect

Acknowledging Individual Strengths:

Descriptive language can be used to recognize and celebrate the diverse strengths of each student, fostering a respectful classroom culture.

- Example: "I see how your analytical mind works, piecing together complex problems like a master puzzle-solver. Your ability to think critically enriches our discussions and inspires your peers."

This not only builds students' confidence but also shows that the teacher respects their unique contributions.

Valuing Student Opinions:

Teachers can use descriptive phrases to affirm the importance of student input, creating an atmosphere of mutual respect.

- Example: "Every time you raise your hand, it's like a spark lighting a candle in our classroom. Your thoughts illuminate the path for others, and I value the light you bring to our discussions."

4. Promoting Friendliness

Fostering a Sense of Community:

Descriptive language can create a friendly atmosphere that encourages collaboration and camaraderie among students.

- Example: "As we embark on this group project, let's imagine our team as a vibrant garden, where each of you is a unique flower, bringing your own colors and fragrances. Together, we can create a beautiful masterpiece!"

This metaphor emphasizes the importance of teamwork and helps students feel more connected to each other.

Encouraging Peer Support:

Teachers can describe the benefits of collaboration using friendly language that promotes inclusivity.

- Example: "In this classroom, we're like a family, always ready to lend a helping hand. Let's lift each other up, just like the roots of a tree support its trunk. Together, we can reach great heights!"

5. Expressing Well-Wishing

Highlighting Future Success:

Descriptive language can also be used to express well-wishing, helping students to visualize their future successes.

- Example: "As you prepare for your next exam, picture yourself walking confidently into the testing room, armed with knowledge and skills. I believe in you, and I can already see the bright future you are crafting for yourself."

Such encouragement can boost students' self-esteem and inspire them to strive for excellence.

Using Encouraging Imagery:

When discussing student progress, descriptive language can help communicate the teacher's genuine hopes for their future.

- Example: "With each lesson you master, you are planting seeds of success that will bloom into a garden of opportunities. Your hard work will bear fruit, and I am excited to see what you will achieve."

6. Adopting the Role of a Philosopher

Promoting Critical Thinking:

Teachers can use descriptive language to frame questions and concepts in a way that encourages philosophical reflection and critical thinking.

- Example: "Consider the choices you make as pathways in a dense forest. Each decision can lead you to a different clearing, each with its own beauty and challenges. What do you hope to find on your journey?"

This encourages students to think deeply about their learning and the implications of their choices.

Fostering Curiosity:

Descriptive language can also inspire curiosity, prompting students to ask questions and seek deeper understanding.

- Example: "Imagine standing before a grand library filled with endless books, each one a doorway to new worlds and ideas. What questions do you want to explore today, and how will you unlock the mysteries within these pages?"

Chapter 3: Learning and Teaching Are Difficult

To speak, see, dance, and play are intrinsic aspects of our human nature. These actions are not merely learned behaviors; they arise spontaneously in response to our environment and experiences. Engaging with the world through our senses fosters a natural learning process, allowing us to understand and interact with our surroundings. Moreover, the desire to relate to others and feel equivalent within our social structures is an inherent drive.

Conversely, activities such as reading, writing, and calculating represent a divergence from instinctive behavior. The capacity to plan and predict future outcomes or to analyze historical events requires a level of abstraction that is not innate. This tendency to reflect on the past and strategize for the future is not found in the same manner among non-human animals. Furthermore, the pursuit of excellence—training ourselves to outperform others—becomes unnatural when basic needs are satisfied. This pursuit emphasizes the distinctive nature of human capacity, which enables us to achieve accomplishments beyond mere survival instincts. It is this unique capability for complex thought, creativity, and self-improvement that sets humans apart from the animal kingdom, shaping our cultural and intellectual landscapes.

Is a teacher required?

In one of my classes, I posed a question to my students: "In the modern world of artificial intelligence and robotics, professions are diminishing, with job cuts and layoffs in diverse fields. Do you think the profession of teaching will also vanish?" Most students answered, "Yes, teachers will also lose jobs." I agreed and then posed another question: "You all know English, you all have access to the internet, and all materials are available online, often for free. How many of you would go and learn by yourselves?" There was a moment of silence, and then nobody raised their hand. From this, two important messages emerge. First, the role of the teacher is to make students learn. Second, the teaching profession is here to stay for a long time—until direct neuro-implantable knowledge technology is invented. Teachers have to inculcate the motivation and trainability in students to learn; that is the primary job of a teacher.

The relationship between the need for a teacher and the motivation or trainability of a student is inherently reciprocal. When students possess high levels of motivation, they are often self-driven and require less direct intervention from a teacher. In such cases, the student may simply need access to resources—such as books, videos, or research materials—alongside explanations to facilitate independent learning. The teacher's role diminishes as the student actively engages with learning materials on their own, driven by their internal curiosity and determination.

However, in reality, many students face challenges related to motivation, trainability, or prior knowledge. Motivation is the internal drive to pursue learning, and without it, even the best resources may go unused or misunderstood. Trainability refers to a student's openness and ability to absorb and apply new information, which can vary significantly from one individual to another. Additionally, gaps in prior knowledge can hinder a student's capacity to comprehend advanced concepts, making the learning process more difficult.

Therefore, in most cases, the presence of a teacher becomes essential. The teacher not only facilitates the transfer of knowledge but also nurtures the student's motivation, addresses gaps in prior learning, and adapts instruction to fit the student's learning style and capacity. In this way, the teacher's role transcends merely providing information; it involves guiding the student's intellectual evolution, offering personalized support, and cultivating an environment where learning can flourish.

"When the student is ready, the teacher will appear. When the student is truly ready, the teacher will disappear." -Lao Tzu, Chinese Philosopher.

Is a Teacher Still Required in the Modern Age?

Since the origin of humans, knowledge levels, thinking skills, and technology have evolved dramatically, reflecting the progression of human civilization. Early humans relied on basic survival skills and passed down knowledge orally. Over time, the development of language, tools, and agriculture signified monumental leaps in understanding and capability. The emergence of writing systems allowed knowledge to be recorded and transmitted across generations, laying the foundation for formal education.

As human societies advanced, thinking skills became more sophisticated. Philosophical inquiry in ancient civilizations like Greece and India and scientific thought during the Renaissance greatly expanded human understanding. The Industrial Revolution accelerated technological innovation, reshaping how humans learned and interacted with the world. The rise of computers and the internet in the 20th century has exponentially increased access to knowledge, transforming education and the acquisition of skills.

Looking forward, each generation will face new frontiers—artificial intelligence, genetic engineering, space exploration—requiring continuous learning. The explosion of information will demand higher levels of critical thinking and adaptability. Humans will discover new ways, new knowledge, and new levels of intelligence. That is the nature of the human mind. People will generate more information about both microscopic and cosmic realms, as well as about distant pasts and futures. In this ever-evolving landscape, teachers remain essential as guides, helping students navigate vast, complex realms of knowledge. The role of educators will not diminish but grow in importance as they nurture intellectual curiosity and prepare future generations for unforeseen challenges.

The role of the teacher has long been fundamental in shaping intellectual, moral, and social development. In the past, the teacher was often the primary—if not the sole—source of knowledge, serving as the conduit through which students accessed information. However, with the advent of digital technologies, the accessibility of knowledge has vastly expanded. Online platforms, educational videos, books, and tutorials can now be accessed instantly, leading many to question whether the role of the teacher is still necessary, especially in the modern age. This essay argues that while access to information has become more democratized, the role of the teacher remains indispensable due to their irreplaceable functions in fostering motivation, facilitating the transfer of knowledge, addressing individual learning needs, and guiding the evolution of intelligence.

The Explosion of Information Access

With the rise of the internet and various educational platforms, students today have unprecedented access to information. From massive open online courses (MOOCs) to YouTube tutorials and academic databases, the knowledge once reserved for classrooms is now readily available to anyone with an internet connection. This has led to the belief that a motivated individual can learn independently, with resources serving as sufficient substitutes for a traditional teacher. Indeed, for highly motivated and self-driven learners, this claim holds some merit. For students who are already equipped with a strong foundation and high levels of intrinsic motivation, learning can occur effectively through self-directed engagement with these resources. I uploaded my lectures to YouTube, and they are watched less than a cat video during a homework marathon! Sure, there are fantastic lectures and dazzling animations by top professors out there. But even when the most crucial and entertaining videos are posted, students still prefer to skip them and show up to class as if it's a surprise event.

Students, with their diverse challenges and unique learning styles, deserve our understanding and support as they navigate the complexities of their academic journey and strive to achieve their full potential. Motivation and prior knowledge are not uniformly distributed among learners; many students lack the internal drive to tackle complex subjects or have gaps in their foundational understanding, which can hinder their independent learning efforts. This highlights a critical aspect of the teacher's role: not only as a transmitter of knowledge but also as a guide who cultivates motivation and provides structured support tailored to each student's unique needs.

The Transfer of Knowledge and Evolution of Intelligence

Another argument for the necessity of teachers in the modern age lies in their capacity to facilitate not just the transfer of knowledge but the evolution of intelligence. Learning is not a passive act of absorbing information; it involves critical thinking, problem-solving, and the ability to apply knowledge in novel situations. A teacher helps students move beyond rote memorization to develop higher-order thinking skills. Through guided instruction, questioning, and interactive dialogue, teachers cultivate students' analytical abilities and encourage them to engage deeply with the material.

Moreover, teachers help students navigate the process of "learning, unlearning, and relearning"—a critical aspect of intellectual growth. While self-directed learners may excel in accumulating information, they may struggle with the necessary process of unlearning outdated or incorrect knowledge and relearning in response to new insights. Teachers guide students through this process by providing feedback, helping them discern credible sources of information, and fostering intellectual humility. The teacher's role in this regard cannot be easily replaced by passive learning resources.

The Human Touch: Emotional and Social Dimensions of Learning

Beyond intellectual development, learning has a significant emotional and social dimension. Teachers play a vital role in creating supportive, inclusive learning environments where students feel safe to express themselves, ask questions, and make mistakes. This emotional connection fosters trust, which is crucial for deep learning. Students often feel more comfortable challenging their own assumptions and exploring new ideas when they have a positive rapport with a teacher. Digital resources, while valuable, cannot replicate this relational aspect of learning.

Additionally, the social dynamics within a classroom, led by a teacher, help students develop interpersonal skills that are crucial for their future professional and personal lives. These include collaboration, communication, and emotional intelligence—skills that are learned through interaction with both teachers and peers. Thus, the teacher's role extends far beyond simply delivering information; they help shape well-rounded individuals who can navigate both intellectual and social challenges.

While the modern age has provided unprecedented access to knowledge, the role of the teacher remains as crucial as ever. Motivation, trainability, and the evolution of intelligence require more than just access to information—they require the presence of a skilled, compassionate teacher who can adapt to students' needs, inspire them to learn, and guide them through the complexities of both knowledge and life. While motivated individuals may be able to learn independently, the vast majority of students benefit enormously from the structure, support, and guidance that a teacher provides. Far from being rendered obsolete by the digital age, teachers remain indispensable in shaping the intellectual, emotional, and social development of future generations. As long as knowledge and skills cannot be directly embedded into individuals, and as long as humans continue to govern their own lives, the teaching profession will remain indispensable and will not go extinct.

Teaching: an art or science?

The question of whether teaching is an art or a science has long been debated by educators, philosophers, and psychologists. On one side of the argument, proponents of teaching as a science emphasize the systematic, evidence-based methods that underpin effective teaching practices. On the other side, those who view teaching as an art highlight the creativity, intuition, and emotional intelligence that teachers bring to the classroom. Both perspectives have merit, as teaching involves elements of both science and art. However, the unique and humanistic aspects of teaching ultimately suggest that it should be viewed more as an art—a subject deeply rooted in the humanities.

Teaching as a Science: The Systematic Approach

Teaching as a science is grounded in the application of research-based strategies and methodologies to optimize learning outcomes.

This perspective emphasizes the importance of instructional design, assessment techniques, and the application of cognitive and developmental psychology. For example, the use of formative assessments, scaffolding, and differentiated instruction are all scientific approaches that have been shown to enhance student learning. These methods rely on data and research to inform decisions, ensuring that teaching practices are effective and aligned with the latest educational theories.

Moreover, the science of teaching includes the study of how students learn, which informs the development of teaching strategies that cater to different learning styles and cognitive abilities. The growing field of educational neuroscience, for instance, explores how the brain processes information, helping teachers design instruction that aligns with students' natural learning processes. This scientific understanding of teaching enables educators to implement structured approaches that maximize learning efficiency and effectiveness.

Teaching as an Art: The Human Connection

While the scientific aspects of teaching are essential, they do not capture the full complexity of the teacher-student relationship. Teaching as an art emphasizes the personal, emotional, and intuitive elements of the profession. Every classroom is a dynamic environment where the teacher must adapt to the unique needs, personalities, and learning styles of each student. This requires a high degree of emotional intelligence, empathy, and creativity— qualities that are difficult to quantify or systematize.

The art of teaching lies in the ability to inspire, motivate, and connect with students on a personal level. This often involves storytelling, humor, and the ability to make abstract concepts relatable and engaging. Teachers who excel in the art of teaching are able to create a learning environment that feels supportive and stimulating, fostering a love of learning that goes beyond the mere acquisition of knowledge. They are also adept at improvisation, adjusting their teaching methods in real time to respond to the needs and moods of their students.

The Intersection: Art and Science in Teaching

In reality, effective teaching requires a blend of both science and art. The scientific aspect provides a foundation of proven strategies and methods, while the artistic aspect allows teachers to apply these methods in ways that resonate with their students. For example, a teacher might use a scientifically supported technique like spaced repetition to help students retain information, but they will need to adapt the implementation of this technique based on the specific dynamics of their classroom, the subject matter, and the individual students.

However, it is the artistic side of teaching that often proves most crucial in bridging the gap between knowledge and understanding. While scientific methods provide the "what" and "how" of teaching, the art of teaching provides the "why," giving meaning and context to the learning experience. This art is inherently personal and relational, shaped by the teacher's personality, experiences, and the unique characteristics of each student.

Given the inherent individuality of both teachers and students, teaching should be regarded as an art deeply embedded in the humanities. Each teacher brings a unique set of skills, experiences, and perspectives to the classroom, just as each student brings their own background, learning style, and personality. The interaction between teacher and student is not merely a transaction of knowledge; it is a complex human connection that requires creativity, empathy, and adaptability.

Teaching, therefore, transcends the realm of pure science and enters the domain of the humanities, where the focus is on understanding and nurturing the human experience. The skills of teaching and learning are inextricably linked with the skills of connecting, communicating, and networking. These are not just technical skills but deeply human ones, requiring a teacher to engage with students not just as learners but as individuals with their own stories, challenges, and aspirations.

While scientific principles can guide effective teaching practices, it is the art of teaching that truly brings education to life. It is in this art that teachers find the flexibility and freedom to inspire their students, foster curiosity, and ignite a lifelong passion for learning. In this light, teaching is not just a profession; it is a craft, a calling, and a vital part of the human journey.

Of course, if the learner possesses immense motivation, drive, energy, imagination, training, and time, they can indeed master knowledge independently through books, videos, or self-guided experimentation. In such cases, the role of a teacher might seem redundant, as the learner's intrinsic qualities propel them towards understanding without external guidance. This scenario, however, is an idealized exception rather than the norm. Most learners benefit from the structure, guidance, and personal interaction that a teacher provides, which helps them navigate the complexities of knowledge and the subtleties of learning. Without the nuanced support of a teacher, many learners might struggle to reach their full potential. Therefore, while self-learning is possible for the highly motivated, the discussion of whether teaching is an art or science remains relevant for the vast majority of learners who thrive within a more collaborative and guided educational environment.

Teaching as the art of coercing others to learn

Teaching, often perceived as a noble pursuit of imparting knowledge and fostering understanding, can also be examined through the lens of coercion. In this context, coercion refers to the strategic influence teachers exert to motivate, guide, and sometimes compel students to engage with and absorb the material being taught. This artful form of coercion is not about force or intimidation but rather about skillfully navigating the psychological dynamics between teacher and student to foster learning and growth.

The psychological underpinnings of coercion in teaching involve understanding the balance between authority and empathy. Teachers may use various strategies to gently encourage students to meet expectations and achieve their potential. For example, setting clear goals, providing structured guidance, and employing motivational techniques are all forms of coercion that help students align their efforts with learning objectives. The art lies in ensuring that these strategies are perceived as supportive rather than punitive, maintaining a positive and constructive learning environment.

Effective coercive techniques in teaching also involve recognizing and adapting to individual student needs and motivations. By tailoring approaches to fit diverse learning styles and addressing students' intrinsic and extrinsic motivators, teachers can influence students' behaviors and attitudes toward learning. This form of coercion respects students' autonomy while guiding them toward academic success, embodying the delicate balance between influencing and respecting individual agency in the learning process.

Selling knowledge to unwilling students

Enticing, Convincing, and Motivating Unwilling Learners to Embrace Knowledge

1. Create an Engaging Pitch: Just as a salesperson tailors their pitch to the customer's interests, present knowledge in a way that aligns with students' interests and real-world applications. Highlight how the subject matter is relevant to their lives and future goals to spark curiosity and engagement.

2. Demonstrate Value: Show the practical benefits and value of the knowledge being offered. Illustrate how mastering the subject can lead to tangible advantages, such as improved problem-solving skills, career opportunities, or personal growth.

3. Use Persuasive Storytelling: Employ storytelling techniques to make the content more relatable and compelling. Share anecdotes or case studies that illustrate the impact and significance of the knowledge, making it more memorable and appealing.

4. Offer Personalized Solutions: Just as a salesperson addresses individual customer needs, adapt your teaching methods to cater to different learning styles and preferences. Provide tailored support and resources to meet students where they are and address their specific challenges.

5. Build Trust and Credibility: Establish yourself as a knowledgeable and trustworthy guide. Demonstrate your expertise and passion for the subject, and show that you genuinely care about students' learning and success.

6. Highlight Success Stories: Share stories of past students who have successfully applied the knowledge or benefited from the subject matter. Success stories can serve as powerful testimonials that motivate and inspire current students.

7. Create a Sense of Urgency: Instill a sense of urgency by emphasizing the importance of timely learning and the potential risks of missing out. Encourage students to take advantage of the opportunity to gain valuable knowledge while it is available.

8. Incentivize Learning: Offer incentives such as rewards, recognition, or opportunities for advancement to motivate students. Acknowledge and celebrate achievements to reinforce the value of their efforts and encourage continued engagement.

9. Foster an Interactive Experience: Engage students through interactive and dynamic learning experiences. Incorporate activities, discussions, and hands-on projects that make learning enjoyable and actively involve students in the process.

10. Provide Ongoing Support and Follow-Up: Just as a salesperson provides customer support, offer continuous guidance and encouragement throughout the learning process. Provide feedback, answer questions, and be available for additional support to help students stay motivated and on track.

By adopting these strategies, teachers can effectively "sell" the value of knowledge, inspire reluctant learners, and create a more engaging and motivating educational experience.

Learning is hard, and teaching is harder. Do them hard but with a smile.

The primary purpose of a teacher is to attract the learner's attention. Knowledge transfer is the ultimate goal, and this can be achieved through a willingness on the part of both sides, the teacher and the learner. Therefore, the prerequisite to the teaching-learning process is willingness. The teachers are paid to teach, and the learner's parents or guardians pay to teach their ward.

Lack of attention is a lack of education.

Teaching is an intricate and dynamic process that extends far beyond the mere transmission of information. It encompasses a continuous cycle of optimization and iteration revolving around three key pillars: Teach, Evaluate, and Encourage. This cyclical framework serves as the foundation for effective pedagogy, fostering a holistic learning environment that nurtures both knowledge acquisition and personal growth.

The first phase, Teaching, is the initiation of the educational cycle. It involves the deliberate and strategic delivery of information by the educator. Effective teaching goes beyond conveying facts; it encompasses the art of inspiring curiosity, igniting a passion for learning, and providing context that makes information relevant and meaningful to the learners. In this phase, the teacher employs diverse instructional methods, adapts to various learning styles, and leverages technology to create an engaging and inclusive classroom environment.

Teaching is not a one-size-fits-all endeavor. It requires flexibility and responsiveness to the evolving needs of students. The optimization of teaching involves refining instructional techniques based on feedback, staying abreast of educational innovations, and tailoring content to cater to the unique characteristics of each learner. As the educational landscape evolves, teachers must continually assess and refine their teaching strategies to ensure maximum effectiveness.

Following the Teaching phase is Evaluation, a critical component that gauges the understanding and progress of learners. Evaluation involves various assessment methods, including quizzes, exams, projects, and discussions. This phase serves as a diagnostic tool, offering insights into the effectiveness of the teaching methods employed. Evaluation is not solely about assigning grades but is a means to identify areas of strength and weakness, allowing for targeted interventions to enhance the learning experience.

The iterative nature of the teaching process is evident in the Evaluation phase. Teachers assess student performance, analyze the results, and adjust their teaching strategies accordingly. This ongoing feedback loop ensures that teaching remains a responsive and adaptive endeavor. It allows educators to identify areas for improvement, refine instructional approaches, and tailor content to address the specific needs of individual learners. The optimization of evaluation methods, such as incorporating formative assessments and peer evaluations, contributes to a more comprehensive understanding of student progress.

Encouragement is the third pillar of the teaching cycle, providing the necessary motivation and support to learners. Beyond the formal assessment, encouragement involves recognizing effort, celebrating achievements, and fostering a positive learning environment. Encouragement is a powerful tool that instills confidence, resilience, and a growth mindset in students. It acknowledges that learning is a journey marked by both successes and setbacks and underscores the importance of perseverance in the face of challenges.

Optimizing the Encouragement phase requires a teacher to cultivate a supportive and inclusive classroom culture. This involves fostering a sense of community, promoting peer collaboration, and acknowledging the unique strengths and contributions of each learner. Encouragement extends beyond academic achievements to encompass personal and social growth, emphasizing the holistic development of students.

The synergy of Teach, Evaluate, and Encourage creates a continuous and dynamic educational loop. Each phase informs and refines the others, fostering a culture of continuous improvement in both teaching practices and student outcomes. The cyclical nature of this process recognizes that education is not a static endeavor but a dynamic and evolving journey.

Teaching as a process of optimization and iteration revolves around the interconnected pillars of Teach, Evaluate, and Encourage. This cyclical framework emphasizes the importance of adaptability, responsiveness, and a holistic approach to education. By continually refining teaching methods, assessing student progress, and fostering a supportive learning environment, educators can optimize the educational experience, empowering learners to thrive academically, personally, and socially.

Personality development of students

Teaching can be viewed through three essential lenses: informative, transformative, and reformative, each contributing uniquely to student development.

Informative teaching focuses on transmitting knowledge. It equips students with facts, concepts, and skills necessary for understanding the world. The goal is to ensure students grasp fundamental knowledge that forms the basis of further inquiry and intellectual growth. This type of teaching is foundational, providing the building blocks of learning.

Transformative teaching goes beyond merely delivering information; it aims to change the way students think, view, and interact with the world. It fosters critical thinking, encouraging students to question, analyze, and evaluate information. Transformative teaching helps students develop new perspectives, broaden their horizons, and challenge pre-existing beliefs. It's a deeper form of education, cultivating intellectual autonomy and encouraging lifelong learning.

Reformative teaching addresses societal issues and drives change. It emphasizes teaching students to not only understand the world but to engage with it constructively, seeking improvement and innovation. This approach instills values of social responsibility, urging students to apply their knowledge in ways that challenge the status quo, promote equity, and solve global problems.

Together, these three modes of teaching prepare students to acquire knowledge, transform their thinking, and actively contribute to societal progress. The development of personality in students extends far beyond the acquisition of knowledge and skills. It encompasses the formation of traits and characteristics that enable students to make meaningful contributions in both their local communities and on a global scale. The ultimate goal is to shape individuals who possess a robust personality and persona capable of exerting immediate and long-term impacts. This complex process requires a concerted focus on cultivating productivity, excellence, and motivation, which are critical for shaping effective local and global citizens.

Local and Global Impact

To be effective local and global citizens, students must develop personalities that align with both immediate and distant objectives. Locally, this involves engaging with and contributing to community needs, while globally, it requires understanding and addressing broader challenges. A well-rounded personality facilitates this dual impact by fostering qualities such as empathy, resilience, and adaptability. These traits enable students to respond effectively to local issues and to collaborate with diverse groups on a global scale. By encouraging students to engage in both community service and international perspectives, educators can help them build a personality that is versatile and impactful.

Building Desired Traits

Instilling desirable traits such as productivity, excellence, and motivation in students is a challenging yet essential task. Personality development involves not only the enhancement of cognitive and emotional competencies but also the nurturing of behavioral attributes that drive success. Productivity is fostered through goal-setting and time management, excellence through continuous improvement and high standards, and motivation through intrinsic and extrinsic incentives. Teachers and mentors play a crucial role in guiding students towards these traits by setting high expectations, providing constructive feedback, and offering support and encouragement.

Challenges and Strategies

Changing and developing a student's personality requires a nuanced approach, as it involves addressing individual differences and needs. It is a challenging endeavor because it demands sustained effort and a deep understanding of each student's unique background and potential. Strategies to facilitate personality development include personalized mentorship, experiential learning opportunities, and reflective practices. Personalized mentorship helps address specific developmental needs, experiential learning provides practical application of skills, and reflective practices encourage self-awareness and growth.

The development of a student's personality is a multifaceted process that requires a strategic approach to integrate local and global perspectives. By focusing on building traits such as productivity, excellence, and motivation, educators can help students become effective and impactful individuals. While the task is demanding, the rewards of nurturing well-rounded personalities that contribute positively to society are profound and far-reaching.

Personality as a Life Skill

Personality is often regarded as a life skill that transcends the mere accumulation of knowledge. While specific knowledge may become obsolete or less relevant over time, the traits associated with a strong personality—such as productivity, excellence, and success—hold enduring value. These traits are crucial for navigating various life scenarios and achieving long-term goals. Individuals who cultivate these qualities are better equipped to adapt to changing circumstances, seize opportunities, and create significant impact in their personal and professional lives.

The Invaluable Nature of Personality Traits

Traits such as productivity, excellence, and success are foundational to achieving meaningful outcomes. Productivity involves the effective use of time and resources to achieve goals, excellence denotes a commitment to high standards and continuous improvement, and success reflects the realization of one's potential and ambitions. These traits are not only invaluable in their own right but also serve as catalysts for personal and professional growth. People who embody these qualities often find themselves well-positioned to take advantage of opportunities, make innovative contributions, and navigate challenges with resilience and adaptability.

The Power of Timing and Placement

The true power of personality traits is often realized when they are coupled with the right timing and placement. Individuals with strong personality traits can leverage their skills and attributes to maximize their impact, especially when they align their efforts with appropriate opportunities and contexts. Timing and placement play a crucial role in determining how effectively these traits can be applied to achieve desired outcomes. When combined with a keen sense of timing and strategic positioning, personality traits can lead to extraordinary achievements and innovations that benefit both individuals and society.

While knowledge may be transient, the development of personality traits such as productivity, excellence, and success provides a timeless advantage. These traits enable individuals to navigate life's complexities, capitalize on opportunities, and achieve remarkable results. By focusing on cultivating these enduring qualities, educators and mentors can equip students with the skills necessary for long-term success and impact, ensuring that they are prepared to make meaningful contributions in an ever-changing world.

Chapter 4: Types of learners and classrooms

In every classroom, a single teacher stands before a diverse group of students, each bringing their own unique background, experiences, and characteristics. No two students are the same, and the diversity in learning stems from a multitude of factors: age, gender, cultural heritage, race, socioeconomic status, parenting styles, sibling dynamics, personality traits such as introversion or extroversion, and even behavioral tendencies like bullishness or passivity. Each of these variables contributes to the distinct way a student perceives, processes, and retains information.

This inherent diversity poses a significant challenge for the educator, who must not only disseminate knowledge but also navigate the complexities of these individual differences. The task becomes even more intricate when considering that the same content is unlikely to be received or understood uniformly by all students. Despite employing best practices in teaching, the inevitable reality remains that students will interpret and internalize information in varied ways, shaped by their unique cognitive, emotional, and social contexts. This diversity in learning styles necessitates a flexible and adaptive approach from educators, one that accommodates the broad spectrum of learners present in the classroom, ensuring that each student has the opportunity to succeed. A teacher has to be sensitive to and acknowledge the diversity of the students.

The learner attributes and constraints

In the absence of immediate necessity, such as survival needs, learners often require motivation or a degree of compulsion to initiate the learning process. Unlike animals, who learn primarily out of necessity, human learners often face a disconnect between what is being learned and its immediate relevance. This disconnect means that learning must be driven by other factors, particularly motivation. Motivation can be sparked by curiosity, personal interest, or long-term goals. When a student is genuinely interested in a subject, they will actively seek knowledge, engaging deeply with the material in ways that transcend mere requirements. Personal goals, such as career aspirations, also provide a powerful motivation that drives the learner to invest time and effort into understanding complex subjects.

On the other hand, learning is sometimes initiated by compulsion or fear, which, while not ideal, can offer an initial push. For instance, the fear of failure in an exam can prompt a student to focus their efforts on studying. Though this form of extrinsic motivation is not as enriching as intrinsic motivation, it can still lead to meaningful learning outcomes. In educational systems where performance is measured and rewarded through assessments, such external pressures are common. However, while effective in the short term, reliance on fear-based motivation rarely sustains long-term intellectual curiosity or passion for learning.

Another crucial factor in the learning process is the ability to maintain attention and focus. Modern learners are often bombarded with distractions that can impair their ability to concentrate. Focused attention, however, is vital for deep learning. Without the ability to block distractions and concentrate on the task at hand, learners will struggle to engage with material at a deeper level, even when motivation is present. Therefore, teaching strategies must aim to create environments that foster focus, enhancing the learner's ability to retain and apply new knowledge.

<u>Types of Student Personalities</u>

Students exhibit a variety of personalities that significantly impact their learning experiences and outcomes. These variations can be categorized based on attributes such as motivation levels, enthusiasm, conformity, discipline, productivity, confidence, self-esteem, and shyness. Understanding these traits, along with their psychological underpinnings, enables educators to tailor their teaching approaches more effectively.

1. **Highly Motivated and Enthusiastic Learners**: These students display a strong drive and excitement towards their studies. Their intrinsic motivation often stems from a deep interest or passion for the subject matter. Psychologically, they are likely to have high self-efficacy, which fuels their enthusiasm and resilience. Teachers can nurture this trait by providing challenging material and opportunities for advanced learning.

2. **Conforming and Disciplined Students**: Conformity in students often reflects a high level of discipline and adherence to rules. These learners are typically motivated by structure and clear expectations. Psychologically, they may find security in predictability and order, making it crucial for educators to maintain a well-organized classroom environment and establish consistent guidelines.

3. **Productive and Self-Disciplined Learners**: These students exhibit high productivity and a strong sense of personal responsibility. Their motivation is often driven by internal goals and a desire to achieve. They tend to have a high level of self-regulation and effective time-management skills. Psychologically, their behavior aligns with the principles of self-determination theory, which emphasizes autonomy, competence, and relatedness.

4. Confident and High Self-Esteem Students: Students with high confidence and self-esteem approach tasks with a positive attitude and are more likely to engage actively in learning. Their self-assurance often leads to higher academic performance and resilience in the face of challenges. Educators should support and encourage these students to further enhance their self-perception and leadership skills.

5. Shy and Reserved Learners: These students may exhibit reluctance in participating and interacting in group settings. Their shyness can stem from a lack of self-confidence or social anxiety. Psychologically, they may require a more supportive and encouraging environment to build their self-esteem and comfort level. Teachers can help by providing a safe space for gradual participation and offering positive reinforcement.

6. Low Motivation and Unenthusiastic Students: These learners may struggle with engagement and often exhibit a lack of interest in academic tasks. Their motivation issues could be related to external factors such as a lack of relevance or personal connection to the material. Psychologically, these students may benefit from strategies that incorporate their interests and provide clearer links between learning and real-world applications.

By recognizing and addressing these diverse personality traits, educators can create a more inclusive and supportive learning environment, catering to the unique psychological needs of each student and fostering their overall academic growth.

In the educational landscape, students exhibit a rich diversity of personalities, each influencing their learning styles, interactions, and academic performance. Understanding these varied personalities, along with their psychological underpinnings, is crucial for tailoring effective teaching strategies.

1. Introverts: These students often prefer solitary activities and may feel overwhelmed in large group settings. They tend to process information deeply and are more reflective. Psychologically, introverts recharge their energy through quiet and alone time, making it essential for educators to provide opportunities for individual work and quiet contemplation.

2. Extroverts: Extroverted students thrive in interactive and dynamic environments. They are generally more vocal and energetic, finding engagement and learning through group activities and discussions. Their psychological needs are met through social interaction and external stimulation, making collaborative projects and frequent class discussions beneficial for their learning.

3. Analytical Thinkers: These students exhibit a preference for logical reasoning and systematic approaches. They are motivated by structured information and clear instructions. Psychologically, analytical thinkers seek coherence and consistency, requiring educators to present material in an organized and logical manner.

4. Creative Thinkers: Creative students are characterized by their imaginative and innovative approaches to problem-solving. They may prefer open-ended tasks and exploratory learning. From a psychological standpoint, creativity involves divergent thinking, which thrives in environments that allow for experimentation and risk-taking.

5. Pragmatic Learners: Pragmatic students focus on practical applications and relevance to real-life situations. They are often goal-oriented and appreciate learning that has immediate utility. Psychologically, they are motivated by practical outcomes and concrete results, requiring educators to link academic content to real-world scenarios.

6. Perfectionists: These students have high standards for themselves and may experience anxiety about making mistakes. They seek excellence and can be highly motivated but may struggle with the fear of failure. Educators should offer constructive feedback and support to manage perfectionistic tendencies and encourage a growth mindset.

Understanding these diverse personalities helps educators create a more inclusive and effective learning environment, addressing the psychological needs and preferences of each student while fostering a supportive educational experience.

Class size and classroom size

Class size, in terms of the number of students, plays a pivotal role in determining the effectiveness of teaching and learning. A class that is too large often results in diminished personal attention, as the teacher must spread their efforts across too many students. This makes it challenging to address individual questions, gauge understanding, and provide personalized feedback. Large classes may also foster anonymity, with some students feeling lost in the crowd, leading to reduced participation and engagement.

On the other hand, a very small class can feel too intimate, potentially limiting the diversity of interactions and perspectives that enrich learning. The ideal class size, while dependent on various factors such as the subject matter and teaching style, typically ranges between 15 to 25 students. This range allows for a balance where the teacher can manage the group while still giving ample attention to individual students.

In cases where class size exceeds the ideal, adjustments can be made. Group work or peer-based learning strategies can help distribute the focus. Incorporating technology, such as online platforms for discussions or assignments, may also relieve some of the pressure. The key lies in striking a balance, ensuring that each student remains engaged and benefits from the educational experience.

The distance between students and the teacher, both physically and metaphorically, is often proportional to the student-to-teacher ratio. In larger classes, students tend to sit farther away, and the personal connection between teacher and student diminishes. This can lead to reduced engagement, less participation, and a more passive learning environment. Conversely, in smaller classes, students are typically closer to the teacher, both in proximity and interaction, fostering a more dynamic, personalized learning experience. The smaller the student-to-teacher ratio, the more direct the communication, leading to enhanced understanding, motivation, and active involvement in the learning process.

The size of a classroom should be proportionate to the number of students occupying it, as both overcrowded and sparsely populated classrooms create challenges that extend beyond physical space. When too many students are crammed into a single classroom, several negative psychological effects arise. The sense of personal space diminishes, leading to discomfort and distractions, while the teacher's ability to offer individual attention decreases. In such an environment, students may feel anonymous, which can result in a lack of motivation and engagement.

Conversely, placing only a few students in a large classroom can also have detrimental effects. A room too large for the number of occupants may create a sense of isolation, causing students to feel disconnected from both their peers and the teacher. The sheer size of the space can dilute the intensity of interaction, making students less inclined to participate. Moreover, auditory issues arise in both scenarios. In an overcrowded room, noise levels escalate, impairing focus and communication. In a sparsely filled room, sound may seem overly dispersed, making it harder to maintain concentration. Creating a balance between classroom and class size ensures that students feel comfortable, connected, and capable of focusing—factors that are crucial for an effective learning environment.

Types of Classroom Heterogeneity

Classroom heterogeneity refers to the diversity of students in a classroom in terms of their characteristics, needs, and behaviors. This diversity can significantly impact teaching strategies and learning outcomes. The main types of classroom heterogeneity in terms of discipline, conformity, motivation, and trainability include:

1. Discipline

Discipline refers to students' adherence to rules, classroom behavior, and self-control. Heterogeneity in discipline can manifest in the following ways:

- Well-Behaved vs. Disruptive Students: Some students consistently follow classroom rules and engage in positive behavior, while others may exhibit disruptive or challenging behaviors. Disruptive students may struggle with self-regulation or have external factors affecting their behavior.

- Motivated vs. Unmotivated Students: Discipline can also vary based on students' motivation levels. Highly motivated students are more likely to adhere to classroom norms and engage in learning activities, whereas unmotivated students may show reluctance to follow rules or participate.

2. Conformity

Conformity refers to the extent to which students adhere to social norms, rules, and expectations within the classroom. Heterogeneity in conformity can include:

- High vs. Low Conformity: Some students naturally align with classroom norms and expectations, contributing to a harmonious learning environment. Others may resist conformity, challenging established norms and potentially disrupting classroom dynamics.

- Cultural and Socioeconomic Differences: Students from diverse cultural and socioeconomic backgrounds may have varying levels of conformity based on their personal experiences and values. These differences can influence how students interpret and respond to classroom expectations.

3. Motivation

Motivation encompasses the drive and enthusiasm students have for learning and achieving their goals. Heterogeneity in motivation can be observed in:

- Intrinsic vs. Extrinsic Motivation: Some students are driven by intrinsic factors, such as personal interest and enjoyment of learning, while others are motivated by extrinsic factors, such as rewards or grades. This difference in motivation can affect students' engagement and persistence.

- High vs. Low Motivation: Students exhibit varying levels of motivation, which can be influenced by factors such as previous experiences, perceived relevance of the material, and individual goals. Highly motivated students are often more engaged and proactive, whereas less motivated students may need additional support and encouragement.

4. Trainability

Trainability refers to students' ability to learn new skills and adapt to instructional methods. Heterogeneity in trainability includes:

- High vs. Low Trainability: Some students readily adapt to new teaching methods and learn new skills quickly, while others may require more time and support to grasp concepts. Differences in trainability can be influenced by cognitive abilities, prior knowledge, and learning styles.

- Learning Disabilities and Special Needs: Students with learning disabilities or special needs may have specific challenges that affect their trainability. These students may require differentiated instruction and tailored interventions to support their learning needs.

5. Prerequisite knowledge

Modern education is a cumulative process, where each layer of knowledge builds on the foundational information beneath it. The vast body of knowledge we teach today is the result of thousands of years of human civilization, progress, and cooperation. However, when a student lacks the prerequisite knowledge, it becomes difficult to grasp more advanced concepts in that subject. This poses a significant challenge for educators, who are often tasked with not only teaching the intended material but also covering the foundational knowledge that students may be missing.

In many cases, students may have the underlying knowledge but struggle to recall or apply it effectively. However, there are always students in each class who lack this foundation altogether. These students are more likely to rely on rote memorization to grasp new concepts rather than truly understanding and engaging with the material. Over time, this leads to a learning approach dominated by memorization, with minimal opportunities for critical thinking, analysis, or creativity. This shift can have long-term consequences, stifling intellectual growth and hindering the development of problem-solving skills that are essential for deeper learning and application of knowledge.

Implications for Teaching

Understanding and addressing the diverse nature of classroom heterogeneity is essential for effective teaching. To manage the variability in discipline, conformity, motivation, and trainability, educators can employ several targeted strategies.

Firstly, differentiated instruction is crucial. By tailoring teaching methods and materials to accommodate the diverse learning needs, preferences, and abilities of students, educators can ensure that each student has access to the resources and support they need to succeed. This approach acknowledges that students learn in different ways and at different paces, requiring flexible and adaptive teaching strategies.

Behavior management is another important aspect. Implementing strategies to address varying levels of discipline and to encourage positive behavior can create a conducive learning environment. Setting clear expectations and providing consistent feedback helps in maintaining order and fostering an atmosphere of respect and engagement.

Motivational strategies also play a significant role. Utilizing a variety of approaches to engage students—such as incorporating their interests, offering relevant and meaningful content, and providing both intrinsic and extrinsic motivators—can enhance student participation and enthusiasm for learning.

Additionally, support services are vital for addressing the needs of students with special requirements or learning disabilities.

Providing individualized education plans (IEPs), resource rooms, or specialized interventions ensures that these students receive the support necessary to thrive. By acknowledging and addressing classroom heterogeneity, educators can cultivate a more inclusive and effective learning environment that meets the diverse needs of all students.

The ideal class and the reality

Properties of a Classroom That Make a Teacher's Job Easier

1. Manageable Class Size: A class size that allows for effective management, ideally between 15 to 25 students, facilitates personalized attention, easier monitoring of individual progress, and more effective classroom management.

2. Homogeneous Motivation Levels: Students with similar levels of intrinsic motivation and enthusiasm for learning enable teachers to implement uniform engagement strategies and reduce the need for varied motivational approaches.

3. Clear Behavioral Norms: Students who consistently adhere to established behavioral expectations reduce the amount of time and energy teachers must invest in discipline, allowing more focus on instruction.

4. Diverse but Balanced Abilities: A class with a well-balanced range of abilities, where students have foundational skills appropriate for the level being taught, simplifies lesson planning and differentiation efforts.

5. Strong Communication Skills: Students who possess effective communication skills enhance classroom discussions and

collaborative activities, making it easier for teachers to facilitate and assess group work.

6. Consistent Attendance: Regular and punctual attendance by students ensures that lessons progress smoothly without frequent interruptions or the need for extensive catch-up sessions.

7. Supportive Environment: An environment where students are actively engaged and supportive of one another fosters a positive atmosphere conducive to learning and reduces the need for extensive individual interventions.

8. Prior Knowledge Alignment: When students enter with a baseline level of prerequisite knowledge relevant to the subject matter, teachers can build on existing understanding rather than spending significant time addressing gaps.

9. Positive Student-Teacher Relationships: A classroom where students respect and respond positively to the teacher facilitates effective instruction and classroom management, promoting a cooperative and productive learning environment.

10. Effective Resource Availability: Access to adequate teaching resources, such as technology, materials, and support staff, enhances the teacher's ability to deliver diverse and effective instruction without undue strain.

These properties collectively contribute to a smoother, more efficient teaching experience, allowing educators to focus on delivering quality education and fostering student development.

The Reality of a Typical Class in an Average Institution

In many average educational institutions, the reality of classroom dynamics often presents a stark contrast to the ideal. Class sizes frequently exceed optimal numbers, with 30 to 60 students per class being common. This large size strains the teacher's ability to provide individualized attention, making it challenging to address each student's unique needs effectively.

Motivation levels among students can vary widely. Teachers often encounter a spectrum of enthusiasm, ranging from highly motivated students eager to engage in learning to those who are disengaged or indifferent. This diversity in motivation necessitates the use of varied teaching strategies and additional effort to inspire and engage less motivated learners.

Behavioral issues are also prevalent, with students sometimes exhibiting inconsistent adherence to classroom norms. Managing disruptive behavior, dealing with frequent absenteeism, and addressing varied levels of discipline can consume significant instructional time and energy.

Academic abilities within a class are often heterogeneous, with some students well-prepared and others lacking fundamental skills. This disparity requires teachers to frequently differentiate instruction, which can be demanding and time-consuming. Additionally, gaps in prior knowledge among students mean that teachers spend considerable time bridging these gaps rather than advancing to new material.

Communication skills among students may also be uneven, with some struggling to articulate their thoughts clearly, impacting group discussions and collaborative projects. Teachers may find themselves needing to invest extra effort in facilitating effective communication and ensuring productive group work.

These challenges create a complex environment where teachers must navigate varying levels of motivation, behavioral issues, and academic readiness. Despite these difficulties, educators strive to create an engaging and supportive learning atmosphere, often going above and beyond to meet the diverse needs of their students.

It is crucial for a teacher's fulfillment and happiness to have a well-composed class, as it makes teaching more straightforward, enjoyable, easy and light. However, the true measure of a teacher's success lies in their ability to engage and educate a class that is less than ideal, particularly when faced with students who may struggle with or resist studying. The real achievement in teaching is not simply honing already sharp skills but transforming a rusted blade into a finely sharpened tool. This process of turning challenges into triumphs exemplifies the essence of effective teaching and demonstrates the profound impact a teacher can have.

Chapter 5: Types of teachers and teaching

Teaching is a delicate profession where personal, professional, and social spheres intertwine significantly. This blending arises from the extensive number of interactions with students, the prolonged duration of these engagements, and the frequent nature of these exchanges. Teachers invest substantial time and effort in each student, shaping their learning experiences while simultaneously navigating their personal and social lives. The frequent and sustained interactions within the classroom environment necessitate a balance between maintaining professional boundaries and fostering meaningful connections. Consequently, teachers often find their personal values and social behaviors influencing their teaching practices, creating a unique and integrated professional identity.

In the personal sphere, teachers often bring their own experiences, emotions, and biases into the classroom. These personal attributes can significantly influence their teaching style and their interactions with students. For instance, a teacher's emotional state, personal values, and life experiences shape their approach to discipline, motivation, and support. This blending of personal and professional spheres means that teachers must navigate their own vulnerabilities and strengths while maintaining a professional demeanor, which can be both challenging and rewarding.

In the professional sphere, teaching demands a high level of skill and expertise in subject matter, pedagogy, and classroom management. However, the profession extends beyond mere instructional delivery to encompass the teacher's role in fostering a supportive and inclusive learning environment. The social sphere further complicates this dynamic, as teachers must interact with students, parents, and colleagues, each bringing their own expectations and perspectives. Teachers must balance the demands of their professional responsibilities with the need to build positive relationships and address the social and emotional needs of their students. This intersection of personal, professional, and social spheres creates a complex and intricate framework within which teaching occurs, highlighting the multifaceted nature of the profession.

Teaching is a profession characterized by the continuous and often prolonged interaction between teachers and students, wherein intellectual engagement is paramount. Unlike professions focused primarily on physical labor, teaching relies on the cognitive and emotional capacities of both the teacher and the student. This daily, immersive engagement requires a deep, sustained focus on the mental and emotional development of students, making the profession inherently complex and multidimensional.

Students are deeply intertwined with their parents' lives, and this connection extends into the classroom. Parents' expectations, values, and concerns influence students' behavior and academic performance, creating a significant overlap between the educational environment and the home sphere. Teachers, in turn, navigate not only their relationships with students but also their interactions with parents, school management, and their own families. This intricate web of relationships blends the personal, professional, and social spheres.

The nature of these interactions—whether in resolving conflicts, discussing student progress, or addressing educational goals— often mirrors those within personal relationships. For example, a teacher's interaction with a student may reflect dynamics similar to those in a family setting, such as providing support, setting boundaries, and offering encouragement. Similarly, communication with parents and school administrators may involve elements of personal rapport and professional responsibility. The fusion of these spheres creates a dynamic environment where personal feelings, professional obligations, and social interactions are continuously interwoven, making the teaching profession uniquely complex. This fusion demands that teachers adeptly manage and harmonize these various aspects of their professional and personal lives, underscoring the profound impact of teaching on both their own lives and those of their students.

The education 'system'

Systems thinking is a holistic approach that emphasizes understanding the interactions and interdependencies within a complex system. When applied to the teaching profession, this approach allows for a comprehensive view of how various components of the educational ecosystem interact and affect one another. This perspective is invaluable for recognizing the multifaceted nature of teaching and the interconnected dynamics between teachers, students, parents, and educational institutions.

Components of the Educational System

1. Teachers: At the core of the educational system, teachers play a pivotal role. They are responsible for delivering instruction, fostering learning environments, and managing classroom dynamics. Their effectiveness is influenced by their skills, experience, and personal attributes, such as empathy, communication skills, and resilience. Teachers are also impacted by external factors like institutional policies, societal expectations, and professional development opportunities.

2. Students: Students are the primary recipients of educational efforts and the most important people in the institution. Their learning outcomes are shaped by individual characteristics such as prior knowledge, motivation, learning styles, and cognitive abilities. Students are also influenced by their social context, including family support, peer interactions, and extracurricular activities. The reciprocal nature of the teacher-student relationship means that students' responses and progress directly affect teaching strategies and approaches.

3. Parents and Guardians: The role of parents and guardians extends beyond supporting students' academic efforts; they are integral to the educational system. Their involvement can influence students' attitudes towards learning, provide additional support, and affect teachers' ability to implement educational strategies. Effective communication and collaboration between teachers and parents can enhance student outcomes and foster a supportive learning environment.

4. Educational Institutions: Schools and educational institutions provide the framework within which teaching occurs. This includes the physical environment, resources, curriculum, and administrative support. Institutional policies and procedures influence teachers' practices, student experiences, and overall educational quality. Institutions are also affected by external factors such as government regulations, funding, and community involvement.

5. Society and Culture: The broader societal and cultural context impacts the educational system. Cultural values, societal expectations, and economic conditions shape educational priorities, standards, and practices. Teachers and students are influenced by these external factors, which can affect curriculum content, teaching methods, and educational goals.

Interactions and Feedback Loops

In a systems thinking approach, understanding the interactions between these components is crucial. For instance:

- Teacher-Student Interaction: Teachers adjust their instructional methods based on students' responses and progress, creating a feedback loop that impacts both teaching and learning outcomes. Positive student engagement can enhance teaching effectiveness, while challenges in student understanding may lead to adjustments in teaching strategies.

- Teacher-Parent Interaction: Effective communication between teachers and parents can lead to better student support and a more cohesive approach to addressing educational challenges. Parents' feedback and involvement can inform teachers' practices and contribute to improved student performance.

- Institutional Impact: Institutional policies and resources influence teachers' ability to implement educational strategies and provide support. Inadequate resources or restrictive policies can hinder teaching effectiveness, while supportive environments and professional development opportunities can enhance teaching quality.

- Societal Influence: Societal changes and cultural shifts impact educational priorities and practices. Teachers must adapt to these changes, balancing traditional educational goals with evolving societal expectations.

The challenge of teaching lies in its inherent complexity: educators must engage a diverse array of students, each with unique preferences, learning styles, and interests, within a limited timeframe. This diversity presents a significant hurdle, as students often have varying levels of motivation and enthusiasm for academic activities compared to more entertaining or recreational pursuits.

Understanding and Engaging Diversity in the Classroom

Understanding diversity is crucial for effective teaching, as every student brings a unique set of experiences, learning styles, and cognitive abilities. Recognizing these individual differences allows teachers to address each student's strengths, challenges, and preferences, ensuring meaningful engagement with the material. Additionally, students often have varied interests outside the classroom, such as sports and social interactions. Balancing these interests with academic content requires creativity and adaptability, making learning relevant and appealing.

Creating an inclusive learning environment is essential, involving differentiated instruction to accommodate diverse needs. Tailoring lessons with various teaching methods—such as visual aids and hands-on activities—allows for more personalized instruction. Utilizing flexible grouping strategies enables students to collaborate based on abilities and interests, fostering peer learning and support.

Engaging students is further enhanced by connecting academic content to real-life applications, demonstrating relevance to their lives. Incorporating active learning techniques—like interactive discussions and problem-solving activities—encourages participation and transforms traditional learning into dynamic experiences.

Effective time management and building positive relationships with students are vital. Structured planning and efficient teaching practices ensure that diverse needs are met while establishing rapport, which fosters an empathetic environment that motivates student participation and promotes a growth mindset, ultimately enhancing engagement and resilience in the classroom.

Teaching and parenting

Teaching and parenting stand as the key pillars of civilization, playing a pivotal role in shaping the future of societies. These interconnected roles are indispensable for the holistic development of individuals and the well-being of communities. The impact of effective teaching and nurturing parenting reverberates across generations, influencing the social fabric, values, and the overall progress of civilizations. This essay will delve into the profound significance of teaching and parenting, exploring specific examples that highlight their crucial contributions to the foundation and continuity of our civilizations.

Parents play an essential role in shaping a child's early behavior and social conduct within the home, extended family, and immediate neighborhood. This is where children first learn the foundational aspects of social interaction, such as respect for elders, basic manners, and the ability to navigate personal relationships. The home environment provides a secure space where children can observe and model behavior, making it the primary place for early socialization. The psychological underpinning here lies in attachment theory, where children form secure or insecure attachments with their caregivers, influencing their ability to interact with others. This early learning sets the groundwork for emotional regulation and self-conduct.

However, as children grow and enter broader social environments, much of their personality development transitions to the realm of schools. Schools become the platform where children learn to navigate more complex social structures, interact with peers, and understand authority beyond the family unit. Educational institutions hold a significant responsibility to shape how children conduct themselves in society and foster dignity, respect, and social competence. Here, the focus shifts from familial bonds to the development of self-esteem, peer relationships, and the ability to assert oneself respectfully in different social settings. Schools, therefore, don't just impart academic knowledge; they play a crucial role in cultivating emotional intelligence, social responsibility, and character formation, preparing children to function with dignity and respect in the outside world. This transition is essential in the broader context of moral and social development, shaping future citizens who contribute meaningfully to society.

The aphorism "if you are a teacher, you are a parent, and if you are a parent, you are a teacher" encapsulates the profound interconnectedness between the roles of educators and parents in shaping the lives of individuals. This statement reflects the shared responsibility both teachers and parents bear in nurturing, educating, and guiding the next generation.

At its core, the idea acknowledges that the influences on a person's development extend beyond the confines of the classroom or the home. Teachers, in their role as educators, often become surrogate parents during school hours. They provide not only academic guidance but also emotional support, encouragement, and a sense of structure akin to what a parent offers within the family environment. In this way, teachers step into the nurturing role typically associated with parents, impacting students' holistic growth.

While we engage in the multitude of tasks that drive the mission of teaching, it is the approach and attitude we bring to the classroom that truly defines our impact. The energy, passion, and understanding we exude shape the learning environment far more than any structured curriculum. A teacher who does not embrace the role of a parent, with its inherent kindness, care, and attentiveness, falls short of nurturing the full potential of students. Likewise, a parent who does not ensure learning—both academically and emotionally—neglects the essential responsibility of guiding their child's development. A teacher who doesn't parent and a parent who doesn't teach are underperforming in their respective roles.The roles of teacher and parent are intertwined, each requiring a balance of compassion and discipline. A teacher must see the individuality of each student, supporting their growth with empathy. At the same time, a parent must have the strength to enforce the necessary boundaries and lessons. Both roles, in their essence, shape not just minds but entire futures.

Parents inherently take on the role of teachers within the home. From the earliest stages of a child's life, parents are the primary educators, imparting foundational skills, values, and knowledge. The home environment becomes a microcosm of learning, where parents teach essential life skills, moral values, and societal norms. This teaching is not confined to formal lessons but extends to everyday interactions, modeling behavior, and fostering a love for learning.

The reciprocal nature of these roles is evident in the similarities between effective teaching and parenting practices. Both involve mentorship, where guidance is provided to support the development of well-rounded individuals. Teachers and parents alike strive to instill a love for learning, curiosity, and a growth mindset that propels individuals to seek knowledge and overcome challenges.

Moreover, effective communication is a cornerstone of both teaching and parenting. Teachers convey complex ideas, foster understanding, and create a positive learning environment. Similarly, parents communicate values, expectations, and emotional support to nurture their children's overall well-being. In both contexts, open dialogue and active listening are crucial components for building trust and meaningful connections.

The roles of teacher and parent converge in their shared commitment to creating a structured and supportive environment. Teachers establish academic expectations and behavioral boundaries, while parents reinforce these expectations at home. This dual reinforcement contributes to the holistic development of individuals, providing consistency and stability across various facets of their lives.

The influence of teachers and parents is not confined to the early years but extends throughout a person's life. The foundation laid by parents in early childhood significantly shapes a child's approach to learning. As individuals progress through formal education, teachers continue to play a pivotal role in honing critical thinking skills, fostering a love for knowledge, and preparing students for the challenges of adulthood.

Increasingly, the teachers' role has become more crucial than ever in shaping the lives of students. To accomplish the vision of SUPC, the teacher has to extend beyond the transfer of knowledge alone. The teacher has to build the productive and confident personality of each student.

Mentorship and Guidance in Teaching and Parenting

Mentorship serves as a cornerstone in both teaching and parenting, as both roles involve guiding individuals through their formative years. In teaching, a high school teacher exemplifies this by not only imparting knowledge but also mentoring students in life choices, personal development and instilling values that extend beyond academics. Similarly, parents provide guidance on academic matters while also supporting their children's life choices and personal growth.

Effective communication is another shared aspect of teaching and parenting. A college professor creates an open and inclusive classroom environment that encourages students to express their thoughts and ideas freely. This active listening fosters a supportive environment that values each student's voice. In parenting, effective communication manifests when parents engage with their children, creating a space for emotions and opinions to be valued, thereby laying the groundwork for positive emotional and intellectual development.

Setting expectations and boundaries is also evident in both domains. A high school teacher defines academic goals and standards, while parents establish behavioral norms at home. Both roles aim to create structured settings that promote growth, responsibility, and accountability.

Moreover, the ability to adapt to unique needs is essential in both contexts. Teachers recognize diverse learning styles, tailoring instructional methods accordingly, while parents adapt their guidance to their children's individual characteristics.

Emotional dimensions play a critical role, as teachers and parents provide empathy and support. Finally, both teaching and parenting emphasize lifelong learning, fostering an enduring love for education and intellectual curiosity in students and children alike. Thus, educators and parents share a profound responsibility not only in imparting knowledge but also in shaping character and navigating complex dynamics while fostering resilience and emotional well-being. This dynamic places teachers in a precarious position. They must balance strictness with leniency, maintaining discipline without alienating students. Too much rigidity can distance students, while too much flexibility can weaken the learning process. Teachers must regulate their own emotions while managing the classroom atmosphere, fostering an environment of respect, trust, and academic rigor. Unlike parents whose emotional bond with their children is enduring, teachers must work harder to build emotional connections without the assurance of affection. Their role demands patience, emotional intelligence, and a commitment to both intellectual and personal development, ensuring that students are not only educated but also supported in their growth.

Types of teachers

Teachers exhibit diverse psychological profiles that influence their communication styles, including their biases, preferences, inclinations, beliefs, and adherence to cultural and religious rules. Understanding these psychological types helps in tailoring teaching strategies to different contexts and student needs. Here, we explore several psychological types of teachers and their associated communication characteristics.

1. Authoritarian Teachers

Characteristics: Authoritarian teachers tend to have a structured and controlling approach to communication. They prefer clear, directive communication and often emphasize adherence to rules and procedures. Their communication style is generally top-down, with a focus on maintaining order and discipline in the classroom.

Biases and Preferences: Authoritarian teachers may exhibit biases towards traditional methods and a preference for established norms. They may be less open to student input and innovative ideas, favoring a rigid structure over flexibility.

Inclinations and Beliefs: They typically believe in the importance of authority and control in the learning environment. Cultural and religious rules may influence their emphasis on respect for hierarchy and obedience.

Impact on Students: This style can create a well-ordered classroom but may also stifle creativity and limit student autonomy. Students may feel less empowered to express their opinions or engage in open dialogue.

2. Democratic Teachers

Characteristics: Democratic teachers use a collaborative communication style that values student input and encourages participation. They foster an environment where students are involved in decision-making processes and contribute to the direction of their learning.

Biases and Preferences: They may show biases towards student-centered approaches and innovative teaching methods. They prefer flexible and adaptive strategies that accommodate diverse student needs.

Inclinations and Beliefs: Democratic teachers believe in the value of shared responsibility and mutual respect in the classroom. Their approach is often influenced by cultural beliefs in egalitarianism and inclusivity.

Impact on Students: This style promotes engagement, autonomy, and a sense of ownership in students. It encourages open communication and fosters a collaborative learning environment.

3. Nurturing Teachers

Characteristics: Nurturing teachers focus on emotional support and personal development. Their communication is empathetic, supportive, and attentive to students' emotional needs. They prioritize building strong, trusting relationships with their students.

Biases and Preferences: They may have a bias towards emotional and relational aspects of teaching, valuing student well-being over strict academic achievement. They prefer methods that promote emotional growth and personal connection.

Inclinations and Beliefs: Nurturing teachers believe in the importance of emotional support and positive reinforcement. Cultural and religious values related to compassion and care often influence their approach.

Impact on Students: This style helps build self-confidence and emotional resilience in students. It creates a safe and supportive learning environment but may sometimes prioritize emotional needs over academic rigor.

4. Innovative Teachers

Characteristics: Innovative teachers are characterized by their willingness to embrace new ideas and technologies. Their communication is often dynamic and forward-thinking, incorporating modern tools and methods to enhance learning.

Biases and Preferences: They may exhibit biases towards cutting-edge practices and unconventional methods. They prefer an adaptive and experimental approach, often challenging traditional norms.

Inclinations and Beliefs: Innovative teachers believe in the importance of staying current with educational trends and technology. Their approach may be influenced by cultural and religious beliefs that value progress and change.

Impact on Students: This style encourages creativity and adaptability in students. It can make learning more engaging and relevant but may require students to adjust to frequent changes in methods and tools.

5. Traditional Teachers

Characteristics: Traditional teachers adhere to conventional teaching methods and communication styles. Their approach is often characterized by a focus on established curricula, direct instruction, and a respect for academic traditions.

Biases and Preferences: They may show biases towards time-tested methods and a preference for structured, lecture-based teaching. They value historical educational practices and often resist new methods.

Inclinations and Beliefs: Traditional teachers believe in the importance of preserving educational heritage and maintaining high standards. Cultural and religious influences may shape their respect for tradition and formality in communication.

Impact on Students: This style provides stability and clarity in learning objectives. While it maintains a clear structure, it may limit opportunities for innovation and student-centered learning.

6. Reflective Teachers

Characteristics: Reflective teachers engage in continual self-assessment and introspection regarding their teaching practices. Their communication is thoughtful and often involves soliciting feedback from students to improve their methods.

Biases and Preferences: They may exhibit biases towards evidence-based practices and a preference for ongoing professional development. They value feedback and self-improvement over rigid adherence to pre-established methods.

Inclinations and Beliefs: Reflective teachers believe in the importance of adaptability and personal growth in teaching. Their approach may be influenced by cultural beliefs in self-improvement and lifelong learning.

Impact on Students: This style fosters a learning environment where feedback is valued and teaching practices are continuously improved. It promotes a responsive and adaptable approach to student needs.

7. Inspirational Teachers

Characteristics: Inspirational teachers aim to motivate and energize their students through passionate communication and enthusiasm. They often use storytelling, personal experiences, and motivational techniques to engage students.

Biases and Preferences: They may exhibit biases towards motivational and engaging methods. They prefer strategies that inspire and captivate students, often focusing on the affective domain of learning.

Inclinations and Beliefs: Inspirational teachers believe in the power of motivation and enthusiasm to drive student success. Their approach may be influenced by cultural values related to charisma and personal influence.

Impact on Students: This style can significantly enhance student motivation and engagement. It creates an emotionally charged learning environment but may sometimes overshadow the importance of academic rigor.

8. Culturally Sensitive Teachers

Characteristics: Culturally sensitive teachers are attuned to the diverse cultural backgrounds of their students. Their communication is respectful of cultural differences and incorporates inclusive practices that honor students' cultural identities.

Biases and Preferences: They may show biases towards culturally inclusive practices and a preference for methods that recognize and celebrate diversity. They value cultural competence and sensitivity in their teaching approach.

Inclinations and Beliefs: Culturally sensitive teachers believe in the importance of respecting and integrating students' cultural contexts into the learning process. Their approach is often influenced by cultural and religious values of inclusivity and respect.

Impact on Students: This style fosters an inclusive and respectful learning environment, promoting cultural awareness and acceptance. It enhances students' sense of belonging and can improve educational outcomes by addressing diverse needs.

9. Rule-Based Teachers

Characteristics: Rule-based teachers emphasize adherence to strict guidelines and procedures in their communication. They value consistency and order, often using clear rules and expectations to manage the classroom.

Biases and Preferences: They may exhibit biases towards structured and regulated approaches to teaching. They prefer methods that uphold established rules and norms, ensuring a predictable learning environment.

Inclinations and Beliefs: Rule-based teachers believe in the importance of discipline and structure in education. Their approach may be influenced by cultural and religious values related to lawfulness and order.

Impact on Students: This style provides clarity and consistency, helping students understand expectations and procedures. However, it may limit flexibility and responsiveness to individual student needs.

10. Holistic Teachers

Characteristics: Holistic teachers focus on the overall development of students, including their intellectual, emotional, social, and moral growth. Their communication integrates various aspects of student development into the learning process.

Biases and Preferences: They may show biases towards integrative and comprehensive teaching approaches. They prefer methods that address multiple facets of student growth, often incorporating interdisciplinary and experiential learning.

Inclinations and Beliefs: Holistic teachers believe in the interconnectedness of different aspects of student development. Their approach may be influenced by cultural and religious beliefs that emphasize the importance of nurturing the whole person.

Impact on Students: This style supports well-rounded development and personal growth, creating a learning environment that values the holistic development of students. It promotes balance and integration but may require careful management to address diverse educational goals.

Teaching, like many other professions, serves a critical societal function, working on the cognitive development of individuals, much like doctors work on physical health. It involves not only imparting knowledge but also shaping the skills and productivity of students, who are in a tender and formative stage of life. Psychologically, this process requires a delicate balance of care, as the teacher-student relationship influences not only intellect but also personal growth and self-concept.

In this context, teachers can adopt two broad attitudes: a closed attitude and an open attitude. These attitudes reflect the degree of personal engagement and openness in their interactions with students, ultimately shaping the learning environment and student outcomes.

The closed attitude is characterized by a structured and transactional approach. A teacher with this attitude focuses solely on the technical aspects of the job—imparting knowledge, teaching skills, and evaluating students. From a psychological standpoint, this approach offers clarity and predictability, both for the teacher and the student. It provides a stable framework within which students can learn, with clear boundaries that might appeal to more task-oriented individuals. However, while this method fulfills the basic requirements of education, it often lacks the emotional engagement necessary for deeper personal development.

A closed attitude minimizes interactions beyond the curriculum, reducing opportunities for students to develop soft skills such as communication, emotional intelligence, and social adaptability. Students, especially those who are introverted or shy, may find it difficult to express their difficulties, fears, or aspirations in such an environment. The limited emotional connection may cause students to feel isolated or unsupported, particularly when facing personal challenges that affect their academic performance.

In contrast, the open attitude involves going beyond the minimum requirements of teaching. This approach emphasizes openness to interaction, accessibility, and a commitment to fostering a deeper teacher-student relationship. From a psychological perspective, an open attitude allows for the creation of a more inclusive and supportive learning environment, which is essential for fostering student confidence, motivation, and emotional well-being. Being approachable and encouraging interaction can make a significant difference in the lives of students, especially those who are naturally shy or hesitant to seek help.

Teachers with an open attitude view their role not just as educators but as mentors. They strive to cultivate the whole student—intellectually, emotionally, and socially. This attitude aligns with the principles of self-determination theory, which posits that individuals need three key elements for psychological growth: competence, autonomy, and relatedness. The open attitude fosters these elements by helping students feel connected to their teacher, which enhances their motivation and engagement. It provides students with a safe space to step outside their comfort zones, explore new ideas, and develop a sense of autonomy in their learning process.

The open approach also addresses the importance of personality development. Education is not merely about acquiring information but about forming a well-rounded individual capable of navigating complex social, emotional, and intellectual landscapes. By encouraging interaction, fostering curiosity, and engaging with students on a personal level, teachers play a critical role in shaping students' confidence, social skills, and resilience. This kind of engagement can be particularly beneficial for students who might struggle with self-expression or lack confidence in their abilities.

However, adopting an open attitude comes with its challenges. It requires emotional labor from teachers, who must balance their personal and professional lives while being open to students' needs. Not all teachers may feel comfortable with this level of involvement, and psychological factors such as teacher burnout can become a risk when boundaries are not clearly defined. Additionally, teachers must be careful not to blur professional boundaries, as too much emotional involvement could lead to dependency or other complications in the teacher-student dynamic.

There are advantages to both attitudes, and they often reflect a teacher's personality, comfort levels, pressures, and priorities. Some teachers may naturally gravitate towards a more reserved, closed approach, while others may prefer the warmth and interaction of an open approach. The key is for teachers to find a balance that works for them and their students, ensuring that they can offer effective education while also fostering a supportive environment for growth.

Personally, I prefer the open attitude, especially because of the shy and reserved students. I believe that education should go beyond imparting knowledge and skills to include personality development, which can only be achieved through consistent interaction and encouragement. Shy students, in particular, benefit from an environment that pushes them beyond their comfort zones, where they can grow not only intellectually but also personally. By helping students develop these traits, teachers contribute to the overall vision of creating socially useful productive citizens (SUPCs), where teaching is not only about learning facts but about molding capable, empathetic, and socially responsible individuals.

The open attitude in teaching promotes a holistic approach to education, one that nurtures students' intellectual and emotional development. It encourages personality growth, which is crucial for preparing students to face the world with confidence, empathy, and a well-rounded sense of self. Through open interaction and encouragement, teachers can help students achieve their full potential, both as learners and as individuals, with the ultimate goal of transforming them into socially useful, productive citizens (SUPCs).

Inculcating an open attitude as a teacher requires conscious effort in expressions, body language, language, and interactions. Below are ten methods that can help foster this open attitude:

1. Warm and Inviting Expressions

Maintain a soft, approachable facial expression with regular smiles. A genuine smile signals warmth and openness, making students feel comfortable approaching you. Nod in affirmation when students speak to show that their thoughts are valued and understood.

2. Open Body Language

Stand or sit in a relaxed posture with arms uncrossed and body slightly leaning forward when engaging with students. This conveys that you are fully present, approachable, and interested in what they have to say. Avoid rigid, closed-off body language, as it can create distance.

3. Encouraging Verbal Cues

Use positive reinforcement through language. Phrases like "That's a great question" or "I'm really glad you shared that thought" can help students feel appreciated. Using such language motivates them to participate more freely, knowing their contributions are valued.

4. Inclusive Classroom Interactions

Frequently ask open-ended questions that invite diverse opinions and thoughts. Rather than focusing on right or wrong answers, encourage students to explore different perspectives. This encourages a culture of dialogue where everyone's ideas are valued.

5. Non-judgmental Responses

When a student makes a mistake or gives an incorrect answer, respond with encouragement rather than criticism. Use language like, "That's an interesting approach; let's explore it together," which fosters a learning environment where students feel safe to take intellectual risks.

6. Active Listening

Practice active listening by giving your full attention when a student speaks. Maintain eye contact, avoid interrupting, and paraphrase their comments to show you understand. This helps in building trust and rapport, signaling that you genuinely care about their input.

7. Personalized Feedback

Give individualized feedback that acknowledges both strengths and areas for improvement. Avoid generic responses and focus on each student's unique progress. Personal feedback shows that you see them as individuals, which strengthens the teacher-student bond.

8. Fostering Peer Collaboration

Encourage group activities where students can share ideas and collaborate. As a facilitator, express admiration for teamwork and emphasize that learning is enhanced through shared knowledge. This shows that you value collective effort and are open to different ways of solving problems.

9. Being Approachable Outside Class

Openly invite students to approach you after class or during office hours. Make it clear through your words and demeanor that you are accessible, not just during lectures but whenever they need guidance or a listening ear. A casual, friendly tone when saying, "Feel free to drop by if you ever need help or just want to talk," fosters a welcoming atmosphere.

10. Cultivating Humor and Positivity

Use light humor and positive energy to create an atmosphere of ease. A laugh or smile, when appropriate, helps dissolve barriers and makes students feel at ease around you. This form of expression shows that while learning is serious, the process can also be enjoyable and stress-free.

Try some of these psychologically driven sentences in the classroom.

1. "I'm here to support you not just in your studies but in your personal growth—never hesitate to share your thoughts or concerns with me."

2. "Every question you ask, no matter how small, is important; it shows your willingness to learn, and that's what truly matters."

3. "Mistakes are a part of learning, and together, we'll turn every misstep into a stepping stone towards success."

4. "I believe in your potential, and my role is to help you see in yourself what I already see in you."

5. "Your voice matters in this classroom—whether it's an idea, a concern, or simply a curiosity, I want to hear it."

6. "I'm not just here to teach you the material but to learn from you as well—every one of you has something unique to offer."

7. "You are not competing against each other; you are each competing against your own potential, and I'm here to help you exceed it."

8. "Growth happens when we challenge ourselves, and I encourage you to step outside your comfort zone—you'll be surprised at what you can achieve."

9. "If something isn't clear, I'm always available to explain things in a different way; your understanding is my priority."

10. "This classroom is a space for open dialogue—no ideas are too big or too small, and together, we can explore them all."

Intimidating teacher

During my teaching career, I made efforts to be approachable by smiling, being playful, and treating students with respect while insisting on discipline during lessons. However, managing this balance was challenging, especially with a class size of about 55 students. I may have compounded the difficulty by introducing more complexity into certain concepts than necessary, which could have been intimidating for the average student. This, combined with my stringent evaluations and strict approach to classroom discipline, may have influenced my reputation—not in terms of my teaching quality but in how my approach was perceived by students.

I have observed signs that suggest my reputation as an intimidating teacher: some students avoid eye contact, steer clear of interactions, and even hide from me. Although many students greet me warmly, the avoidance by others is particularly disheartening, especially when I believe my intentions are to support their learning. This situation has led me to reflect on the emotional impact of my teaching methods. Over time, I have learned to manage my emotions and approach these students with increased empathy. I sometimes feel a sense of guilt for any discomfort I may have caused. Building a reputation as a teacher who is both effective and kind remains challenging. To address the impact of disciplinary stringency, I have focused on fostering positive interactions, such as initiating greetings and offering smiles, with the aim of balancing discipline with encouragement to create a more supportive learning environment.

Students, especially those who are shy or less confident, often feel intimidated by various factors when interacting with teachers. One significant source of intimidation is the teacher's depth of knowledge. While expertise is essential for guiding students through complex topics, it can also highlight gaps in their understanding, making them feel vulnerable. The teacher's ability to quickly identify mistakes or probe into areas where a student's knowledge is lacking can increase this sense of vulnerability. Additionally, the use of sophisticated language and advanced vocabulary, while necessary for clarity, can further heighten intimidation, especially if students struggle with the terminology.

Physical appearance and demeanor also shape the student-teacher dynamic. A teacher's tone of voice, facial expressions, and body language can either put students at ease or heighten their anxiety. For instance, a stern tone or serious expression may discourage students from asking questions or engaging fully. Similarly, a teacher's authoritative body language can, while necessary for classroom control, create a sense of unease, making the teacher seem less approachable.

Intimidation is often amplified by perceived differences between the teacher and students, whether intellectual, cultural, or linguistic. Such differences can create psychological barriers, inhibiting participation and questioning. For less confident students, these differences can exacerbate their sense of inadequacy, further distancing them from the learning process.

Moreover, authority, accomplishments, and popularity within the institution can add to the intimidation factor. Teachers in senior positions or with significant academic achievements may appear distant or unapproachable to students, who may fear repercussions for mistakes or feel inadequate in comparison. Popularity can also create pressure, as students might feel compelled to perform at higher standards to meet the expectations associated with the teacher's reputation.

Preconceived notions about a teacher—whether they are known as strict graders, disciplinarians, or brilliant scholars—further compound this issue. Students often enter the classroom with assumptions that shape their behavior, leading to a guarded and less open learning experience.

Recognizing these psychological dynamics, teachers can take deliberate steps to mitigate intimidation. Creating an inclusive classroom atmosphere that encourages open dialogue is essential. Teachers should be mindful of how their demeanor and language might be perceived and strive to be approachable. Normalizing mistakes as part of the learning process and framing them as opportunities for growth can ease student anxiety. Constructive feedback should focus on progress, not failure, fostering a more supportive learning environment.

Managing the pursuit of perfection in teaching is crucial. Teachers should promote a growth mindset, highlighting that progress matters more than perfection. Setting realistic expectations and encouraging students to embrace challenges reduces stress. Collaborative learning fosters shared responsibility, creating an inclusive environment for open discussions. Emotional support and empathy build positive relationships, making teachers approachable rather than intimidating. By balancing authority with warmth, teachers create a classroom where students feel empowered to engage and succeed. This supportive atmosphere encourages students to embrace challenges, leading to deeper learning and personal growth.

To help students see the teacher as a relatable human being while acknowledging their greater age, experience, and knowledge, consider incorporating the following tips:

1. Share Personal Stories: Occasionally share relevant personal anecdotes, including challenges and triumphs from your own learning journey. This demonstrates that you, too, have navigated difficulties and growth, making you more relatable.

2. Acknowledge Your Learning Journey: Discuss your own ongoing learning experiences and professional development. By showing that you are also continuously learning and evolving, you humanize yourself and model lifelong learning.

3. Express Your Passion: Clearly communicate your passion for the subject and for teaching. Share what excites you about the material and why you enjoy teaching it. Passion is contagious and helps students connect with you on a personal level.

4. Show Vulnerability: Occasionally admit when you don't have all the answers or when you make mistakes. This can help students see that it's okay to be imperfect and that learning is a process of growth.

5. Highlight Shared Interests: Engage students in conversations about common interests, hobbies, or activities. Finding common ground can help bridge the gap between you and your students, making you seem more approachable.

6. Be Open About Challenges: Discuss some of the difficulties you've faced in your career or personal life and how you've managed to overcome them. This can make you seem more human and less of an authority figure.

7. Use Humor: Incorporate appropriate humor into your teaching. Light-hearted jokes or amusing anecdotes can create a more

relaxed atmosphere and show students that you have a sense of humor.

8. Show Empathy: Demonstrate understanding and empathy towards students' struggles. Validate their feelings and provide support, showing that you care about their well-being and success.

9. Engage in Personal Reflection: Reflect on your own experiences and insights in class discussions or informal conversations. This helps students see your thought process and personal growth.

10. Encourage Mutual Respect: Emphasize that while you hold a position of authority, you respect your students as individuals with their own unique perspectives and contributions. This fosters a more balanced and respectful relationship.

Sharing Personal Failures and Lessons Learned: A Humanizing Approach for Teachers

Sharing personal stories of failure can significantly enhance a teacher's relatability and foster a supportive classroom environment. When teachers openly discuss their struggles and setbacks, they present themselves as approachable and human. For instance, a teacher who recounts a time when they struggled with a challenging project demonstrates that learning is a continuous journey, not exclusive to students. By narrating their own experiences, educators normalize challenges, illustrating that even experienced professionals encounter obstacles. Such transparency helps demystify the learning process and encourages students to view their difficulties as a natural part of growth. Teachers can highlight their resilience by sharing how they adapted after a lesson didn't go as planned, emphasizing that setbacks can lead to improved methodologies and insights.

Crafting these narratives requires honesty and authenticity, as teachers should candidly acknowledge their mistakes. This honesty builds trust and credibility in the classroom. By focusing on the lessons learned rather than the failures themselves, educators can articulate the steps taken to overcome challenges and refine their approaches. Integrating personal stories into relevant discussions can enhance learning without overshadowing the primary lesson. By encouraging student reflection on their own experiences with failure, teachers create a culture that values resilience, offering support and encouragement that empowers students to embrace challenges and persist in their academic endeavors. This approach ultimately enriches the learning experience and fosters personal and academic growth.

Moral Aggression and Teachers

One day, a student littered a paper on the road. I couldn't stand it and impulsively called the student to pick up the litter and put it in the dustbin. I am sure the student felt humiliated. That student doesn't attend my classes, he doesn't know me, and I don't know him. After the difficult interaction, the student must have hated me, and I felt sorry about it. Should I have confronted the student about littering or not? Why did I do it? That is called moral aggression, and I suffer from it a lot. Moral aggression, in the context of teaching, refers to a teacher's intense emotional response, often leading to strict or punitive actions, when a perceived moral standard is violated. It stems from a deep sense of righteousness or duty to uphold ethical norms within the classroom. While the intent behind moral aggression is often to maintain discipline or instill values, it can sometimes have unintended psychological consequences on students.

From a psychological standpoint, moral aggression arises when a teacher experiences cognitive dissonance between their moral beliefs and the students' behaviors. For instance, if a student cheats or shows disrespect, the teacher may experience frustration or anger, as these actions directly challenge the ethical code they aim to foster. The teacher's response may range from stern reprimands to harsher punitive measures, driven by a need to correct what they perceive as morally deviant behavior. This reaction, however, can lead to a cycle of negative reinforcement.

Psychologically, the repeated use of moral aggression can result in a counterproductive classroom environment. Students may respond to aggressive moral enforcement with fear, resentment, or disengagement. This dynamic inhibits open communication, stifles curiosity, and may foster an atmosphere where students comply out of fear rather than understanding. Moral aggression can alienate students, especially those with divergent perspectives or learning challenges, creating a divide between teacher and learner.

Furthermore, moral aggression can erode the teacher-student relationship, which is critical for effective teaching. According to attachment theory, a nurturing, secure bond fosters a learning environment where students feel safe to explore, make mistakes, and grow. Teachers who rely on moral aggression risk severing this bond, reducing students' intrinsic motivation to learn and develop ethical reasoning.

However, this does not mean that moral standards should be abandoned. Instead, teachers should adopt approaches grounded in empathy, moral reasoning, and restorative practices. Psychological research supports that positive reinforcement, combined with constructive dialogue, encourages moral development more effectively than punitive measures. Teachers can model the behaviors they wish to instill, guiding students toward ethical maturity through example rather than confrontation.

By understanding the psychological underpinnings of moral aggression, teachers can reflect on their disciplinary approaches and create an educational environment where ethical values are nurtured through empathy, reflection, and mutual respect rather than enforced through punitive means.

Pleasures, prides and pains of teaching

The profession of teaching, while inherently challenging, offers profound rewards that sustain and inspire educators. These moments of pride and fulfillment arise from witnessing student success and growth, which serve as a powerful affirmation of a teacher's dedication. Observing a struggling student finally grasp a complex concept or achieve a significant milestone validates the teacher's efforts, reinforcing the impact they can have on their students' lives.

Equally rewarding are the "aha" moments when students experience sudden clarity and understanding, marking the culmination of the teacher's guidance and patience. Such instances create a shared sense of triumph that strengthens the teacher-student bond. Additionally, positive feedback from students, parents, or colleagues can significantly enhance a teacher's sense of purpose. Whether through a simple thank-you or a heartfelt note of appreciation, these gestures of gratitude reinforce a teacher's commitment and sense of accomplishment, particularly when expressed by students who have been positively impacted.

Moreover, teachers derive immense satisfaction from igniting curiosity and passion within their students. When students express genuine interest in a subject or engage in insightful questioning, it indicates the teacher has succeeded in fostering a love for learning. This sense of awakening curiosity is among the most fulfilling experiences for educators. The relationships that teachers cultivate with their students further enrich their professional journey. As these relationships develop into mutual respect and trust, they create a positive and supportive learning environment. Teachers take pride in being trusted guides and mentors, and knowing they have made a difference in a student's life is profoundly rewarding.

Another significant aspect of teaching is witnessing students evolve into independent thinkers. When students begin to apply critical thinking skills and form their own opinions, it signals that the teacher has effectively empowered them. This intellectual independence represents a key educational goal and is a source of pride for educators. Additionally, teachers find satisfaction in their role in shaping the future. Every lesson imparted and skill taught contributes to the development of future leaders and innovators, adding a layer of pride to their profession.

The shared celebrations of achievements—such as graduations or successful projects—further solidify the joy of teaching. These moments recognize the collective efforts of both teachers and students, creating cherished memories that highlight hard work and perseverance. Ultimately, the pride and pleasure derived from teaching are intricately tied to the successes and happiness of students, providing educators with the motivation to navigate the profession's challenges.

However, the teaching profession is not without its challenges. Emotional exhaustion often arises from the substantial emotional investment teachers make in their students' development. This investment can be particularly draining when faced with disengaged or struggling students. Balancing a supportive classroom environment with the emotional labor required can lead to burnout. Furthermore, the administrative demands of teaching—such as lesson preparation, grading, and classroom management—can detract from the primary mission of education, contributing to feelings of being overwhelmed.

The pressure to continuously adapt to changing educational standards while addressing diverse student needs adds another layer of difficulty. Insufficient resources and support can lead to frustration, impacting teachers' morale and effectiveness. Additionally, external criticism from students, parents, and colleagues can accumulate, contributing to feelings of isolation and inadequacy. Teachers may face resentment from students regarding grading or discipline, as well as parental disagreements regarding teaching methods. These external pressures can erode job satisfaction and contribute to negative sentiments.

Moreover, systemic issues in the educational environment, such as inadequate resources and unrealistic demands, can exacerbate these challenges. The accumulation of negative feelings can affect teachers' morale and overall effectiveness. Addressing these issues is crucial for maintaining a positive teaching atmosphere and ensuring the well-being of educators. Despite the complexities and emotional toll of teaching, the enduring rewards serve as powerful motivators, reinforcing the critical role that teachers play in shaping the future.

Chapter 6: Teacher the philosopher and psychologist

Philosophy and psychology together form the cornerstone of effective teaching. Philosophy guides the content and objectives of what should be taught, grounding the curriculum in fundamental principles and values. It shapes the overarching goals and intellectual framework of education. On the other hand, psychology informs the methodologies and strategies of how to teach. It provides insights into learning processes, motivation, and student behavior, helping educators tailor their approaches to meet diverse needs. Thus, while philosophy directs the direction and purpose of education, psychology optimizes the methods and practices for delivering knowledge effectively.

Teaching Philosophy

Everything we study is philosophy at its core because all knowledge seeks to understand fundamental truths about existence, reality, and the principles governing human thought, behavior, and the natural world. In the realm of philosophy, a distinction must be made between various types of philosophical inquiry. Here, we focus on what could be termed "bare naked philosophy," which strips away religious, cultural, or regional biases to address the core aspects of truth. This approach delves into the fundamental questions of what constitutes truth, how to discern it, and why its dissemination is paramount. It operates under a framework of rigorous doubt and empirical inquiry rather than faith or tradition.

At its essence, bare naked philosophy is not concerned with religious dogmas or culturally specific beliefs. Instead, it pursues a universal quest for truth, seeking to understand reality in its most unadulterated form. It does not adhere to any preconceived notions or biases but rather starts with a blank slate, asking fundamental questions about the nature of existence and knowledge. This approach aligns with the philosophical principle of skepticism, epitomized by René Descartes' famous dictum, "*Dubito ergo cogito, cogito ergo sum*" (I doubt, therefore I think, I think, therefore I am). This statement underscores the process of self-reflection and doubt as foundational to the pursuit of knowledge. Would you prefer to believe first and then doubt, or doubt first and then believe? Embracing doubt as the initial step is a more rigorous path to uncovering the truth. By questioning and challenging assumptions before settling on beliefs, we engage in a thorough examination of validity. This approach, though arduous, demands critical thinking and rigorous scrutiny, paving the way for more authentic understanding. Belief without doubt often leads to unexamined acceptance, whereas doubt fosters a deeper pursuit of truth through careful evaluation and analysis. Thus, while doubting may be difficult, it is the pathway to genuine and reliable knowledge.

Young students, being impressionable, often face significant indoctrination, which discourages questioning and fosters blind acceptance. This approach stifles deeper learning and critical thinking. As educators, our responsibility extends beyond mere instruction; we must guide students to rediscover the essence of genuine inquiry. We need to help them break free from imposed beliefs and encourage them to seek knowledge actively and independently. By reopening their minds to exploration and doubt, we counteract the limitations of indoctrination and foster a more profound and authentic understanding of the world. This process is crucial for developing thoughtful, inquisitive learners.

Finding and Evaluating Truth

The quest for truth in bare naked philosophy begins with doubt—an essential tool for peeling away layers of assumptions and misconceptions. Doubt forces us to question the veracity of our beliefs and the reliability of our sources of information. This process involves rigorous analysis and critical thinking, where the goal is not merely to accept information at face value but to scrutinize its validity through logical reasoning and empirical evidence.

To find truth, bare naked philosophy employs a methodical approach that includes observation, experimentation, and logical deduction. It seeks to understand reality through objective means, minimizing the influence of subjective biases and personal beliefs. The evaluation of truth is thus grounded in evidence and rational analysis rather than in preconceived ideologies or emotional responses. This method ensures that the pursuit of knowledge remains focused on objective realities rather than subjective interpretations.

Spreading Truth and Its Importance

Once truth is discerned, the next step is to spread it. The dissemination of truth serves several critical functions in society. It fosters intellectual growth, promotes informed decision-making, and helps build a more rational and just world. Spreading truth is not merely about imparting knowledge but about encouraging a culture of inquiry and critical thinking. It challenges individuals to think independently, question assumptions, and engage in meaningful dialogue.

The importance of spreading truth lies in its role in advancing human understanding and progress. When individuals and societies base their actions and beliefs on verified truths rather than falsehoods or unfounded opinions, they contribute to a more enlightened and equitable world. This process helps combat misinformation and fosters a more informed public, which is crucial for addressing complex global issues and fostering constructive societal change.

Bare naked philosophy represents a pursuit of truth that is free from religious, cultural, or regional constraints. It emphasizes the use of doubt and empirical inquiry to find and evaluate truth, and it underscores the importance of spreading truth for the betterment of society. By adhering to the principles of skepticism and rational analysis, bare naked philosophy offers a robust framework for understanding reality and contributing to a more informed and equitable world. In this quest, the focus remains on the essence of truth itself, unencumbered by extraneous factors, allowing for a clear and objective exploration of the fundamental nature of existence and knowledge.

Philosophy serves as the foundational framework that shapes and guides the educational process, transcending mere abstraction to influence every aspect of teaching and learning. To fully appreciate the significance of teaching, one must explore the philosophical underpinnings that give it purpose and direction. At its essence, philosophy tackles fundamental questions regarding knowledge, reality, and values, prompting inquiries such as: What constitutes knowledge? How do we ascertain what we know? What are the aims of education? Engaging with these inquiries empowers educators to deliver content effectively while inspiring students to seek deeper understanding.

To teach without philosophy is to miss the essence of what it means to educate. Philosophy breathes life into teaching, providing it with meaning, direction, and depth. Moreover, a teaching philosophy involves reflective consideration of the values and goals that guide educational practices. By contemplating questions about what educators aim to achieve and which values they wish to instill in students, teachers can clarify their educational purpose. This clarity is crucial for creating meaningful learning experiences. Without a philosophical foundation, education risks devolving into a series of disconnected tasks, rendering it mechanical and devoid of deeper significance. Philosophy encourages critical thinking, allowing educators to challenge established norms and innovate their methods. Ultimately, a teacher who engages with philosophy transcends the role of mere instructor to become a mentor, fostering a dynamic learning environment where both educator and student embark on a journey of discovery and growth.

Teaching with psychology

Psychology, the scientific study of the mind and behavior, provides crucial insights into how students learn, develop, and interact. Without this foundational knowledge, a teacher's ability to connect with and effectively educate their students can be significantly hindered. At its heart, psychology illuminates the intricate processes underlying learning and development. It offers valuable perspectives on cognitive functions, emotional regulation, motivation, and social interactions—each of which plays a critical role in the educational experience. A teacher who is unaware of these psychological principles may struggle to address the diverse needs of their students, potentially leading to ineffective teaching practices and diminished student engagement.

Teaching is the only profession that consistently involves engaging with a large number of people over extended periods. If teachers genuinely connect with each student, their influence becomes significant. Over time, the teacher develops an ability to read students—understanding their motivations, challenges, and potential. While this reading may not be flawless, the likelihood of accurately assessing a student's needs, strengths, and weaknesses improves as the relationship evolves. This ongoing interaction allows teachers to adjust their approach, enhancing the overall learning experience and fostering meaningful connections that can shape the student's personal and academic growth. Consider the diverse range of learning styles and cognitive processes that students bring into the classroom. Psychological theories, such as Howard Gardner's Multiple Intelligences or Jean Piaget's stages of cognitive development, provide teachers with frameworks to understand and accommodate these variations. By integrating these insights, educators can tailor their teaching methods to better align with students' individual learning preferences, thus enhancing their educational experience.

Motivation, another crucial psychological factor, greatly influences student engagement and performance. Understanding motivational theories, such as intrinsic versus extrinsic motivation or self-determination theory, enables teachers to design strategies that foster a deeper commitment to learning. For instance, incorporating elements that tap into students' interests and providing opportunities for autonomy can significantly boost their motivation and enthusiasm for the subject matter.

Additionally, psychological insights into emotional and behavioral development are vital for creating a supportive learning environment. A teacher who recognizes the impact of emotional well-being on learning can better address issues such as anxiety, self-esteem, and interpersonal conflicts. Implementing strategies to support emotional resilience and positive self-concept can facilitate a more inclusive and conducive learning atmosphere.

Classroom management, an essential component of effective teaching, also benefits from psychological understanding. Techniques informed by psychological research, such as positive reinforcement, setting clear expectations, and understanding behavioral triggers, can help maintain a respectful and productive classroom environment. By addressing the root causes of misbehavior and promoting positive interactions, teachers can create a space where all students feel valued and motivated to learn.

Furthermore, psychology offers insights into developmental stages, helping teachers tailor their approaches to the cognitive and emotional capacities of different age groups. Recognizing that younger students may require more concrete and guided instruction while older students benefit from abstract thinking and independent problem-solving allows teachers to adapt their strategies effectively.

The integration of psychological principles into teaching practices transforms the educational experience from a one-size-fits-all approach to a more nuanced and responsive process. It equips teachers with the tools to understand and meet the diverse needs of their students, fostering an environment where learning is both effective and enriching.

The knowledge of psychological principles is not merely supplementary but integral to the art and science of teaching. It empowers educators to connect more deeply with their students, to address their diverse needs, and to create a learning environment that promotes growth, engagement, and success. Embracing psychology in teaching is not just an enhancement—it is a fundamental necessity for those who aspire to inspire and educate effectively.

Overcoming Biases, Beliefs, and Norms

What we see is often shaped by what we want to see, revealing the complex relationship between sensing and perception. Sensing is the raw, unfiltered experience of stimuli from the external world, but perception is where interpretation happens, colored by personal desires, emotions, and immediate needs. Our perception tends to align with our self-interest in the present moment, skewing our understanding of reality. This bias is a natural inclination rooted in our evolutionary history as animals.

Like other animals, human brains are wired for immediate survival, driven by instincts to address present needs and threats. However, human evolution has brought culture and civilization, requiring long-term, collective thinking. This creates tension between our instinctual responses and the expectations of society, which values objectivity and future-oriented decision-making.

Biases, natural cognitive shortcuts, help us navigate the world but distort reality when unchecked. In professional settings like medicine, education, or law, biases undermine fairness and rationality. Recognizing this conflict between instinct and societal expectations is crucial for balanced decision-making and maintaining personal and professional integrity.

Biases are an inherent part of human nature. We naturally favor those who resemble us, share our identity, or are familiar to us. While people are quick to recognize biases in others, they often overlook their own, akin to criticizing others' outfits while unaware of a stain on their own shirt. Despite believing we've conquered bias, it resurfaces regularly, making self-awareness crucial.

In professional settings, especially for teachers, managing biases is essential. Teachers shape the developing minds of students, influencing their perceptions of learning and fairness. If a teacher unconsciously favors certain students, it can skew academic experiences, affecting students' self-esteem and reinforcing inequality. A biased learning environment diminishes fairness and limits educational outcomes, perpetuating stereotypes.

Thus, teachers must actively acknowledge and address their biases to foster an equitable, supportive atmosphere. This vigilance ensures all students receive equal attention and opportunities, shaping both their academic and social development. By doing so, teachers uphold the principles of fairness and merit, helping to build a more inclusive, thoughtful learning environment that supports the growth of all students. The long-term effects of bias-checking are profound, contributing to better learning outcomes and a more just society.

In my early years of teaching, there was a student who constantly misbehaved in class—talking during lessons, distracting others, and showing little respect for the rules. Naturally, I became biased against him. I was stricter with him than with others, always anticipating disruption and almost expecting failure. My teaching style toward him became more about maintaining discipline than fostering learning. I justified it at the time, thinking I was keeping the class in order, but looking back, I realize I was letting my frustration dictate my response.

This went on for a few weeks, and while I felt justified in my actions, something gnawed at me. I noticed that while other students were improving, this particular student remained stagnant, disconnected, and perhaps even more unruly. It dawned on me that my bias was not helping him—it was perpetuating the cycle of negativity. It took time, but I learned to approach each day with a fresh perspective. I made a conscious effort not to carry the past into the present. Every day became a new opportunity for each student, regardless of past behavior. With this shift, I began seeing changes. The once disruptive student started engaging more, slowly but surely. Over time, it was clear I had not conceded but won him over. What seemed like leniency at first was actually the beginning of a better teacher-student relationship. My bias had blinded me, but by giving him a fair chance each day, I allowed him to show his potential, and in doing so, I felt better. But I have to remind myself and check on my biases every day!

Problems of Overcoming Biases

Teachers, like all individuals, are influenced by cognitive biases, which skew judgment and decision-making. For example, confirmation bias can cause educators to favor information that aligns with their beliefs, neglecting diverse perspectives. Emotional investment in teaching methods and personal beliefs can also create resistance to change, as cognitive dissonance arises when these are challenged. This resistance is often exacerbated by a bias toward traditional methods, which hinders the adoption of innovative teaching strategies. Additionally, deep-seated cultural, religious, or moral values may influence teaching styles, potentially clashing with the need for inclusive education. Teachers must learn to separate personal beliefs from their professional responsibilities to offer a balanced learning environment. Ethical dilemmas, especially when personal beliefs conflict with educational content, add to this complexity, requiring careful navigation between integrity and duty. Finally, teachers' perceptions of authority and discipline can further complicate the integration of progressive, student-centered approaches into modern classrooms.

Problems of Overcoming Norms

Cultural and institutional norms heavily influence teaching practices, often creating barriers to innovation. Teachers may struggle to challenge these norms due to societal expectations or institutional pressures, such as the emphasis on rote learning and standardized testing. Fear of repercussions, including concerns about job security, professional reputation, or conflicts with colleagues, can further discourage deviation from established practices. This apprehension can stifle the adoption of progressive teaching methods. Additionally, the lack of institutional and peer support can lead to isolation and frustration, making it difficult for educators to embrace new ideas or challenge outdated norms effectively.

Psychological Turmoil for Teachers

Cognitive dissonance occurs when teachers encounter evidence that contradicts their established beliefs, causing internal conflict and stress. This can lead to emotional strain as they confront biases feeling insecure as they integrate new ideas into their teaching. Professional uncertainty also arises when teachers deviate from norms, often leading to self-doubt and fear of criticism. Furthermore, identity conflict may emerge as teachers struggle to align their personal values with professional responsibilities. These challenges require emotional resilience, openness to new perspectives, and institutional support to foster professional growth and contribute to a more progressive educational environment.

Should the Teacher Teach Truth or Stick by Belief or Bias?

The question of whether a teacher should prioritize teaching truth or adhere to personal beliefs and biases is a complex and multifaceted issue that touches on ethical, pedagogical, and psychological dimensions. This discussion involves examining the roles and responsibilities of educators in fostering a rigorous and objective learning environment while navigating their own personal convictions and potential biases.

The Case for Teaching Truth

1. Academic Integrity: Educators must provide accurate, evidence-based information, fostering critical thinking and ensuring academic integrity. This objectivity enables students to evaluate information independently.

2. Intellectual Growth: Teaching truth promotes curiosity and solid intellectual foundations, preparing students to engage with complex issues in an informed manner.

3. Ethical Responsibility: Teachers have an ethical duty to avoid misinformation. Presenting evidence-based knowledge fosters trust and upholds professional standards.

4. Adapting to Change: Truth-centered teaching encourages adaptability, ensuring that educators remain updated with evolving knowledge and emerging discoveries.

The Case for Sticking by Belief or Bias

1. Personal Integrity: Teachers' personal beliefs can shape their teaching style. For some, adhering to these beliefs reflects authenticity and integrity in their professional practice.

2. Cultural Sensitivity: Cultural and contextual factors influence beliefs, requiring teachers to respect community norms while balancing educational content and cultural diversity.

3. Motivational Factors: Personal convictions can inspire students, allowing teachers to create an engaging and passionate learning environment that fosters interest in the subject matter.

4. Ethical Dilemmas: Teachers may face challenges balancing personal beliefs with professional duties, particularly when handling controversial topics objectively.

Reflective Methods to Pursue Truth in Teaching

Pursuing truth in teaching requires a multifaceted approach that emphasizes critical self-assessment and engagement with diverse perspectives. Critical self-assessment involves regularly evaluating one's teaching practices, content delivery, and the accuracy of the information presented. For instance, after each class, educators can review lecture notes alongside student feedback to identify inaccuracies or biases in the content. This ongoing reflection allows teachers to make necessary adjustments, ensuring that their lessons align with established facts and evidence. Engaging in peer review further enhances this process. By collaborating with colleagues to observe each other's classes and critique teaching materials, educators can gain valuable insights into their methodologies. Participation in a peer observation program fosters an environment of constructive feedback, allowing teachers to refine their approaches and correct potential biases.

Incorporating diverse perspectives is essential for presenting a balanced understanding of subjects, particularly when addressing controversial topics. Teachers can enhance their curriculum by integrating multiple viewpoints and encouraging student inquiry, creating a classroom atmosphere where students are invited to ask questions and explore alternative explanations. Utilizing evidence-based resources, such as recent academic journals and reputable textbooks, reinforces the integrity of the content delivered. Maintaining a reflective journal enables educators to document their thoughts and observations throughout the semester, facilitating a deeper understanding of their teaching effectiveness. Furthermore, soliciting regular student feedback through anonymous surveys helps address any issues related to clarity and relevance, promoting a culture of open dialogue. By challenging personal biases through self-examination and bias training, teachers can ensure their instruction remains objective. Ultimately, these reflective methods not only enhance the pursuit of truth but also foster an educational environment that prioritizes critical thinking and continuous improvement.

Chapter 7: The Purposeful Showmanship

Showmanship

Teaching is as much about performance as it is about imparting knowledge. The concept of showmanship in teaching involves employing various strategies that engage students, enhance learning, and make the educational experience memorable and impactful. Rooted in psychological principles, these strategies can transform a standard lecture into a dynamic and interactive experience.

"Good teaching is one-fourth preparation and three-fourths pure theater" - Gail Godwin.

Don't tell me you don't know how to act. We are all actors. We have been practicing deception and pretension since we were about two years old. We persuade others to get what we want or to conceal our desires. Acting is part of life, often driven by self-interest. There is nothing wrong with it as long as it doesn't harm others. As teachers, however, we must elevate our acting—not for self-interest but to help learners absorb the knowledge we impart. This kind of acting is more challenging and less natural, as it requires selflessness. Like actors on stage, we can develop this skill through practice. Initially, it feels awkward and may even lead to embarrassment, but once we overcome that phase and shed our shyness and ego, acting becomes natural, forming part of the teacher's persona.

Showmanship involves arousing emotions in varying degrees based on the context, using actions, speech, expression, and body language. Like a magician, a teacher must master the art of guiding focus and directing attention to key points. Just as a magician mesmerizes with a sleight of hand and leaves the audience in awe, a teacher can captivate students, making learning an experience of wonder and curiosity.

One day in a class, I was describing the enormous amounts of food humans consume. I said, "I am not an avid eater or particularly obsessed with food. I just need something to fill my stomach, as long as it has some texture and doesn't taste bad. I rarely eat at the canteen; I usually bring food from home. However, last week, I visited the campus canteen. There was a sale of a new dish, limited to only 100 servings. Somehow, the placard caught my attention, and I was intrigued. I can't remember the name of the dish; the name sounded exotic. I had recently read some motivational lines about how one wouldn't know without trying something new, so I pushed myself to step out of my comfort zone. Normally, I stick to my usual choices to avoid surprises, but that day, I encouraged myself to take a chance on this novel dish. With only eight servings left, I was lucky to get one. I collected my food and sat down. The dish looked exotic—truly mouthwatering. When I cut into it, juices flowed over the knife. That was all fine, but the first bite—well, that was something else. I've never tasted anything so exquisite in my life. It was like my long-dormant taste buds came alive, dancing to techno music. The second bite only amplified the experience, drowning me in the luxury of flavors. I'm not sure how or when it happened, but my plate was empty, and I was left stunned, craving more."

I used this fabricated food story to captivate my students, making them drool over a dish that never existed. As I described the dish—its exotic look, the juices flowing, the first bite that awakened long-dormant taste buds—I noticed their attention shifting from the lesson to the imaginary plate of food. Their eyes widened, and I could almost see their mouths watering. By crafting the vivid details with care, I tapped into their senses, knowing well that even a simple story, if told passionately, could make them crave something purely imaginary. The power of words alone created that hunger. You can evoke emotions in students by talking about almost anything, real or fictional. The key lies in how the story is told—whether it resonates with them on a deeper level. I often use real-life stories because they naturally carry authentic emotions and relatable experiences. When these stories are shared with sincerity, students connect to the underlying humanity, which makes the lesson more impactful. For instance, when discussing diseases, I use images of real patients (without identities) and their suffering. This not only captures their attention but also cultivates empathy. Such visuals and narratives are powerful tools to help students grasp the gravity of the issues at hand, fostering a personal connection to the subject. Over time, these emotional triggers serve as motivational drivers, encouraging students to pursue their studies with the intent to make meaningful contributions. By linking facts to emotions, the classroom becomes a space for learning and emotional engagement.

(i) In the Use of Arms and Fingers:

1. Expressiveness: Use hand gestures to emphasize key points. Wide, open gestures convey excitement or importance, while subtle movements can guide students' focus.

2. Precision: Pointing with a single finger can direct attention to specific items or areas on the board or screen, ensuring clarity in explanation.

3. Variety: Avoid repetitive gestures. Change up your hand movements to keep the audience visually engaged.

4. Visualizing Concepts: Use your hands to "illustrate" ideas or concepts. For example, show contrast by spreading your arms wide or indicate connection by bringing your fingers together.

5. Inclusiveness: Sweep your arms across the room occasionally to make the whole class feel included, symbolically inviting everyone into the discussion.

(ii) In the Tone and Voice:

1. Volume Control: Adjust the volume of your voice for different effects. Louder tones signal importance or urgency, while softer tones invite reflection or emphasize intimacy.

2. Pacing: Vary your speech speed. Slower pacing builds suspense and allows students to digest complex information, while faster pacing can energize the class.

3. Pauses: Strategic pauses create anticipation and give students time to process information. Silence can be as powerful as words.

4. Pitch Variation: Use higher pitches to express excitement or curiosity and lower pitches to convey seriousness or authority.

5. Clarity: Enunciate clearly, especially when introducing new terms or complex ideas. This ensures students grasp every concept you're delivering.

(iii) In the Movements of the Legs:

1. Purposeful Movement: Walk around the classroom to engage different parts of the room and create an interactive atmosphere. Don't stand still for too long.

2. Anchoring: Occasionally, stand still during critical explanations to give the impression of stability and focus. It signals that this is a moment to pay close attention.

3. Pacing: Slow, deliberate pacing during explanations can show deep thought, while more dynamic movements can suggest enthusiasm and energy.

4. Positioning: Shift positions to maintain the attention of all students, especially those sitting in the back or corners of the room. Moving closer to students can also create a sense of intimacy.

5. Balance: Maintain a balanced posture to project confidence. Avoid fidgeting or unnecessary leg movements that could distract from your message.

(iv) In the Eyes:

1. Eye Contact: Make frequent eye contact with individual students to engage them directly. This conveys confidence and encourages participation.

2. Scanning: Regularly scan the entire room with your eyes to ensure all students feel seen and included, preventing any feeling of detachment.

3. Focus: Use focused eye contact to emphasize key points. When delivering critical information, lock eyes on specific students to enhance the impact.

4. Expression: Use your eyes to express emotions. Wide eyes can show excitement or surprise, while narrowed eyes may indicate focus or seriousness.

5. Observation: Continuously observe students' facial expressions and body language to gauge their understanding and adjust your delivery accordingly.

(v) In the Persona:

1. Confidence: Cultivate a confident persona by projecting assurance in your body language and speech, which makes students more likely to trust and follow your lead.

2. Authenticity: Be genuine in your interactions. Students can sense authenticity, and being true to yourself creates a more meaningful connection.

3. Adaptability: Adjust your persona based on the situation. Sometimes, you may need to be a strict authority figure, while at other times, a relaxed, humorous approach may be more effective.

4. Positivity: Maintain a positive demeanor, even in challenging moments. A positive attitude fosters a more productive and open learning environment.

5. Empathy: Show empathy in your tone and body language. A teacher who cares about their students' emotions and struggles builds trust and encourages engagement.

These tips aim to enhance a teacher's ability to create an engaging, memorable, and effective learning experience through conscious control of body language, voice, and presence.

A teacher should embody the spirit of a child while engaging with students, fostering an environment of curiosity, playfulness, and exploration. By adopting this approach, the teacher connects with students on their level, breaking down formal barriers that can hinder active learning. However, unlike a child who plays for fun, the teacher has a singular objective: to inspire and motivate students to learn. This requires the teacher to balance the spontaneity of play with the structured intention of guiding students toward knowledge.

When a teacher becomes an active participant in the learning process, mirroring the students' energy and enthusiasm, it creates a more dynamic and engaging atmosphere. The students are more likely to open up, ask questions, and explore new ideas. At the same time, the teacher steers the play towards learning outcomes, ensuring that the students remain focused on the educational goals, all while enjoying the process.

Showmanship Tips for Teachers Based on "Becoming the Child"

1. Mirror Student Energy: Match the enthusiasm and curiosity of your students. Use animated expressions, gestures, and playful language to engage them, making learning feel more like an adventure than a task.

2. Create Playful Scenarios: Turn lessons into games or challenges. Encourage students to approach problems like puzzles to be solved, fostering a fun yet focused atmosphere.

3. Use Humor Strategically: Light humor and jokes can break the ice and make the learning environment more comfortable. A well-timed joke or playful remark can relieve tension and keep students' attention. In the initial stages of teaching, our humor may fail us. But we have to practice it, and over time, it becomes natural.

4. Encourage Open Exploration: Just as a child explores without fear of failure, create an environment where students feel safe to try, fail, and learn. This builds their confidence and willingness to engage with challenging topics.

5. Be Spontaneous Yet Purposeful: Act spontaneously in your interactions, but always guide the conversation or activity towards the lesson's objectives. Maintain a balance between the joy of discovery and structured learning.

Below are ten key techniques that educators can incorporate into their teaching practice to maximize effectiveness.

1. Storytelling

Storytelling is a powerful tool in teaching, as it engages students' emotions and cognitive faculties simultaneously. Stories have the unique ability to make abstract or complex concepts more relatable and memorable. When teachers integrate storytelling into their lectures, they not only capture students' attention but also facilitate deeper understanding and retention of the material.

2. Emotional Engagement

Emotional engagement is essential for fostering a connection between the student and the subject matter. When teachers convey enthusiasm and passion for the topic, students are more likely to mirror those emotions, leading to increased motivation and interest in the learning process. This emotional connection can also help students develop a lasting affinity for the subject.

3. Gestures and Body Language

Non-verbal communication, including gestures and body language, plays a crucial role in teaching. Effective use of hand movements, facial expressions, and posture can reinforce verbal communication and convey enthusiasm. This dynamic form of expression helps maintain student attention and reinforces key teaching points.

4. Vocal Modulation

The way a teacher uses their voice can significantly impact student engagement. By varying tone, pitch, and pace, teachers can emphasize important information, create suspense, and maintain student interest throughout the lecture. This vocal variety keeps the content from becoming monotonous, ensuring that students remain attentive.

5. Interactive Techniques

Interactive techniques, such as posing questions, encouraging discussions, and using group activities, promote active learning. These methods engage students directly, encouraging them to think critically and participate in the learning process. Interaction also helps students feel more connected to the material and to their peers, fostering a collaborative learning environment.

6. Appearance and Dress

A teacher's appearance can influence how they are perceived by students. Dressing professionally and appropriately commands respect and establishes authority. It also sets a positive tone for the classroom environment. While appearance should not overshadow content, it contributes to the overall impression a teacher makes, which can impact student engagement and respect.

7. Positive Expression

Facial expressions and body language that exude positivity can create a welcoming and encouraging atmosphere in the classroom. A teacher who smiles, makes eye contact, and demonstrates enthusiasm for the subject matter can inspire similar attitudes in students. This positivity not only makes the classroom a more enjoyable place but also encourages student participation and openness to learning.

8. Odor and Hygiene

Personal hygiene and the use of a subtle, pleasant fragrance can contribute to a comfortable learning environment. While often overlooked, these aspects are important as they ensure that the teacher's presence is not a distraction but rather a complement to the learning experience. A well-groomed appearance and attention to personal scent can enhance the overall classroom ambience .

9. Use of Humor

Humor, when used appropriately, is a powerful tool in the classroom. It helps to reduce stress, creates a more relaxed atmosphere, and makes the learning process more enjoyable. Humor can also serve as a mnemonic device, helping students remember concepts associated with funny or surprising moments in the lecture.

10. Clear Structure and Analogies

A well-organized presentation reduces cognitive load, making it easier for students to process and retain information. Clear structure, combined with the use of analogies and metaphors, simplifies complex concepts by linking them to familiar ideas. This approach not only aids comprehension but also makes learning more accessible and less intimidating for students.

"Show without showing" is a pedagogical strategy that employs descriptive language and emotion to evoke vivid imagery and deep understanding in students. By using metaphorical expressions and emotional resonance, teachers can engage learners' senses and imagination, fostering a richer comprehension of concepts while encouraging personal connections to the material.

1. Literature Analysis: Instead of stating that a character is sad, a teacher might describe the character's actions and surroundings: "She stood at the window, watching raindrops race down the glass, her heart heavy as if each droplet carried the weight of her unspoken dreams." This vivid imagery allows students to feel the character's sadness without directly stating it.

2. Science Concept: When explaining the process of photosynthesis, rather than simply stating facts, a teacher might describe it as follows: "Imagine a leaf as a tiny factory, tirelessly converting sunlight into energy. Each green cell hums with life, capturing golden rays and breathing in carbon dioxide, transforming it into sweet sustenance that nourishes the entire plant." This approach brings the concept to life, making it more relatable and engaging.

As teachers, our aim is to nurture students' imagination and critical thinking, not to guide them through every step. If we "peel the banana" for them, we limit their ability to think independently. Instead, we should merely hint at the "banana's" location, encouraging students to explore, discover, and solve problems on their own. This approach fosters self-directed learning, empowering students to take responsibility for their education. By creating an environment that values curiosity and exploration, teachers help shape individuals who are not only knowledgeable but also capable of navigating real-world challenges with creativity and independence.

As teachers, our role is to transform individuals into independent, creative, and driven citizens. This responsibility extends beyond simply transmitting knowledge; it involves shaping students' ability to think critically, solve problems, and approach life with curiosity and initiative. Fostering independence means encouraging students to explore, question, and take ownership of their learning. By providing opportunities for self-discovery and critical thinking, we prepare them to navigate real-world complexities with confidence and competence.

Creativity and drive are equally important. In a rapidly changing world, creative thinkers who can adapt, innovate, and persevere are essential. Teachers play a crucial role in nurturing this creativity by promoting an environment that values exploration, experimentation, and resilience. Additionally, inspiring students with a sense of purpose and connecting their learning to real-world applications instills the drive to pursue personal and academic goals with determination. Ultimately, our teaching shapes not just academically capable individuals but well-rounded citizens who can contribute meaningfully to society.

Instructor presence in the classroom

The power position

In the classroom, a teacher's power position is intricately tied to their stance and presence. This concept transcends mere physical posture and encompasses how a teacher's demeanor and approach can influence classroom dynamics. A teacher's stance—whether authoritative, approachable, or neutral—directly impacts their interaction with students and the learning environment.

When a teacher adopts an authoritative stance characterized by upright posture, deliberate gestures, and steady eye contact, they project confidence and control. This presence establishes a clear boundary of respect and sets the tone for a structured learning atmosphere. Conversely, an approachable stance, often marked by open body language, relaxed posture, and empathetic gestures, fosters an environment of trust and openness. This can encourage student participation and create a supportive learning space.

The power position also involves how a teacher navigates the physical space of the classroom. Moving with purpose and engaging with students individually or in groups helps maintain authority while being accessible. Balancing these elements— assertiveness and approachability—ensures that the teacher's presence is both commanding and inviting. This equilibrium is crucial for managing classroom behavior, promoting engagement, and fostering a productive educational environment.

The mingling

Mingling with students is a vital aspect of teaching that extends beyond traditional instruction. When a teacher actively interacts with students—moving around the classroom, engaging in casual conversations, and showing genuine interest in their lives—it humanizes the learning experience and fosters a sense of connection. This mingling allows teachers to assess individual understanding in real time, offer tailored support, and build rapport. It also encourages students to feel valued and heard, thereby enhancing their motivation and engagement. By integrating this personal interaction into their teaching strategy, educators create a more dynamic and inclusive learning environment that goes beyond mere academic instruction.

The smile and playfulness

The smile is one of humanity's greatest inventions. It immediately conveys that there is no threat or harmful intent, signifying that we are approaching with a friendly gesture. Many conflicts and misunderstandings have been averted at the mere flash of a smile. The smile and playfulness of a teacher are powerful tools that significantly impact the classroom environment. Psychologically, a genuine smile fosters a positive emotional climate, reducing students' anxiety and creating an atmosphere of warmth and approachability. Playfulness, on the other hand, stimulates curiosity and engagement, making learning more enjoyable and less intimidating. This light-hearted approach can break down barriers, encourage creativity, and enhance students' willingness to participate. By incorporating smiles and playful interactions into their teaching, educators not only make the learning experience more pleasant but also strengthen students' emotional and cognitive connections to the material.

The lightness projection

The lightness projection by a teacher refers to the ability to infuse a classroom with a sense of ease and positivity. This involves more than just a cheerful demeanor; it encompasses a genuine, approachable attitude that reduces anxiety and fosters a conducive learning environment. Psychologically, such an atmosphere alleviates stress and encourages students to engage more freely. When teachers project lightness, they diminish the barriers of fear and resistance, making the classroom a space where students feel safe to explore and participate. This projection of lightness not only enhances learning but also builds a positive rapport, which is crucial for effective teaching and student well-being. In a semester, I dedicate two or three hours just to talking about lighter topics related to the course, sometimes even unrelated topics. Just to engage and connect with the students. It is a way for me to yield to the students but make a benefit out of it.

The humility and humbleness in person

Humility and humbleness in a teacher's persona are essential for fostering a supportive and respectful learning environment. Psychologically, these traits create an atmosphere where students feel valued and understood, reducing barriers to communication and learning. When teachers exhibit humility, they acknowledge their own limitations and are open to students' perspectives, which promotes a collaborative and inclusive classroom dynamic. This openness encourages students to engage more freely and take intellectual risks. Humbleness in teaching also builds trust and respect, which is essential for a positive student-teacher relationship. Ultimately, these qualities help in creating a nurturing environment where students feel empowered to learn and grow.

The vastness of knowledge

A teacher's vast knowledge is pivotal in guiding and inspiring students, yet the continuous evolution of information necessitates constant upgrading. Psychologically, a teacher's expansive knowledge base builds credibility and fosters trust, as students perceive their instructor as a competent and reliable source of information. However, the rapid advancement in various fields means that even the most knowledgeable teacher must regularly update their understanding to maintain relevance. This commitment to lifelong learning not only ensures that the teacher remains at the cutting edge of their discipline but also models a growth mindset for students, highlighting the value of ongoing education and intellectual curiosity.

The greatness of intelligence

Intelligence in teaching is not merely about possessing knowledge but about continually honing cognitive and pedagogical skills through consistent practice. Psychologically, intelligence is dynamic and requires active engagement to sustain and enhance its effectiveness. For teachers, this means regularly practicing critical thinking, problem-solving, and adaptive teaching methods to remain effective. Constant practice ensures that teachers can effectively navigate diverse classroom challenges, fostering an environment that stimulates student learning and growth. This iterative process not only sharpens the teacher's intellect but also reinforces their role as a facilitator of knowledge, ultimately benefiting both their professional development and student outcomes.

The openness to learn

Openness to learning, regardless of the source, is a hallmark of effective teaching. Psychologically, this openness is crucial for fostering a growth mindset, which emphasizes the ability to develop intelligence and skills through effort and learning. For teachers, embracing new knowledge from any source—be it students, peers, or even children—encourages intellectual humility and adaptability. This willingness to learn enriches the teacher's understanding and enhances their ability to connect with students on a deeper level.

When teachers remain receptive to learning from students, they not only model lifelong learning but also build a more dynamic and responsive classroom environment. Students often bring fresh perspectives, innovative ideas, and novel approaches that can challenge and expand a teacher's existing knowledge. A teacher who values and integrates these insights demonstrates respect for students' contributions, which can boost student engagement and motivation.

Furthermore, this openness reflects psychological principles of reciprocal learning and social interaction. It fosters a collaborative learning atmosphere where knowledge is shared and constructed collectively. Such an environment not only benefits the teacher's professional growth but also creates a richer, more inclusive educational experience for students, ultimately enhancing the overall teaching and learning dynamic.

Building a persona of the class

Creating a strong and positive academic culture within a class is pivotal for the collective success of the students. The concept of building a "persona of the class" refers to the cultivation of a shared identity, values, and expectations that define the group's approach to learning and collaboration. This collective persona can significantly enhance the academic culture, motivating students to perform better and fostering a supportive and engaged learning environment.

To establish this class persona, a teacher can begin by setting clear and high expectations for academic behavior, effort, and respect for one another. This includes defining what success looks like for the class as a whole—whether it's achieving certain academic milestones, developing critical thinking skills, or engaging in respectful discourse. Encouraging students to take ownership of these expectations can instill a sense of pride and collective responsibility.

Regularly celebrating achievements, both individual and group successes, further strengthens the class persona. This could involve recognizing improvements in grades, effort, or participation in class discussions. By acknowledging and rewarding these behaviors, students are more likely to internalize these values as part of their own identity, thus contributing to a robust academic culture.

Additionally, fostering an environment of collaboration over competition helps build a class persona that values mutual support and shared goals. Group activities, peer teaching, and collaborative projects can encourage students to see themselves as part of a team, where each member's success contributes to the whole.

Finally, the teacher's role as a model of the desired academic culture is crucial. Demonstrating enthusiasm for the subject matter, showing respect for all students, and maintaining a consistent and fair approach to discipline and encouragement will set the tone for the class persona. Over time, as these practices take root, the class will develop a unique identity that emphasizes academic excellence, mutual respect, and a collective drive towards success.

By carefully crafting this persona, teachers can transform their class into a cohesive unit that is not only academically successful but also rich in positive social and intellectual culture.

1. "I'm impressed with how you all support one another in your learning—this collaborative spirit is exactly what we need to achieve great things together."

2. "Your dedication to understanding the material deeply is what makes this class stand out—keep up the excellent work."

3. "The thoughtful questions and discussions you bring to the classroom are a testament to your commitment to learning."

4. "Seeing how you challenge each other respectfully is a clear sign that you're all invested in growing academically."

5. "Your consistent effort to push beyond the basics and explore new ideas is what will set you apart in the future."

6. "I appreciate how you all take responsibility for your learning and hold each other accountable—this is the mark of a strong academic community."

7. "The way you all come prepared and ready to engage every day shows a true commitment to your education."

8. "Your ability to balance focus and creativity in your work is something I truly admire about this class."

9. "The enthusiasm you bring to each lesson is contagious—it's clear that you're all here to make the most of your time and opportunities."

10. "I'm proud of how you've created an environment where everyone feels encouraged to participate and share their thoughts—this is what academic excellence looks like."

Teacher as a well-wishing opponent.

To be the opponent but also root for the student.

"To be the opponent but also root for the student" encapsulates a nuanced teaching strategy that embraces both challenge and support in the educational journey. This duality reflects the dynamic role teachers play as both facilitators of intellectual growth and advocates for the success of their students. It underscores the importance of providing constructive opposition while simultaneously offering encouragement and support.

Being the opponent implies creating challenges, setting high expectations, and pushing students beyond their comfort zones. This aspect of the teaching approach acknowledges the role of adversity in fostering growth. By presenting challenges that require critical thinking, problem-solving, and application of knowledge, educators encourage students to develop resilience, adaptability, and a deeper understanding of the subject matter.

Challenging students can take various forms, such as assigning complex projects, posing thought-provoking questions, or encouraging debate and discussion. The goal is to stimulate intellectual curiosity and prompt students to engage in deeper levels of analysis and synthesis. By being the opponent, teachers cultivate an environment where students learn not only from success but also from overcoming obstacles and grappling with complex concepts.

Simultaneously, the phrase "but also root for the student" emphasizes the vital role of encouragement and support in the learning process. While presenting challenges, teachers must actively champion their students' success. This involves recognizing individual strengths, providing positive feedback, and fostering a belief in the students' capabilities. When students feel supported, they are more likely to approach challenges with confidence, knowing that their efforts are valued.

Rooting for the student goes beyond mere praise; it involves cultivating a positive and inclusive classroom culture. Teachers can create an atmosphere where mistakes are viewed as opportunities for learning, and every student feels that their unique contributions are appreciated. This support extends to acknowledging the diverse learning styles, strengths, and backgrounds of each student, fostering an environment where everyone can thrive.

The duality of being both opponent and supporter embodies a balanced and holistic approach to teaching. It recognizes that learning is a multifaceted journey that involves not only academic challenges but also personal and emotional growth. By providing constructive opposition and simultaneous encouragement, educators prepare students for the complexities of real-world scenarios where success often requires a blend of resilience, critical thinking, and self-belief.

"To be the opponent but also root for the student" represents a teaching philosophy that embraces the dynamic nature of the educator-student relationship. It acknowledges that fostering growth requires a delicate balance between presenting challenges that promote intellectual development and offering unwavering support that nurtures students' confidence and well-being. This teaching tip encourages educators to be intentional in their approach, creating an environment where students can not only overcome academic hurdles but also flourish as resilient, confident, and capable individuals.

Here are some sentences a teacher can utter in the class.

1. "I'm challenging you today because I believe you're capable of more, and I'm here to push you toward that potential."

2. "Think of me as your sparring partner—every challenge I set is designed to make you sharper, not to defeat you."

3. "If I didn't think you could overcome this obstacle, I wouldn't have placed it in front of you."

4. "My goal isn't to beat you in this intellectual battle but to prepare you for the next one."

5. "Every time you stumble, I'm rooting for you to get back up stronger."

6. "I push hard because I see greatness in you, and I won't let you settle for less."

7. "I'll keep testing you because growth happens outside your comfort zone, but I'm always on your side."

8. "When I question your answers, it's not because I doubt you—it's because I know you can think deeper."

9. "I'm your toughest critic, but also your biggest supporter; I challenge you because I care about your progress."

10. "Remember, every time I oppose your answer, it's an invitation for you to grow and surpass the limitations you think you have."

<u>Deep Mentoring</u>

Deep mentoring in the context of teaching extends far beyond the mere transmission of knowledge. It involves cultivating a relationship where the teacher assumes the role of a guide, confidant, and role model, helping students navigate not only their academic challenges but also their personal growth and development. Deep mentoring is about understanding the individual needs, aspirations, and potential of each student and then tailoring guidance to help them achieve their full potential. This process requires patience, empathy, and a genuine commitment to the well-being of the student.

At its core, deep mentoring is characterized by the teacher's ability to listen actively and respond thoughtfully. It involves recognizing the unique strengths and weaknesses of each student, providing constructive feedback that encourages growth, and helping students set realistic goals for their academic and personal lives. The mentor must also foster a sense of trust, creating a safe space where students feel comfortable sharing their struggles and successes. This relationship often goes beyond the classroom, as mentors support their students in developing the skills and resilience needed to face life's broader challenges.

Moreover, deep mentoring is a reciprocal process. While the teacher imparts wisdom and guidance, they also learn from their students, gaining insights into different perspectives and deepening their understanding of the evolving educational landscape. This mutual growth enriches the educational experience for both parties, making deep mentoring a profoundly rewarding aspect of teaching. By engaging in deep mentoring, teachers not only contribute to the intellectual and emotional development of their students but also leave a lasting impact that shapes the students' future trajectories.

Objectives of Deep Mentoring

The primary objective of deep mentoring is to foster holistic growth in students, guiding them not only academically but also personally and professionally. Deep mentoring aims to develop critical thinking, emotional intelligence, resilience, and a sense of purpose in students. It seeks to build a strong mentor-mentee relationship that encourages self-discovery, ethical decision-making, and the ability to navigate complex life situations. Another crucial objective is to help students recognize their potential, set and achieve meaningful goals, and ultimately become self-sufficient learners and responsible individuals.

Methods of Deep Mentoring

1. Personalized Guidance: Deep mentoring involves tailoring advice and support to the unique needs and aspirations of each student. This requires understanding their strengths, weaknesses, interests, and challenges.

2. Active Listening and Empathy: A mentor must practice active listening, showing genuine interest and empathy toward the student's experiences and emotions. This builds trust and encourages open communication.

3. Goal Setting and Planning: Mentors assist students in setting realistic and meaningful goals, both short-term and long-term. They help create actionable plans to achieve these goals, offering guidance and support throughout the process.

4. Reflective Dialogue: Engaging students in reflective conversations encourages them to think critically about their experiences, decisions, and goals. This method helps students gain deeper insights into their own behavior and thought processes.

5. Role Modeling: Mentors serve as role models, demonstrating integrity, perseverance, and a commitment to lifelong learning. By exemplifying these qualities, mentors inspire students to adopt similar values in their own lives.

6. Feedback and Constructive Criticism: Providing honest, constructive feedback is essential in deep mentoring. It should be delivered in a manner that is supportive, helping students recognize

areas for improvement while encouraging them to strive for excellence.

7. Emotional Support and Encouragement: Mentors offer emotional support, helping students manage stress, anxiety, and other challenges. Encouragement and positive reinforcement play a key role in boosting students' confidence and motivation.

Tips for Effective Deep Mentoring

1. Build Trust Early: Establish a strong foundation of trust from the beginning. Be consistent, reliable, and respectful in your interactions with students.

2. Be Patient and Persistent: Deep mentoring is a long-term commitment. Be patient with your mentees as they progress at their own pace, and remain persistent in offering support and guidance.

3. Encourage Independence: While providing guidance, encourage students to take ownership of their learning and decision-making processes. The goal is to empower them to become self-sufficient.

4. Adapt to Individual Needs: Recognize that each student is different, and be flexible in your approach. Adapt your mentoring style to meet the unique needs of each mentee.

5. Foster Open Communication: Create an environment where students feel comfortable sharing their thoughts, concerns, and aspirations. Encourage them to speak openly and honestly.

6. Celebrate Achievements: Acknowledge and celebrate the accomplishments of your mentees, no matter how small. This reinforces positive behavior and motivates them to continue striving for success.

7. Maintain Boundaries: While building a close relationship, it is important to maintain professional boundaries. This ensures that the mentoring relationship remains focused and effective.

8. Incorporate Real-World Experiences: Connect classroom learning with real-world applications. Encourage students to participate in internships, projects, and extracurricular activities that align with their goals.

9. Provide Resources and Opportunities: Offer resources such as books, articles, and workshops that can help students develop their skills and knowledge. Introduce them to networking opportunities and professional connections.

10. Reflect on Your Mentoring Practice: Regularly assess your own mentoring approach. Seek feedback from your mentees and reflect on what is working well and what can be improved. This self-awareness enhances the effectiveness of your mentoring.

Chapter 8: Teaching Tips

<u>Work without Overwhelming Students</u>

Cerebral work, or intellectually demanding tasks, is essential for deep learning and cognitive development. However, such work can be stressful and taxing for students if not managed properly. Teachers play a crucial role in guiding students through these tasks while minimizing stress. Here are effective strategies for encouraging cerebral work in a supportive and engaging manner:

1. Create a Supportive Learning Environment

- Establish Clear Expectations: Clearly outline the goals and expectations for cerebral tasks. Providing students with a roadmap for what is required can reduce anxiety and increase their confidence in tackling complex tasks.

- Foster a Growth Mindset: Emphasize that intellectual challenges are opportunities for growth rather than tests of ability. Reinforce the idea that effort and persistence are key to mastering difficult material.

2. Break Down Complex Tasks

- Divide Tasks into Manageable Chunks: Break down complex tasks into smaller, more manageable parts. This approach helps students focus on one aspect at a time, reducing feelings of overwhelm and making the work seem less daunting.

- Provide Step-by-Step Guidance: Offer step-by-step instructions or a structured approach to problem-solving. Clear guidance helps students navigate complex tasks more effectively and with less stress.

3. Use Active Learning Techniques

- Incorporate Interactive Activities: Engage students with interactive activities such as discussions, debates, and problem-solving exercises. Active learning techniques promote deeper understanding and make cerebral work more engaging.

- Utilize Collaborative Learning: Encourage group work and peer collaboration. Working with others allows students to share ideas, provide support, and approach problems from different perspectives, which can reduce individual stress.

4. Provide Adequate Support and Resource

- Offer Resources and Tools: Provide students with access to resources such as reference materials, study guides, and digital tools. Having the right resources can facilitate their understanding and reduce the cognitive load.

- Be Available for Support: Make yourself available for one-on-one assistance or office hours. Providing individualized support helps students address specific challenges and reduces their stress levels.

5. Promote Effective Time Management

- Encourage Planning and Organization: Teach students effective time management and organizational skills. Encourage them to create study schedules, set goals, and prioritize tasks to manage their workload more effectively.

- Implement Time Limits: Set reasonable time limits for tasks or segments of work. Time constraints can help students focus and work more efficiently, reducing procrastination and stress.

6. Incorporate Varied Learning Modalities

- Use Multiple Modalities: Integrate different learning modalities, such as visual aids, multimedia, and hands-on activities. Varied approaches cater to different learning styles and make cerebral tasks more engaging.

- Encourage Creative Thinking: Promote creative thinking and problem-solving through activities that allow for exploration and experimentation. Encouraging creativity helps students approach complex tasks with a more open mindset.

7. Encourage Self-Reflection and Metacognition

- Promote Self-Reflection: Encourage students to reflect on their learning processes and outcomes. Self-reflection helps them understand their strengths and areas for improvement, fostering a sense of control and reducing stress.

- Teach Metacognitive Strategies: Help students develop metacognitive skills, such as self-monitoring and adjusting strategies. Metacognition enhances their ability to manage their own learning and reduces anxiety about complex tasks.

8. Provide Positive Reinforcement and Feedback

- Celebrate Achievements: Recognize and celebrate students' efforts and achievements, both big and small. Positive reinforcement boosts motivation and confidence, making cerebral work feel more rewarding.

- Offer Constructive Feedback: Provide feedback that is specific, constructive, and focused on improvement. Constructive feedback helps students understand their progress and areas for growth without adding undue stress.

9. Foster a Balanced Approach

- Promote Breaks and Downtime: Encourage students to take regular breaks and engage in activities that relax and refresh their minds. Balancing cerebral work with relaxation helps prevent burnout and maintains overall well-being.

- Encourage Healthy Study Habits: Promote healthy study habits, such as regular sleep, balanced nutrition, and physical activity. A healthy lifestyle supports cognitive function and reduces stress.

10. Model a Balanced Attitude

- Demonstrate a Positive Attitude: Model a positive and balanced attitude towards intellectual challenges. Show that you approach complex tasks with curiosity and resilience, which can inspire students to adopt a similar mindset.

- Maintain Open Communication: Keep open lines of communication with students about their experiences and challenges. Being approachable and supportive helps students feel more comfortable seeking help and managing their stress.

By implementing these strategies, teachers can guide students through intellectually demanding tasks in a way that fosters engagement and reduces stress. Balancing intellectual challenges with support, positive reinforcement, and self-care helps students thrive academically while maintaining their well-being.

Blending heaviness and lightness

Balancing authority, humor, happiness, and knowledge in teaching requires a nuanced approach that blends strong classroom management with a warm, engaging demeanor. Here's how to cultivate these traits:

1. Establish Clear Expectations (Authoritative)

- Set Boundaries: Clearly communicate classroom rules and expectations from the outset. Students should understand the importance of respect, punctuality, and effort.

- Consistent Enforcement: Apply rules consistently and fairly to maintain order. This establishes your authority and ensures students know you mean what you say.

- Confident Body Language: Maintain strong eye contact, a confident posture, and a clear, steady voice. This projects authority and commands attention.

2. Incorporate Humor (Funny)

- Use Light-Hearted Jokes: Integrate subject-related humor or light-hearted jokes to make the class more enjoyable. Ensure the humor is appropriate and inclusive.

- Self-Deprecation: Occasionally laugh at yourself in a way that humanizes you and breaks down barriers between you and your students.

- Spontaneous Wit: Use spontaneous humor to diffuse tension or refocus the class if things get too serious or off-track. This helps keep the atmosphere relaxed.

3. Cultivate a Positive Atmosphere (Happy)

- Show Enthusiasm: Your passion for the subject should be evident. Enthusiasm is contagious and motivates students to engage more deeply.

- Celebrate Successes: Regularly acknowledge student achievements, both big and small. This creates a positive, supportive environment where students feel valued.

- Maintain Optimism: Approach challenges with a positive attitude. Show students that obstacles can be overcome with effort and creativity.

4. Demonstrate Expertise (Knowledgeable)

- Deep Subject Mastery: Continuously expand your knowledge of the subject to confidently address student questions and provide deeper insights.

- Connect Concepts: Relate complex ideas to real-world examples or students' interests. This makes the material more relatable and easier to understand.

- Encourage Curiosity: Foster an environment where questions are welcomed. Encourage students to explore beyond the curriculum, showing them that knowledge is a lifelong pursuit.

5. Blend Traits Seamlessly

- Engage Authentically: Be yourself while teaching. Authenticity allows you to blend authority with humor and happiness naturally, making you relatable yet respected.

- Adapt Your Approach: Recognize that different situations call for different emphases. Sometimes, a more authoritative stance is needed, while at other times, humor or a positive outlook will be more effective.

- Reflect and Adjust: Continuously reflect on your teaching practice. Seek feedback from students and peers to refine your balance of these traits, ensuring you meet the needs of all learners.

Training Vs. Play

Training and play represent distinct approaches to learning, each serving unique purposes in an academic context.

Training is structured, goal-oriented, and focused on mastery of specific skills or knowledge. It involves repetition, feedback, and assessment to ensure learners reach a defined level of competence. For instance, in mathematics, solving algebraic equations repeatedly under guided supervision exemplifies training. Here, precision and progression through a curriculum are key, ensuring students gain proficiency in essential techniques.

On the other hand, play is exploratory and open-ended, encouraging creativity and experimentation without rigid objectives. Play allows learners to engage with content in a more relaxed, imaginative way, fostering intrinsic motivation and joy in learning. In a science class, play might involve students designing their own experiments or exploring a scientific concept through hands-on activities without the pressure of assessment. This approach cultivates curiosity, allowing students to connect ideas freely.

While training builds competence and ensures measurable outcomes, play nurtures creativity, problem-solving, and emotional engagement. Both are essential in learning: training develops discipline and expertise, while play fosters innovation and a deeper understanding of concepts. Effective education balances both, enabling students to master core skills while also exploring new ideas in a dynamic, engaging manner.

Learning is a multifaceted process that involves the acquisition of both knowledge and skills. However, this journey is often characterized by effort, and learners may perceive it as a mundane or even boring endeavor. It is crucial to recognize that while training and play are distinct approaches to learning, each contributes uniquely to the educational experience. Learning can occur through both training and play, with each method offering its own set of advantages and challenges.

Learning, whether it involves acquiring knowledge or honing skills, often demands effort and perseverance. The mental exertion required for understanding complex concepts or the physical practice needed to master a skill can be arduous. Students may encounter challenges that test their patience and resilience, and it is during these moments that the perception of learning as tedious or boring may emerge. Acknowledging the effortful nature of learning is a crucial step in devising effective educational strategies that engage and motivate learners.

Training and play represent two distinct approaches to learning, each with its own set of characteristics. Training is akin to preparation, involving the deliberate and systematic development of muscle memory, neural connections in the brain, and the ability to tolerate discomfort. It encompasses the discipline of handling delayed gratification, enduring the discomfort of effortful practice, and persisting in the face of failure. Training is a process of building the foundations necessary for competence and mastery.

Contrastingly, play is characterized by enjoyment, interaction, and immediate gratification. It involves the application and enjoyment of existing knowledge or skills in a dynamic and often spontaneous manner. Play taps into the intrinsic joy of discovery, exploration, and creative expression. It is a context where learners engage with what they already know, reinforcing understanding and skill proficiency in a relaxed and enjoyable atmosphere. The interactive and gratifying nature of play makes it a powerful tool for reinforcing and consolidating learning.

While training and play have distinct qualities, they are not mutually exclusive. Learning can seamlessly integrate both approaches, creating a comprehensive and balanced educational experience. Training provides the necessary structure and discipline for skill development, ensuring that learners build the foundation required for proficiency. On the other hand, the play offers a context for the application of acquired knowledge and skills, fostering creativity, spontaneity, and a deepening of understanding through enjoyable experiences.

Success, expertise, skill, and experience are the fruits of consistent and disciplined training rather than mere play. While play serves as a valuable tool for introduction, motivation, and easing into a new skill or discipline, it lacks the depth and rigor required to achieve true mastery. Play is inherently gratifying and enjoyable, offering immediate rewards such as social interaction, fun, and a sense of accomplishment. However, it is often unstructured and lacks the repetitive, focused intensity that training demands. Training, on the other hand, is a deliberate and systematic process designed to push an individual beyond their current capabilities. It is characterized by effort, stress, and often discomfort, as it requires one to engage deeply with both body and mind in the pursuit of long-term goals.

The distinction between play and training lies in the nature and purpose of each activity. Play is fundamentally about interaction, enjoyment, and exploration; it is often social and designed to engage multiple senses in a light-hearted manner. In contrast, training is an individual pursuit, often solitary, where the focus is on repetitive practice, refinement, and pushing personal limits. Training involves reps and sets—whether in physical exercise or mental practice—aimed at building muscle memory, improving technique, and enhancing cognitive skills. The process is often challenging and can be painful, both physically and mentally, but it is through these challenges that true growth occurs. The mind is trained to endure, focus, and strive for improvement despite the absence of immediate gratification. This delayed gratification, a hallmark of effective training, is what ultimately leads to expertise, skill, and success. Without the rigorous demands of training, play alone cannot cultivate the discipline and perseverance required to achieve lasting proficiency.

Training instills in learners the ability to handle challenges such as pain, delayed gratification, and failure, fostering resilience and perseverance. These attributes are essential not only in the educational context but also in real-world scenarios where individuals must navigate obstacles and setbacks. Training contributes to the development of a growth mindset, where setbacks are viewed as opportunities for learning and improvement.

Play, with its immediate rewards and enjoyable experiences, serves as a motivational force. It allows learners to see the practical relevance and applicability of what they have learned, reinforcing the joy of discovery. The balance between training and play creates a dynamic and holistic learning environment that acknowledges the effortful nature of learning while providing avenues for enjoyment, interaction, and immediate gratification.

The concept of play in teaching-learning is a powerful tool, but if overdone, it can lead to unintended consequences. While integrating play into education can make learning more engaging and enjoyable, an excessive focus on play may cause learners to become more accustomed to the entertainment aspect rather than the learning itself. It is essential to remember that education is fundamentally about training the mind, which requires active cognitive participation and critical thinking. Balancing play with rigorous intellectual engagement ensures that students not only enjoy the learning process but also develop the mental discipline necessary for deep understanding and lasting knowledge. The goal of the teacher and education is to make the student feel that even training is enjoyable. That is a success for the teacher and student.

The ultimate goal of teaching and education is to create an environment where students find joy even in the rigor of training, for it is through training that real progress is made. Whether it's mastering a difficult concept or refining a skill, training is the pathway to growth. A successful teacher understands that learning, though challenging, should not feel burdensome; instead, it should be seen as an enriching process that sparks curiosity and motivation. When both the teacher and the student embrace training with enthusiasm, learning becomes not just effective but deeply fulfilling, marking true success for both.

"Success is forged in the quiet, relentless hours of training; medals are merely the acknowledgment of what has already been earned long before the competition."

Learning is a nuanced process that involves effort, resilience, and the potential for perceived boredom. Training and play represent two complementary approaches to learning, each contributing distinct qualities to the educational journey. Recognizing the value of both training and play allows educators to design learning experiences that are not only effective in building knowledge and skills but also engaging, enjoyable, and motivating for learners. By leveraging the strengths of each approach, education can become a dynamic and fulfilling endeavor that fosters a lifelong love for learning.

Status quo and change

"All that is present is not right/good, and all the new is not wrong/bad."

The statement "All that is present is not right/good, and all the new is not wrong/bad" reflects a nuanced understanding of human thinking and progress, grounded in both psychological and philosophical perspectives. It challenges the tendency toward cognitive biases, such as status quo bias, where individuals assume that what currently exists or has been long-established is inherently superior or correct, and the inverse resistance to new ideas, often labeled as neophobia or fear of change.

From a psychological standpoint, humans have an innate tendency to cling to familiar concepts, practices, and beliefs. This is rooted in cognitive conservatism—the tendency to preserve mental effort by relying on established frameworks, patterns, or routines. Such cognitive biases can foster an unwarranted belief that what exists in the present is "right" or "good" simply because it is familiar, accepted, or has stood the test of time. However, this may overlook evolving contexts, changing needs, and new knowledge that could challenge outdated notions.

Similarly, psychological aversion to change, or neophobia, can result in an automatic dismissal of new ideas, technologies, or social innovations. This resistance can stem from fear of the unknown, anxiety about failure, or discomfort with uncertainty, leading to the false assumption that what is new is inherently "wrong" or "bad." However, psychological research emphasizes that openness to experience—a key personality trait associated with creativity and innovation—enables individuals to adapt to change and embrace new possibilities for progress.

Progress and Human Thinking

Human progress is deeply rooted in the ability to question established norms while also evaluating new ideas on their own merits. Historically, many societal advancements have come from those who challenged the status quo and embraced new paradigms.

For instance, scientific revolutions often arose from rejecting outdated models that were once considered unquestionable truths. This dynamic process of learning, unlearning, and relearning enables societies to grow, evolve, and overcome inherent limitations.

While tradition provides continuity and a sense of stability, progress requires a willingness to reconsider long-held beliefs and engage with the new. The key is maintaining a balanced approach—evaluating the present not through complacency but through critical thought and assessing new developments not with unthinking rejection but through open-minded inquiry.

In the context of academics, teaching, and the learning process, the statement "All that is present is not right/good, and all the new is not wrong/bad" serves as a critical reminder of the need for ongoing evaluation and adaptation. Education, as both a practice and an institution, is not immune to the human tendencies that favor the status quo and resist change. However, fostering a progressive, adaptive mindset is essential for both teachers and students to succeed in an ever-evolving intellectual landscape.

Traditional vs. Progressive Approaches in Academics

Traditionally, academic institutions have relied on well-established methods, curricula, and standards. These structures provide a sense of continuity and reliability in the teaching and learning process. However, the persistence of certain long-standing practices, though comfortable and familiar, may not always serve the best interests of students in a rapidly changing world. For instance, rote memorization, once considered an essential learning tool, is now increasingly questioned in favor of critical thinking and problem-solving skills that better prepare students for modern challenges.

At the same time, new methods of learning and technology-driven tools, such as online education platforms, active learning techniques, and flipped classrooms, have often faced skepticism from traditional educators. The fear is that these innovations may compromise academic rigor or personal engagement, although research increasingly supports the benefits of incorporating such tools to enhance student engagement and understanding. This underscores the danger of dismissing new approaches simply because they deviate from conventional academic norms.

Psychological Factors in Teaching and Learning

From a psychological perspective, students and educators alike may be inclined to rely on familiar methods, resisting change even when newer approaches might be more effective. Teachers, for example, may feel a sense of security in using the same textbooks, lectures, and assessments year after year, assuming that since these methods have worked in the past, they must still be the best approach. This reluctance to innovate may stem from cognitive biases like the aforementioned status quo bias or from fear of failure in implementing untested techniques. Students, too, may prefer sticking to traditional learning methods that feel safe, even if they are not the most conducive to long-term understanding and creativity.

However, research in educational psychology emphasizes the importance of flexibility, adaptability, and critical thinking. The ability to question, explore, and adopt new teaching methodologies can invigorate the learning environment and meet the diverse needs of today's learners. This might involve introducing project-based learning, integrating technology, fostering interdisciplinary connections, or incorporating real-world applications into the curriculum. All these approaches acknowledge that traditional methods, while valuable, may not always be the best fit for every student or every context and that openness to innovation is critical to achieving more effective educational outcomes.

Philosophical Underpinnings of Academic Change

Philosophically, the tension between the old and the new in education reflects a broader debate about the nature of knowledge and progress. Is knowledge static, something to be passed down unchanged, or is it dynamic, constantly evolving and subject to reinterpretation? The constructivist approach to education argues that knowledge is not simply transmitted from teacher to student but co-constructed through experience, reflection, and dialogue. This requires both educators and learners to be flexible and open-minded, recognizing that the "right" way to teach and learn is not fixed but adaptive to the needs of the time.

Furthermore, the philosophy of pragmatism, as articulated by figures like John Dewey, highlights that education should be geared toward preparing individuals to navigate and contribute to an ever-changing world. Learning is not merely the acquisition of facts but the development of critical faculties that enable students to evaluate, adapt, and innovate. In this light, the resistance to new methods in education is not just a practical issue but a philosophical one. It calls into question whether the purpose of education is to replicate the past or to prepare students to face and shape the future.

Balancing Tradition and Innovation

In sum, the teaching and learning process requires a delicate balance between preserving effective traditional methods and embracing innovative approaches that meet the demands of a changing world. As educators, it is vital to recognize that what has always been done may not always be the best solution and that the new, while unfamiliar, may offer transformative opportunities for learning. The psychological inclination to stick with what we know must be countered with a conscious effort to reflect, adapt, and grow.

By being open to both continuity and change, teachers can cultivate a learning environment that encourages students to think critically, adapt to new information, and be flexible in their pursuit of knowledge. This balance ensures that education remains relevant, dynamic, and capable of preparing students for the complexities of the modern world. Ultimately, the process of learning is not about choosing between old and new but about integrating both in a way that best serves the intellectual and personal growth of the learner.

Methods to Train Students to Embrace Nuanced Thinking and Overcome Cognitive Biases

The statement "All that is present is not right/good, and all the new is not wrong/bad" challenges students to critically assess established norms and new ideas, encouraging a more balanced and open-minded approach to knowledge. This requires training that addresses cognitive biases and fosters a deeper understanding of both psychological and philosophical perspectives. Here are ten methods to achieve this:

1. Critical Thinking Exercises

- Method: Implement activities that encourage students to evaluate arguments and evidence critically. Use case studies, debates, and structured analysis tasks to challenge students to assess both traditional and innovative viewpoints.

- Purpose: Helps students recognize and question biases, such as status quo bias and neophobia, by promoting rigorous examination of all perspectives.

2. Diverse Perspectives in Discussions

- Method: Facilitate discussions that include multiple viewpoints, particularly those that contrast with students' existing beliefs. Encourage students to explore and articulate the strengths and weaknesses of various perspectives.

- Purpose: Exposes students to a range of ideas, reducing cognitive biases by broadening their understanding and fostering empathy for differing viewpoints.

3. Historical and Philosophical Contextualization

- Method: Provide historical and philosophical context for current ideas and practices. Show how concepts have evolved over time and how new ideas have challenged established norms.

- Purpose: Illustrates that both established and new ideas have merit and helps students understand the dynamic nature of knowledge and progress.

4. Bias Awareness Training

- Method: Educate students about common cognitive biases, including status quo bias and neophobia. Use exercises and examples to help them recognize these biases in their own thinking.

- Purpose: Raises awareness of biases and encourages students to actively counteract them in their decision-making and evaluations.

5. Encouraging Innovation and Experimentation

- Method: Create opportunities for students to engage in innovative projects and experiments. Encourage them to test new ideas and reflect on their outcomes.

- Purpose: Fosters an open-minded attitude towards new ideas and helps students experience firsthand the benefits and limitations of innovation.

6. Role of Skepticism and Open-Mindedness

- Method: Teach students to balance skepticism with open-mindedness. Encourage them to question established ideas while remaining receptive to new information and perspectives.

- Purpose: Develop a nuanced approach to evaluating ideas, recognizing that both established and new concepts can be valid.

7. Reflective Practices

- Method: Incorporate reflective journaling and self-assessment exercises. Ask students to reflect on their own cognitive biases, learning experiences, and how their views may have changed over time.

- Purpose: Promotes self-awareness and critical reflection, helping students recognize their biases and embrace a more balanced perspective.

8. Case Studies of Successful Change

- Method: Analyze case studies where new ideas or innovations have successfully challenged the status quo. Focus on how these changes were implemented and the impact they had.

- Purpose: Provides real-world examples of how new ideas can be beneficial, countering resistance to change and encouraging a more open approach to innovation.

9. Structured Problem-Solving Sessions

- Method: Engage students in problem-solving activities where they must consider both traditional and innovative solutions.

Facilitate group discussions to evaluate the pros and cons of each approach.

 - Purpose: Encourages students to assess ideas critically and to consider multiple approaches, reducing the influence of cognitive biases on their decision-making.

10. Exposure to Contradictory Evidence

 - Method: Present students with evidence that contradicts widely accepted beliefs or practices. Encourage them to analyze and debate this evidence, considering its implications.

 - Purpose: Challenges existing biases and assumptions, promoting a more open and critical evaluation of both established and new ideas.

Training students to navigate cognitive biases and appreciate the complexity of human thinking requires deliberate and multifaceted approaches. By incorporating critical thinking exercises, promoting diverse perspectives, and encouraging reflection and experimentation, educators can help students develop a more nuanced understanding of progress and change. These methods collectively foster an environment where students are better equipped to evaluate ideas objectively, appreciate the value of both established and new concepts, and contribute thoughtfully to ongoing dialogues in their academic and personal lives.

<u>Vocabulary building</u>

The capacity for language is a fundamental aspect of human biology, deeply embedded in our species' evolutionary heritage. This intrinsic ability, often referred to as the biological endowment of language, underpins our remarkable aptitude for complex communication. From an early age, humans exhibit an inherent predisposition for language acquisition, characterized by the ability to learn and use intricate linguistic structures with remarkable ease. This biological capacity is supported by specialized neural structures in the brain, such as Broca's and Wernicke's areas, which facilitate the production and comprehension of language. The universal presence of language in all human cultures, combined with the consistent developmental trajectory of language acquisition across diverse populations, underscores its biological foundation. Language's deep-rooted role in human evolution highlights its significance not merely as a cultural artifact but as a critical, biologically ingrained mechanism that enables sophisticated interaction, thought, and social organization.

In teaching, especially in technical or specialized fields, students are often introduced to new vocabulary specific to the subject matter. These terms, if taught effectively, should become part of the student's technical vocabulary, serving as conceptual tools to unlock deeper understanding. However, when these words are not adequately explained—when their meanings, origins, and relevance to the subject are overlooked—they risk becoming empty jargon. This is a significant concern in education, as it can create psychological barriers to learning and comprehension.

From a psychological perspective, learning new vocabulary involves more than just associating sounds with spelling. It requires creating meaningful connections between the new term and the student's existing cognitive framework. The cognitive load theory suggests that working memory has limited capacity, and when students are bombarded with unfamiliar terms without proper context or explanation, they are forced to use their cognitive resources inefficiently. When a new word is not described properly, the student may know the sound and spelling of the word but not the meaning of the word. Instead of understanding the word in relation to the larger concept, they resort to memorization. This disconnection between vocabulary and meaning creates a superficial layer of knowledge that cannot support long-term retention or application.

Moreover, the lack of meaningful understanding can lead to a form of cognitive dissonance. When students encounter words repeatedly without grasping their significance, they may experience confusion or frustration. Over time, this leads to a psychological disengagement from the subject. The brain, as part of its defense mechanism, may begin to associate the subject with negative emotions, fostering aversion rather than curiosity. This can seriously hinder motivation, a key psychological driver in learning.

In addition, without clear ontological grounding—without understanding where the word fits into the broader conceptual framework—students fail to see the relevance of these terms in real-world applications. This further diminishes their interest in the subject, reducing both intrinsic and extrinsic motivation. For instance, a biology student who merely memorizes terms like "mitosis" or "homeostasis" without knowing their functional relevance within biological systems will struggle to integrate these concepts into broader biological understanding.

Therefore, when teaching, it is critical for educators to provide more than just the spelling and pronunciation of a term. They must delve into the ontology of the word—its role and place within the conceptual structure of the discipline. Explaining why a word is relevant and how it connects to the concept being taught helps students make meaningful associations. This approach aids in deep learning, where the student not only recalls the term but understands its application and significance.

Enhancing language skills and employing diverse learning and delivery methods are pivotal for improving educational outcomes. By focusing on these areas, educators can create a more effective and engaging learning environment that caters to varied learning styles and fosters deeper understanding.

Enhancing Language Skills

1. Vocabulary and Communication:

 - Explicit Instruction: Incorporate targeted vocabulary instruction into the curriculum to build students' lexicons. Use techniques such as word maps, semantic gradients, and context clues to deepen understanding.

 - Active Use: Encourage students to actively use new vocabulary in written and spoken communication through discussions, debates, and presentations. This practice helps reinforce language acquisition and improves fluency.

 - Reading and Writing: Promote extensive reading and writing across disciplines. Diverse reading materials, including fiction, non-fiction, and academic texts, enrich vocabulary and enhance comprehension. Writing assignments that require critical analysis and synthesis of information also improve language skills.

2. Language Across the Curriculum:

 - Integrated Approach: Apply language skills across various subjects by integrating reading and writing into all areas of study. For example, students might write scientific reports, analyze historical texts, or engage in mathematical problem-solving with written explanations.

 - Cross-disciplinary Projects: Design projects that require students to research, communicate, and present information in multiple formats. This approach reinforces the application of language skills in different contexts and disciplines.

Employing Diverse Learning and Delivery Methods

1. Differentiated Instruction:

- Tailored Strategies: Implement differentiated instruction to address the diverse needs of learners. Use various teaching methods, such as visual aids, auditory materials, and hands-on activities, to cater to different learning styles.

- Flexible Grouping: Utilize flexible grouping strategies to provide targeted support and enrichment. Group students based on their skill levels or interests for specific tasks, allowing for personalized instruction and collaborative learning.

2. Technology Integration:

- Digital Tools: Leverage educational technology tools, such as interactive whiteboards, educational apps, and online resources, to enhance learning experiences. These tools can provide interactive and multimedia elements that engage students and support diverse learning needs.

- Blended Learning: Incorporate blended learning models that combine face-to-face instruction with online components. This approach allows for personalized pacing and access to a variety of resources and instructional methods.

3. Active Learning Strategies:

- Engagement Techniques: Employ active learning strategies, such as problem-based learning, case studies, and simulations, to actively involve students in the learning process. These methods promote critical thinking and the application of knowledge in real-world scenarios.

- Collaborative Learning: Foster collaborative learning environments where students work together to solve problems, conduct research, or complete projects. Collaborative activities enhance communication skills, teamwork, and collective problem-solving abilities.

4. Assessment for Learning:

- Formative Assessments: Use formative assessments, such as quizzes, polls, and peer reviews, to gauge student understanding and provide timely feedback. Formative assessments help identify areas for improvement and guide instructional adjustments.

- Authentic Assessments: Implement authentic assessments that mirror real-world tasks and challenges. Projects, presentations, and portfolios provide a comprehensive view of student learning and allow for the demonstration of language and content mastery.

Enhancing language skills and adopting diverse learning and delivery methods are crucial for optimizing educational outcomes. By focusing on explicit language instruction, integrating language across the curriculum, and employing differentiated, technology-enhanced, and active learning strategies, educators can create a dynamic and effective learning environment. These approaches not only improve language proficiency but also foster deeper understanding, critical thinking, and engagement among students, ultimately leading to more successful educational experiences.

Textbook reading or Notes?

When it comes to teaching, a common dilemma faced by educators is whether to make students read adapted standard textbooks or provide them with prepared notes. Each approach has its own set of advantages and disadvantages, impacting the students' learning experiences and overall educational outcomes.

Advantages of Making Students Read Adapted Standard Textbooks

1. Comprehensive Coverage of the Subject: Textbooks, especially adapted standard ones, are structured to cover topics in a systematic and in-depth manner. They provide a broad understanding of a subject, often including examples, case studies, and exercises that expose students to different facets of the material. This comprehensive approach can ensure students are well-versed in the subject.

2. Development of Reading and Analytical Skills: Encouraging students to read textbooks helps in developing critical academic skills. Textbooks are often complex, requiring students to break down, analyze, and synthesize information. Over time, this practice can improve reading comprehension, note-taking, and analytical thinking—skills that are essential for academic success.

3. Engagement with Source Material: By reading textbooks, students engage directly with the original material rather than a filtered or condensed version. This gives them a chance to form their own interpretations and understand the subject matter in its intended context.

4. Reference Material for Further Study: Textbooks serve as lasting references that students can return to when needed. They provide well-organized information that students can rely on for future studies, ensuring a stable knowledge base beyond exams or assignments.

5. Preparation for Higher Studies: University-level education and beyond often require students to read multiple sources, including complex textbooks. Familiarizing students with standard textbooks

early on equips them with the habits and skills necessary for future academic or professional pursuits.

Disadvantages of Making Students Read Adapted Standard Textbooks

1. Time-Consuming: Textbooks can be dense and time-consuming to read. Students with limited time or those who struggle with reading comprehension might find it difficult to keep up with the assigned readings. This may lead to frustration or disengagement from the learning process.

2. Difficulty in Understanding: Even adapted versions of standard textbooks can be challenging for students, especially those who are new to a subject or have weaker backgrounds in certain areas. The language used may be too technical or the concepts too abstract, leading to confusion rather than clarity.

3. Not Always Aligned with Course Objectives: Sometimes, textbooks may cover material that is not entirely relevant to a specific course or may provide too much detail on certain topics while skimming over others. This can create a misalignment between what is taught in class and what students are expected to learn from the textbook.

4. Limited to the Author's Perspective: While textbooks are usually well-researched, they reflect the perspective and interpretation of their authors. Depending exclusively on one textbook can limit students' exposure to alternative viewpoints or interdisciplinary insights.

5. Resource-Intensive: Textbooks, particularly for specialized or higher-level subjects, can be expensive and not easily accessible to all students. This financial burden can be a disadvantage, especially in under-resourced schools or developing countries.

Advantages of Providing Notes

1. Condensed Information: Notes are typically a more concise version of the material, focusing on the most important points. This makes them more accessible and less time-consuming for students to read and understand, especially when they are pressed for time.

2. Tailored to Course Objectives: Teachers can design notes to directly reflect the learning goals of the course, ensuring that students focus on the most relevant topics. This alignment between classroom instruction and provided notes helps students stay on track.

3. Clarification of Difficult Concepts: Teachers often include simplified explanations in notes, making complex ideas more understandable. This can help students grasp challenging concepts more quickly than if they were reading a more comprehensive textbook.

4. Time Efficiency: Providing notes allows students to focus on critical content without spending hours wading through dense textbooks. This efficiency is particularly beneficial during exam preparation when time is of the essence.

5. Customizability: Teachers can update notes to reflect new developments, tailor them to the class's needs, or provide additional resources such as diagrams, summaries, and practice questions, which might not be available in textbooks.

Disadvantages of Providing Notes

1. Lack of Depth: Notes are often a distilled version of the material and may omit important details or context that a textbook would provide. This could result in a superficial understanding of the subject, particularly for students who rely solely on notes for their study.

2. Over-Dependence on Teacher's Interpretation: When students are given notes, they may become reliant on the teacher's interpretation of the material rather than developing their own critical thinking and problem-solving skills. This can limit their intellectual autonomy.

3. Missed Skill Development: By providing ready-made notes, teachers may inadvertently discourage students from engaging with the material more deeply. This can lead to a loss of valuable skills like independent research, critical reading, and self-assessment.

4. Limited Exposure to Comprehensive Learning Resources: Notes, by their nature, are not comprehensive. Students miss out on the opportunity to practice sifting through detailed information and may not develop the stamina required for deeper academic reading.

5. Short-Term Focus: Notes tend to emphasize what is immediately necessary for exams or assessments. This short-term focus may hinder the development of a lasting understanding or appreciation for the subject.

Both textbooks and notes serve distinct purposes, and the choice between them depends on the educational goals, the complexity of the subject, and the students' needs. A balanced approach that combines both methods may often provide the best learning experience. In the end, a teacher's role extends beyond preparing students for exams; it is to instill the habit of reading for the sheer joy of gaining knowledge. True education lies in nurturing a curiosity that drives students to read and learn during relaxed moments, not solely for the purpose of scoring marks. By cultivating this habit, the teacher fosters lifelong learners who are motivated by a genuine desire for intellectual growth rather than short-term academic success. This deeper connection with knowledge ensures that students engage with learning in a meaningful, sustained way throughout their lives.

The Critical Role of Attention and Focus

Success in any teaching-learning scenario is fundamentally rooted in the dynamics of attention and focus. As a teacher, the level of attention you receive from your students is directly proportional to the attention you devote to them. This reciprocal relationship forms the bedrock of effective teaching. However, the challenge arises as the number of students increases, leading to a natural dilution of the attention you can allocate to each individual student.

The Impact of Class Size on Attention

In a larger classroom, it becomes increasingly difficult for a teacher to give personalized attention to every student. This diffusion of focus can hinder the teacher's ability to gauge individual understanding, address specific needs, and foster a strong connection with each learner. However, while the challenge is significant, it is not insurmountable.

Enhancing Attention Through Authority, Talent, and Reputation

Teachers can counterbalance the limitation of divided attention through the cultivation of authority, talent, and reputation. Authority, when exercised with fairness and empathy, can command the attention of the entire classroom, ensuring that students remain engaged. Talent—whether in the form of subject matter expertise, storytelling, or the ability to make complex ideas accessible—naturally draws students' attention. Similarly, a strong reputation, built on consistency, dedication, and positive outcomes, can predispose students to be more attentive and receptive.

The Role of Humor and Physical Presence

Humor is another powerful tool in the teacher's arsenal. When used appropriately, it can lighten the classroom atmosphere, making learning more enjoyable and thus increasing student focus. Humor also humanizes the teacher, making them more approachable and relatable, which can enhance student engagement.

Physical presence, including body language, voice modulation, and movement within the classroom, also plays a critical role. A teacher who moves around the classroom, maintains eye contact, and uses gestures effectively can command attention and foster a dynamic learning environment.

The Complex Role of Physical Attraction

Physical attraction can indeed play a role in garnering attention, but it comes with significant caveats. While attraction might temporarily motivate students to engage more or follow instructions, it can also have unintended consequences. When students are attracted to a teacher for reasons beyond their academic abilities or personality, it can lead to distractions, reduce the focus on learning, and complicate the teacher-student relationship. Moreover, reliance on physical attraction undermines the cognitive and professional foundations of teaching, as it shifts the focus from intellectual engagement to superficial aspects.

Using attraction as a tool to motivate students can lead to serious complications, including the blurring of boundaries and ethical dilemmas. A teacher's role is to foster a learning environment based on respect, intellectual curiosity, and mutual growth, not to manipulate emotions for compliance.

Success in teaching-learning scenarios is deeply intertwined with how attention is managed and maintained. While larger classrooms present challenges, they can be mitigated by cultivating authority, talent, reputation, and the strategic use of humor. However, it is essential to avoid relying on physical attraction, as it can undermine the cognitive engagement and professionalism that are central to effective teaching. By focusing on these elements, teachers can create a more attentive, focused, and ultimately successful learning environment.

Chapter 9: Managing Students

<u>Discipline, reprimanding and punishments</u>

Discipline is a cornerstone of effective learning and plays a critical role in shaping the overall academic ambience of a classroom. A disciplined classroom environment provides the structure necessary for students to focus on their studies, engage deeply with the material, and interact respectfully with both their peers and the teacher. Without discipline, the learning process can be easily disrupted, leading to a chaotic atmosphere where meaningful education is compromised.

Effective discipline in the classroom fosters a sense of order and predictability, which is essential for students to feel secure and supported in their learning journey. When students understand the expectations and consequences within the classroom, they are more likely to adhere to the rules, thereby creating an environment where all learners can thrive. Discipline ensures that time is used efficiently, minimizes disruptions, and allows for the smooth progression of lessons, all of which contribute to better learning outcomes.

The teacher's role in maintaining discipline is paramount. Teachers set the tone for the classroom, establishing clear expectations for behavior and consistently enforcing them. By modeling appropriate behavior, providing clear instructions, and responding to misconduct in a fair yet firm manner, teachers create an atmosphere of mutual respect. Moreover, the teacher's ability to balance authority with empathy is crucial; while it is important to uphold discipline, it is equally important to understand the individual needs of students and to address behavioral issues with compassion and insight.

In sum, discipline is not merely about control but about creating an environment conducive to learning. It allows students to develop self-regulation, respect for others, and a sense of responsibility—qualities that are essential not only for academic success but also for their future lives. The teacher, as the leader of the classroom, plays an instrumental role in assuring that discipline is maintained, thereby enhancing both the learning experience and the overall academic atmosphere.

In the context of classroom discipline, understanding what constitutes indiscipline can be nuanced and subjective, often varying from teacher to teacher. For instance, some might view behaviors like sitting improperly, sleeping, or yawning as minor and not disruptive to the learning environment. These actions might reflect fatigue, discomfort, or boredom, but they do not necessarily indicate a lack of respect or engagement. Others, however, such as talking during class, giggling, using mobile phones, or frequently looking outside, can be more disruptive. These behaviors tend to break the flow of the lesson, distract other students, and signify a lack of focus or respect for the learning process.

As a teacher, it's essential to strike a balance between tolerance and firmness. Developing a "thick skin" to certain behaviors allows you to maintain your composure and focus on teaching without being overly distracted by minor disruptions. However, being sensitive to more disruptive behaviors is also necessary to uphold a standard of respect and engagement in the classroom. Each teacher has their own threshold for what they consider disruptive, and it's important to establish clear expectations with students while also being adaptable to different situations.

Effective discipline is not about rigid enforcement of rules but about creating an environment where learning can thrive. This means recognizing when to let minor infractions slide and when to intervene to maintain order. It also involves understanding the individual needs and behaviors of students, offering them guidance rather than punishment, and fostering a classroom atmosphere where both respect and engagement are cultivated.

In the context of global education, cultural differences significantly influence the perception and practice of discipline within classrooms. In Western countries, teachers often face limitations on how much they can enforce discipline, with a strong emphasis on students' rights and autonomy. Conversely, in many Eastern and developing regions, teachers traditionally wield more authority, often demanding respect and sometimes employing fear as a tool for maintaining order. Despite these differences, the core challenge for teachers remains universal: how to balance these cultural norms with the overarching goal of fostering student development.

Navigating this delicate balance requires teachers to be adaptable, respecting the legal frameworks, professional ethics, and cultural expectations of their environments while also ensuring that discipline serves its true purpose—promoting a positive learning atmosphere. In the West, this might involve more subtle forms of influence, such as building rapport and using positive reinforcement, whereas in the East, a teacher might be expected to take a more direct approach to guiding student behavior. Regardless of the method, the ultimate aim remains the same: to create an environment conducive to learning, where students are motivated, engaged, and developing their personalities in a positive direction.

The teacher's role is to deliver effective education while remaining sensitive to the cultural and legal context in which they operate. This requires a nuanced understanding of the local expectations and a commitment to fostering a classroom environment where discipline supports, rather than hinders, student growth. The success of this approach lies in the teacher's ability to balance firmness with empathy, ensuring that students not only acquire knowledge but also develop the motivation and character necessary to thrive both in and out of the classroom.

Structuring Stringency in Discipline: Psychological and Philosophical Underpinnings

Inculcating discipline within an educational setting is a delicate balance that must be thoughtfully structured to support the overall development of students. The stringency of discipline imposed by a teacher can be strategically varied over the course of a student's academic journey, as well as throughout the duration of a specific course or semester. This approach aligns with both psychological principles and philosophical considerations that recognize the evolving nature of student maturity and autonomy.

Psychological Underpinnings

1. Developmental Stages and Cognitive Growth:

Psychologically, students undergo significant cognitive and emotional development over the course of their academic programs. Early in their education, students may benefit from a more structured and stringent approach to discipline, as this provides a clear framework within which they can understand expectations, develop self-regulation, and build foundational habits. According to developmental theories, such as those proposed by Jean Piaget, younger students are still solidifying their operational thinking and require external guidance to navigate the complexities of academic and social norms.

As students progress through their educational journey, they gradually develop higher-order thinking skills, greater self-regulation, and an increased capacity for abstract reasoning. In later years, and as the semester advances, students can handle more autonomy and a relaxed approach to discipline. This shift mirrors their cognitive and emotional readiness to take on more responsibility for their actions, fostering independence and critical thinking.

2. Operant Conditioning and Gradual Release of Responsibility:

The principles of operant conditioning, as described by B.F. Skinner also supports this graduated approach. In the early stages of learning, consistent reinforcement—both positive and negative—helps establish desired behaviors and expectations. Stringent discipline at the outset can be viewed as a form of clear, consistent feedback that helps students understand the consequences of their actions. As they internalize these behaviors, the need for external reinforcement diminishes, allowing for a gradual relaxation of disciplinary measures. This gradual release of responsibility helps students transition from extrinsic to intrinsic motivation, which is crucial for their long-term success and independence.

3. Building Trust and Autonomy:

Stringent discipline early in a course or program also helps establish trust between the teacher and students. By setting clear boundaries and expectations, students learn to trust the teacher's guidance and the structure provided. As trust is built and students demonstrate their ability to self-regulate, the teacher can gradually relax their approach, signaling to students that they are trusted to manage their own behavior. This transition fosters a sense of autonomy, which is essential for developing self-directed learners.

Philosophical Considerations

1. Aristotelian Ethics and the Doctrine of the Mean:

Philosophically, the approach to discipline can be informed by Aristotle's concept of the "Doctrine of the Mean," which advocates for balance in all things. Stringency in the discipline should neither be excessive nor deficient but should strike a balance that is appropriate for the students' level of maturity and the specific context of their learning. Early stringency serves as a necessary boundary to cultivate virtue and good habits, while the relaxation of discipline over time reflects a recognition of the students' growing competence and moral autonomy.

2. Humanistic Education and Respect for the Individual:

Humanistic educational philosophies, such as those espoused by Carl Rogers, emphasize the importance of respecting the individual learner and fostering their inherent potential. Stringent discipline early on can be seen as a form of guidance that respects the students' need for structure, but as the students grow, the relaxation of discipline respects their individuality and autonomy. This approach aligns with the view that education should be a process of self-actualization, where the role of the teacher evolves from a strict guide to a supportive facilitator of learning.

3. Confucian Philosophy and the Role of the Teacher:

Confucianism, with its emphasis on the teacher-student relationship, provides a framework for understanding the gradual relaxation of discipline. In the early stages of learning, the teacher is seen as a strict mentor who imparts wisdom and moral guidance. As students internalize these lessons, the teacher's role shifts to one of mutual respect and guidance, reflecting the Confucian ideal of "ren" (benevolence) and the importance of harmonious relationships. This gradual shift in disciplinary approach aligns with the Confucian belief in the cultivation of moral character and the development of a virtuous life.

A Balanced Approach to Discipline

The structuring of discipline in educational settings should be dynamic, evolving in response to the developmental stages of students and the progression of the course or semester. Early stringency provides the necessary structure for students to develop foundational skills and habits, while the gradual relaxation of discipline reflects their growing maturity, autonomy, and capacity for self-regulation. This approach is supported by psychological theories of cognitive and emotional development, as well as philosophical principles that emphasize balance, respect for the individual, and the evolving role of the teacher. By adopting a flexible and responsive approach to discipline, teachers can effectively support the holistic development of their students, fostering both academic success and personal growth.

Reprimanding

Reprimanding a student can have a profound psychological impact, with the potential to induce emotions such as fear, guilt, hate, and anger. The specific effects vary depending on the context in which the reprimand is delivered—whether in private or in public—and on the individual student's personality and emotional resilience.

Reprimanding can evoke fear, especially when done in an authoritative manner, as students may perceive a threat to their well-being. Public reprimands heighten this fear due to the embarrassment of being singled out, which can create anxiety and inhibit future participation. Guilt arises when students realize their behavior violated norms, prompting introspection and a desire to amend their actions. While private reprimands can foster constructive guilt, public ones may lead to shame and withdrawal. Reprimanding may also provoke anger or resentment if perceived as unjust or harsh, potentially leading to defiance or disengagement, disrupting the learning process further.

The effects of reprimanding in private versus public settings differ significantly. In private, teachers can address behavior calmly and constructively, fostering a sense of respect and understanding in the student. This approach minimizes emotional fallout and encourages accountability. Conversely, public reprimands can lead to humiliation and alienation, heightened by peer judgment. This may damage the student's relationship with the teacher and classmates while instilling a fear-driven atmosphere focused on avoiding punishment rather than learning. Thus, while reprimanding is essential for discipline, teachers must balance authority with empathy, carefully considering the context and potential emotional consequences for students.

In the realm of effective teaching, it is imperative to adhere strictly to principles of professionalism and respect when addressing student behavior. It is crucial to maintain a focus solely on the behavior or misdeed in question, avoiding any comments or implications about the student's personal attributes, background, ethnicity, or activities outside the classroom. Here's why this approach is essential and how it should be implemented:

Professionalism and Respect

1. Focus Exclusively on Behavior: When addressing misbehavior, the conversation should center exclusively on the specific issue at hand—whether it is talking during a lecture, using a mobile phone, or any other classroom disruption. By concentrating solely on the behavior, the teacher avoids making the students feel targeted or judged based on their personal characteristics. For instance, a

teacher might say, "Using mobile phones during class distracts others and disrupts the lesson," rather than making any personal remarks. This approach ensures that the feedback is relevant, objective, and directly related to classroom conduct.

2. Avoid Personal Comments: It is vital never to make comments about a student's appearance, background, ethnicity, or personal life. Such comments can be perceived as discriminatory or insensitive, potentially causing emotional harm and reinforcing negative stereotypes. For example, if a student's behavior is problematic, focusing the discussion on how their actions affect the class, rather than any personal attributes, maintains a respectful and supportive atmosphere. This helps prevent the discussion from veering into areas that are irrelevant to academic performance and behavioral expectations.

3. Positive Reinforcement: When discussing student behavior, it is more productive to highlight positive attributes or improvements rather than focusing on negative aspects. Acknowledging positive behaviors, such as participation or improvement, can encourage continued good conduct without delving into sensitive areas. For example, "I appreciate your recent efforts in participating actively during discussions. Let's continue focusing on staying engaged and minimizing distractions." This method fosters a constructive environment and motivates students to adhere to expected behaviors.

4. Addressing Only the Issue at Hand: By strictly addressing the misbehavior or offense, teachers create a focused and fair environment where students understand that the issue is about their actions, not their identity. This approach prevents students from feeling personally attacked and helps them concentrate on modifying their behavior. For instance, if a student is speaking out of turn, the teacher should address the specific disruption, such as,

"Please wait until I finish speaking before contributing. This will help everyone stay on track."

Maintaining a professional demeanor by focusing solely on the behavior, avoiding personal comments, and emphasizing positive reinforcement helps in creating a respectful and effective learning environment. By adhering to these principles, teachers can manage classroom behavior constructively, fostering a positive and supportive atmosphere that promotes academic success and personal growth.

1. "I see you're distracted—let's focus on the lesson now so you don't miss anything important."

2. "Using your phone during class takes away from your learning experience; let's put it aside for now."

3. "Your conversation seems interesting, but let's save it for after class so everyone can concentrate."

4. "I need your full attention to make sure you're getting the most out of this lesson."

5. "It's important to stay engaged; let's respect our time here by keeping distractions to a minimum."

6. "I understand you might have something on your mind, but let's focus on the lesson to ensure we're all on the same page."

7. "We all benefit when everyone is fully present in class—please put your phone away."

8. "Your participation is valuable to the class, so let's keep the focus on the lesson."

9. "I appreciate your enthusiasm, but let's channel it towards the lesson right now."

10. "We're all here to learn, so let's make sure our behavior reflects that by avoiding distractions."

Provoking the guilt

1. "When you interrupt, it disrupts the entire class's learning experience and affects everyone."

2. "Your actions take away from the collective focus we need to make this class productive for everyone."

3. "By talking during the lesson, you're not just distracting yourself—you're disrespecting your peers' right to learn."

4. "When you use your phone during class, it sends a message that the lesson isn't important, which isn't fair to your classmates."

5. "Your interruption shows a lack of respect for the effort everyone else is putting into their learning."

6. "The time and focus we're dedicating to this lesson are valuable—let's not undermine it by distracting the group."

7. "When you disrupt the class, it affects everyone's ability to concentrate and learn."

8. "Your behavior takes away from the shared goal of making this class a space for effective learning."

9. "When you don't give your full attention, it diminishes the respect we owe each other as a learning community."

10. "Interruptions like this disrespect the time and energy your classmates are investing in their education."

Keep the punishments positive.

Positive punishments, also known as constructive or educational consequences, are designed to correct behavior while fostering personal growth and maintaining a positive classroom environment. Unlike traditional punitive measures, positive punishments aim to engage students in a way that encourages reflection, responsibility, and improvement. Here are some strategies for implementing positive punishments effectively:

My new invention of positive punishment: As a lighthearted consequence for arriving late, students can be encouraged to sing a cheerful song in front of the class, turning a potentially negative experience into a memorable moment of laughter and camaraderie. This fun punishment not only fosters a positive classroom atmosphere but also helps build confidence and community among classmates. To avoid singing, some students race me into the class!!

1. Educational Tasks

- Short Research Assignments: For minor infractions like being late, assign a brief research task related to the subject matter. For example, if a student is late, they could be asked to write a short paragraph on a related topic, demonstrating their understanding.

- Classroom Presentations: Have the student prepare and present a short talk on a topic relevant to the class. This can be a valuable learning experience and help them contribute positively to the class.

2. Creative Tasks

- Creative Performances: For coming late, students could be asked to perform a brief, fun activity such as singing a song, reciting a poem, or performing a skit. Ensure the activity is light-hearted and not humiliating.

- Art Projects: Assign a small art project related to the subject. For instance, drawing a concept map or creating a visual representation of a recent lesson.

3. Classroom Contributions

- Helping with Setup: Assign the student to help with setting up or tidying up the classroom. This fosters a sense of responsibility and contributes positively to the classroom environment.

- Leading an Activity: Have the student lead a small class activity or discussion. This can be a constructive way for them to re-engage with the material.

4. Reflection Activities

- Writing Reflections: Ask the student to write a reflection on their behavior and how it affects their learning and the classroom environment. This encourages self-awareness and accountability.

- Behavior Logs: Maintain a log where students track their own behavior and set goals for improvement. Review it periodically with the student to discuss progress.

5. Community Building

- Positive Peer Interaction: Encourage the student to engage in a positive activity with peers, such as organizing a group study session or leading a team-building exercise.

- Classroom Helper Role: Assign the student a role that involves helping others, such as distributing materials or assisting with classroom tasks.

6. Skill Development

- Public Speaking Practice: For minor infractions, such as tardiness, students could be asked to give a short, informal talk in front of the class, which helps build public speaking skills.

- Organizational Tasks: Have the student assist with organizing classroom materials or resources, helping them develop organizational skills.

7. Volunteering

- Classroom Volunteering: Involve the student in voluntary tasks like helping with a class project or preparing materials for the next lesson.

- Community Service: If appropriate, involve the student in a small community service project related to the school or class.

8. Interactive Learning

- Educational Games: Incorporate educational games or quizzes that the student must participate in as a consequence of their behavior. This makes the consequence engaging and beneficial.

- Peer Teaching: Have the student teach a concept to their peers. This can be a valuable learning experience and a way to reinforce their understanding.

9. Positive Reinforcement

- Reward Systems: Combine positive punishments with reward systems where students earn rewards for improved behavior. This encourages them to view the consequence as part of a broader system of growth and recognition.

- Celebration of Improvement: Acknowledge and celebrate improvements in behavior or performance, reinforcing positive changes.

10. Involvement in Goal Setting

- Goal Setting: Have the student set personal goals related to their behavior and academic performance. Monitor their progress and offer positive reinforcement when goals are met.

Managing Tough Situations in Teaching

Getting mad or angry at students is, unfortunately, a part of the teaching profession. Despite our best efforts, situations may arise that test our patience and composure. However, how we handle these moments and recover from them can significantly impact both the classroom environment and our relationship with students. Below are five strategies to get out of an anger-induced situation and ten tips to recover and rebuild after such events.

Five Strategies to Get Out of an Anger-Induced Situation

1. Pause and Breathe:

- When you feel anger rising, take a moment to pause. Close your eyes, take a few deep breaths, and allow yourself to regain composure. This brief pause can prevent you from saying or doing something you might regret.

2. Step Away Temporarily:

- If the situation allows, step out of the classroom for a moment. Inform the students that you need a brief break. This physical distance can help you calm down and gain perspective.

3. Refocus on the Task:

- Redirect the class's attention to a specific task or activity. Shifting the focus from the conflict to something constructive can diffuse tension and help you regain control of your emotions.

4. Acknowledge Your Feelings:

- It's okay to be human in front of your students. Acknowledge your frustration without lashing out. You might say, "I'm feeling a bit frustrated right now, and I need a moment to collect my thoughts."

5. Use a Calming Technique:

- Implement a calming technique such as counting to ten, visualizing a peaceful scene, or repeating a calming mantra. These methods can help you quickly reduce the intensity of your anger.

Ten Tips to Recover from Tough Situations

1. Apologize if Necessary:

- If your anger led to harsh words or actions, apologize to the students. A simple, sincere apology can go a long way in rebuilding trust and showing that you are committed to maintaining a respectful environment.

2. Reflect on the Situation:

- Take time to reflect on what triggered your anger. Was it something specific a student did, or was it a buildup of smaller frustrations? Understanding the root cause can help you prevent similar situations in the future.

3. Discuss the Incident Calmly:

- After the situation has cooled down, address it with the students. Discuss what happened, why it led to frustration, and how everyone can work together to avoid such incidents.

4. Seek Feedback:

- Engage with your students by asking for their feedback on how the situation was handled. This can provide valuable insights and help you adjust your approach.

5. Practice Forgiveness:

- Forgive yourself for losing your temper. Holding onto guilt can negatively affect your teaching. Acknowledge that everyone makes mistakes and focus on moving forward.

6. Rebuild Relationships:

- Spend time rebuilding relationships with students who may have been affected. Engage with them individually or as a group to show that you value them and are committed to a positive classroom experience.

7. Use Humor to Lighten the Mood:

- After the incident, using humor can help lighten the atmosphere and show that you've moved past the situation. However, be mindful that the humor is appropriate and does not undermine the seriousness of the earlier conflict.

8. Reinforce Positive Behavior:

- Focus on reinforcing positive behavior in the days following the incident. Praise students for their efforts and cooperation, which can help shift the classroom dynamic back to a positive one.

9. Adjust Your Teaching Strategies:

- Consider whether changes to your teaching methods or classroom management strategies could reduce stress and prevent future conflicts. This might include varying your approach to discipline, using more engaging activities, or altering the pace of the lesson.

10. Practice Self-Care:

 - Take care of your mental and emotional well-being. Engage in activities that help you relax and recharge, such as exercise, meditation, or spending time with loved ones. A well-rested and calm teacher is less likely to experience intense anger in the classroom.

Anger in the classroom is inevitable, but it does not have to define your teaching experience. By employing strategies to de-escalate at the moment and taking thoughtful steps to recover afterward, you can maintain a positive and productive learning environment. These experiences also offer valuable opportunities for growth, both for you as a teacher and for your students, as you demonstrate resilience, self-awareness, and the ability to navigate challenges constructively.

Mirroring as a classroom management tool

The psychological basis of mirroring behaviors lies in the activation of mirror neurons, which are specialized brain cells that respond both when we perform an action and when we observe someone else performing the same action. These neurons play a critical role in empathy, social learning, and understanding others' emotions and intentions. By unconsciously mimicking the body language, facial expressions, and emotional states of others, individuals create a sense of connection and mutual understanding.

The effect of mirroring behaviors is profound in fostering social bonding and rapport. When one person mirrors another's behavior, it signals a sense of similarity and empathy, making interactions smoother and more cooperative. This can lead to increased trust, better communication, and a positive feedback loop of reinforcement in both social and professional settings. Mirroring in classroom management is a powerful tool for establishing a reciprocal dynamic of behavior between the teacher and students. By reflecting on the emotional and behavioral tone exhibited by students, teachers can create a clear, consistent link between their actions and the responses they receive, reinforcing the principle that "nice begets nice, and bad begets bad."

When students display positive behaviors—such as attentiveness, respect, or kindness—a teacher can mirror those qualities back by offering praise, encouragement, and a supportive attitude. This positive reinforcement fosters an environment where students feel recognized and appreciated, motivating them to continue behaving well. Conversely, when students exhibit negative behaviors, mirroring those actions through controlled but firm responses helps them understand the consequences of their actions. For example, if a student is disruptive, a teacher might calmly yet firmly respond with clear boundaries, demonstrating that poor behavior will not be tolerated without escalating the situation.

This approach not only encourages students to self-regulate but also builds a reputation for fairness and consistency. Students learn that their actions directly influence the atmosphere of the classroom and that respectful, kind behavior will be met with warmth, while disruptive behavior leads to appropriate corrective measures. Mirroring thus reinforces the concept that behavior, whether positive or negative, yields corresponding outcomes.

Below are five methods of mirroring that can contribute to an efficient and harmonious learning environment:

1. Behavioral Mirroring

- Method: Reflect students' positive behaviors to reinforce them. For instance, if a student is focused and diligent, the teacher can mirror that attentiveness by actively engaging with them, praising their effort, and giving them additional opportunities to contribute.

- Impact: This reinforces that good behavior is valued and reciprocated, encouraging other students to follow suit.

2. Emotional Mirroring

- Method: Reflect students' emotions by matching their tone and energy. If a student is excited about a topic, the teacher can respond with enthusiasm. If a student is frustrated, a calm and empathetic response can help diffuse the tension.

- Impact: This validates students' feelings and fosters a classroom environment where emotional intelligence and mutual respect are practiced.

3. Tone and Language Mirroring

- Method: Match the tone and language students use, particularly when correcting misbehavior. If a student is respectful in a disagreement, the teacher can reciprocate with a respectful tone. If a student is rude, the teacher can mirror them with controlled firmness without hostility.

- Impact: This teaches students the power of language and tone and models how they should communicate respectfully, even during conflicts.

4. Nonverbal Mirroring

- Method: Mirror students' body language and facial expressions. For example, if students are relaxed and focused, a teacher might adopt a similar posture to reinforce the collective mood. If students show disinterest, mirroring with subtle shifts in posture and eye contact can signal attentiveness.

- Impact: This non-verbal communication creates a silent rapport, making students feel understood and helping redirect unspoken classroom dynamics.

5. Work Ethic Mirroring

- Method: Reflect on the work ethic demonstrated by students. If students are engaged and working hard, a teacher can match their effort by offering constructive feedback and investing time in individual progress.

- Impact: By mirroring students' dedication, teachers establish a culture of mutual respect and collaboration, where effort is acknowledged and rewarded.

Effective sentences that can be uttered by the teacher.

1. "I can see that many of you are focused; let's continue this energy throughout the lesson."

2. "You all seem curious about this topic, just like I was when I first learned it. Let's dive deeper together."

3. "I notice some confusion on your faces, and I felt the same when I first studied this. Let's clarify it."

4. "I see a lot of enthusiasm for today's activity, and that makes me excited to guide you through it."

5. "I understand you're feeling frustrated; I've been there too, but we can work through it step by step."

6. "The way you're working hard shows commitment, and it inspires me to push harder for you as well."

7. "Just like you, I'm trying to stay patient with this challenging material. Let's tackle it one part at a time."

8. "I appreciate the respect you're showing each other during discussions. It makes me proud to be your teacher."

9. "Your questions show you're really thinking deeply, which pushes me to give more detailed explanations."

10. "I see many of you are concentrating, and it reminds me how important this topic is. Let's stay focused together."

Randomness in classroom management

Teachers are often tasked with the dual responsibility of discouraging negative behaviors and promoting positive ones, all while ensuring students remain productive. This constant vigilance can be draining, leading to frequent burnout as it depletes energy, patience, and motivation. To maintain effectiveness without the burden of perpetual monitoring, what strategies can be employed to reduce the need for continuous oversight while still achieving optimal results? Introducing randomness in vigilance and responses is an effective strategy. By being unpredictable, it keeps students on their toes, as they are unsure when behaviors will be noticed or addressed. This uncertainty encourages consistent adherence to expectations, fostering a more self-regulated and attentive classroom environment. Maximizing outputs with reduced inputs!

The strategic use of rewards and punishments is a well-established method in pedagogy for promoting desirable behaviors and discouraging undesirable ones. However, the integration of randomness into this process can be a powerful tool, enhancing engagement, reducing stress on both students and teachers, and contributing to a more dynamic and responsive classroom environment. By making the distribution of rewards and punishments less predictable, teachers can foster an atmosphere of attentiveness, motivation, and self-regulation among students.

Here, we shall explore how randomness can be applied effectively in rewarding positive traits and punishing negative ones, focusing on how such practices encourage sustained student engagement while minimizing stress on teachers.

Behavioral Conditioning in Education

At its core, the use of rewards and punishments in education is grounded in behavioral conditioning theories, particularly operant conditioning, as proposed by B.F. Skinner. According to Skinner, behavior can be shaped through reinforcements (rewards) or punishments. Positive reinforcement strengthens desirable behaviors by offering a reward, while negative reinforcement and punishment aim to reduce undesirable behaviors.

However, predictable patterns in reinforcement and punishment can lead to a sense of entitlement or complacency among students. If students know when to expect rewards or punishment, they may only act in accordance with desired behaviors when they believe they are being observed. This predictability can limit the development of intrinsic motivation and long-term behavioral changes, as students may focus more on external rewards than on the inherent value of positive behavior.

In contrast, introducing randomness into this system disrupts expectations and keeps students continuously engaged, not knowing when a reward might come or when a mistake might be called out. This uncertainty encourages consistent effort and attention, as students cannot rely on patterns to guide their actions.

Randomness in Rewarding Good Traits

Randomly rewarding positive behaviors can be a highly effective strategy for promoting desirable student traits such as attentiveness, participation, cooperation, and respect. By not making rewards predictable, students are motivated to display good behavior consistently, as they are unsure when their efforts might be acknowledged.

1. Encouraging Intrinsic Motivation

One of the key benefits of random rewards is that they prevent students from becoming solely dependent on external validation. If rewards are given sporadically and unexpectedly, students learn to value the behavior itself rather than just the reward. For example, a student who consistently participates in class discussions may not receive praise every time but knows that their effort could be recognized at any moment. This intermittent reinforcement helps shift the focus from the reward to the internal satisfaction of contributing to the classroom dynamic.

2. Reducing Stress and Teacher Burnout

A major challenge in classroom management is the pressure on teachers to constantly monitor and reward good behavior. Randomness helps alleviate this burden by removing the expectation that every positive action must be rewarded immediately. Instead, teachers can focus on the overall classroom atmosphere, rewarding good traits occasionally but meaningfully. This reduces the stress associated with continuous reinforcement and creates a more relaxed, less transactional learning environment.

3. Fostering Curiosity and Engagement

When rewards are unpredictable, students are more likely to stay engaged in their learning environment. The element of surprise stimulates curiosity, which in turn enhances attentiveness and participation. A teacher who randomly acknowledges a student's insightful comment or thoughtful question during class discussion keeps the rest of the class alert, as everyone knows that their turn to be recognized might come at any time. This randomness can be particularly effective in encouraging quieter students to participate, as it removes the fear of competition for recognition.

4. Practical Application of Random Rewards

In practice, teachers might use small, tangible rewards such as tokens, stickers, or verbal praise to acknowledge positive behaviors, but on a randomized schedule. For example, if students consistently turn in homework on time, a teacher might choose one or two random students to receive special recognition each week. Alternatively, after a particularly insightful class discussion, the teacher might hand out a small reward to a student who demonstrated critical thinking without prior notice.

This approach can also be adapted to group settings. If the entire class demonstrates collective effort in a group project, the teacher might randomly select one group to receive extra credit or a symbolic reward, ensuring that all groups stay motivated, as any of them could be recognized for their work.

Randomness in Punishing Bad Traits

Randomly applied punishments can also be effective in moderating undesirable behaviors. While consistent discipline is crucial for maintaining order, the element of randomness can prevent students from becoming too comfortable with the boundaries of acceptable behavior. If students are unsure when a transgression might be noticed or punished, they are more likely to regulate their own behavior rather than test limits.

1. Discouraging Complacency

When punishments are applied randomly, students cannot predict when bad behavior will be penalized. This unpredictability prevents students from becoming complacent or attempting to manipulate the system. For example, if a student knows that the teacher only reprimands phone use at certain times, they may become adept at avoiding detection during those times. However, if the teacher occasionally but unpredictably calls out students for inappropriate phone use, students are less likely to risk using their phones in class.

2. Encouraging Self-Discipline

Random punishment encourages students to take greater responsibility for their own actions. In an environment where punishment is not guaranteed but always possible, students must learn to regulate their own behavior rather than simply respond to external controls. This fosters self-discipline, which is a critical skill both in and out of the classroom.

3. Reducing Teacher Stress

Like random rewards, random punishments relieve teachers of the pressure to constantly monitor and discipline students. By establishing an expectation that negative behavior could be noticed and penalized at any time, teachers can step back from constant surveillance. This reduces stress and allows teachers to focus on instruction rather than micromanaging student behavior.

4. Practical Application of Random Punishments

Teachers might adopt a random approach by occasionally enforcing rules more strictly than usual without establishing a predictable pattern. For instance, if students frequently chat during lessons, the teacher might reprimand one or two students randomly on certain occasions, rather than calling out every instance. Over time, students will realize that any instance of misbehavior could be punished, leading to more consistent adherence to classroom rules.

Balancing Randomness with Fairness

A critical concern when implementing randomness in rewards and punishments is maintaining fairness. While randomness can prevent complacency and encourage self-regulation, it should not be perceived as arbitrary or unjust. Students need to understand that while they may not always know when a reward or punishment is coming, the underlying principles are consistent. Good behavior will be recognized, and bad behavior will be addressed — even if the timing is uncertain.

To achieve this balance, teachers should be transparent about the behaviors they value and the consequences of negative actions. Randomness should be applied within a clear framework of expectations, ensuring that students view it as an extension of the teacher's fairness rather than a chaotic or unpredictable element of the classroom environment.

The use of randomness in rewarding and punishing student behavior introduces an element of unpredictability that keeps students engaged, motivated, and self-disciplined. By shifting the focus from external validation to intrinsic motivation, random rewards encourage students to develop a genuine interest in positive behaviors. Similarly, random punishments foster self-regulation, as students cannot rely on predictability to avoid consequences. For teachers, randomness reduces the stress of constant monitoring and provides a more flexible approach to classroom management. Ultimately, this strategy can lead to a more dynamic and balanced learning environment, where both rewards and discipline are tools for growth rather than mere transactional mechanisms.

Here are some of the sentences a teacher could try to infuse randomness.

1. "I could call on anyone at any time, so be ready to share your thoughts whenever you're asked."

2. "Today, we might have a quiz, or maybe not—stay prepared just in case."

3. "I'll be rewarding someone for their effort soon, but I won't say when or who it will be."

4. "Sometimes I let things slide, and sometimes I don't—it depends on how the class is doing overall."

5. "I might check your homework today, or I might not—but it's always best to stay on top of it."

6. "I won't always point out mistakes immediately, but that doesn't mean I won't notice them."

7. "Rewards can come at any moment, even if you don't expect it—keep up the good work consistently."

8. "One of these days, I'll ask a random question from any of our previous lessons, so keep your notes ready."

9. "Sometimes I'm strict about phones, and sometimes I won't say anything—but don't get too comfortable."

10. "I might randomly pick someone to lead a discussion or present today, so make sure you're all prepared."

Boundaries of Freedom in the Classroom

For a teacher, defining the boundaries of freedom is a crucial aspect of classroom management. When done effectively, it helps students understand the limits within which they can exercise their autonomy, fostering a sense of responsibility while still encouraging creativity and independent thinking. The key lies in clearly communicating these boundaries and sincerely allowing students the freedom to explore and express themselves within them.

1. Setting the Stage with Clarity and Respect

- Speech Example: "In our classroom, I want each of you to feel free to express your thoughts, ask questions, and explore new ideas. However, to ensure that everyone has the same opportunity, we have certain guidelines that we all need to follow. These guidelines are not meant to restrict you but to create an environment where everyone can thrive."

- Explanation: This kind of sentence sets a positive tone by framing boundaries as a means of ensuring fairness and mutual respect. It emphasizes that rules are not arbitrary but are in place to benefit the entire class.

2. Empowering Through Responsibility

- Speech Example: "You have the freedom to choose how you approach your assignments, but with that freedom comes the responsibility to meet deadlines and produce your best work. I trust you to manage your time and make decisions that reflect your potential."

- Explanation: Here, the teacher acknowledges the students' autonomy while also reminding them of their responsibilities. This approach empowers students to make choices but within a framework that expects accountability.

3. Encouraging Open Communication

- Speech Example: "If at any point you feel that the boundaries we've set are hindering your learning or creativity, please come talk to me. I'm open to discussing how we can adjust things to better suit your needs while still maintaining the respect and order we need in our classroom."

- Explanation: This sentence encourages students to view boundaries as flexible and open to discussion. It reinforces the idea that the teacher values their input and is willing to negotiate within the established limits.

4. Promoting Positive Freedom

- Speech Example: "You are free to explore different methods in solving problems during our lab sessions. Feel free to experiment and think outside the box, but remember that your safety and the integrity of your work come first. Let's push the boundaries of what we know while respecting the guidelines that keep us on track."

- Explanation: This kind of speech promotes the idea of "positive freedom," where students are encouraged to push their intellectual boundaries within a safe and structured environment. It balances encouragement with caution.

5. Balancing Freedom and Discipline

- Speech Example: "Freedom in this classroom means you have the space to learn in a way that works best for you, whether it's through group work, independent study, or creative projects. But it also means respecting the classroom environment—keeping noise levels down, staying focused, and supporting each other."

- Explanation: This approach clarifies that freedom comes with the expectation of self-discipline. It reinforces that the classroom is a shared space where individual freedoms must align with the collective good.

6. Fostering a Collaborative Environment

- Speech Example: "Within these walls, you are encouraged to collaborate with your peers, share ideas, and even debate differing opinions. The freedom to express yourselves is a cornerstone of our learning experience, but it must be exercised with respect and a willingness to listen to others."

- Explanation: This sentence emphasizes the importance of collaboration and respectful discourse, suggesting that freedom in the classroom is not just about individual expression but also about engaging constructively with others.

7. Encouraging Growth Within Limits

- Speech Example: "Think of these boundaries as the edges of a canvas—you have the freedom to paint anything you like within this space. These limits are here to challenge you and help you focus your creativity and energy. Let's see what masterpieces you can create within the framework we've established."

- Explanation: This metaphorical approach helps students see boundaries as opportunities rather than constraints. It encourages them to view the limits as a space for growth and creative exploration.

In defining and communicating boundaries of freedom, the teacher sets the stage for a classroom environment that fosters both discipline and creativity. By using language that is clear, respectful, and empowering, a teacher can encourage students to explore their potential while understanding the importance of responsibility and mutual respect. These boundaries are not walls but guiding lines that help students navigate their educational journey with confidence and purpose.

Helping a stuck student

When teaching difficult problems, it is essential to employ strategies that facilitate learning and mastery. Three effective approaches are repetition, downgrading the difficulty, and upgrading the difficulty level.

1. Repetition

Purpose: Reinforce understanding and build confidence through practice.

Repetition is a foundational teaching method that enables students to solidify their knowledge and improve their problem-solving abilities. The key is to provide students with multiple opportunities to practice similar problems to strengthen their grasp of the underlying concepts.

- Drill Exercises: Offering repetitive exercises that mimic the difficult problem allows students to internalize the approach needed to solve them. These drills help students gain fluency and become more comfortable with complex topics.

- Review Sessions: Regular review sessions are essential for revisiting challenging concepts and consolidating learning. This continuous reinforcement deepens students' understanding, ensuring that they retain critical information over time.

- Incremental Complexity: Gradually increasing the complexity of problems helps students master each level before moving on to more difficult questions. This scaffolding ensures students are not overwhelmed while still being challenged progressively.

Implementation:

- Quizzes: Incorporating quizzes into the learning process provides students with regular opportunities to practice and reinforces their understanding.

- Homework Assignments: Assign variations of the original problem, allowing students to explore the concept from multiple angles.

- Peer Tutoring: Pairing students for collaborative learning enables them to reinforce their skills by teaching and learning from one another.

2. Downgrading the Difficulty Level

Purpose: Build foundational skills and confidence by simplifying problems.

When students struggle with a complex problem, breaking it down into smaller, manageable components helps them tackle it more effectively. Downgrading the difficulty provides a clear, step-by-step path toward mastering the challenging concepts.

- Scaffolding: By breaking the problem into simpler sub-tasks, students can gradually build up their understanding. Starting with basic problems that focus on individual elements allows students to develop the necessary skills for tackling the larger problem.

- Tiered Practice: Introduce problems with increasing difficulty, beginning with foundational questions that prepare students for more complex challenges.

- Guided Practice: Walk students through simplified versions of the problem with clear, step-by-step guidance. This approach builds confidence and provides a clearer roadmap for solving complex problems.

Implementation:

- Step-by-Step Instructions: Providing detailed instructions for solving simpler problems allows students to focus on understanding the process, one step at a time.

- Interactive Activities: Hands-on learning and manipulatives can simplify abstract concepts, allowing students to engage actively and build their understanding.

- Mini-Lessons: Short, focused lessons on specific components of the problem help students tackle more challenging concepts with a solid foundation.

3. Upgrading the Difficulty Level

Purpose: Stimulate creative problem-solving and encourage higher-order thinking.

Sometimes, when students are stuck on a smaller problem, introducing a more complex challenge can help shift their perspective. As the Russian proverb suggests, "When there is no way out, go deeper." By increasing the difficulty level, students are encouraged to apply their existing knowledge in new ways, prompting breakthroughs and innovative solutions.

Rationale: Engaging students with more advanced problems can help them reframe their approach to the initial challenge, encouraging them to think creatively and analytically.

- Introduce Related Complex Problems: Presenting a more challenging yet related problem encourages students to use their existing knowledge in broader contexts, leading to new insights.

- Provide Advanced Scenarios: Offering case studies or real-world applications of the concept helps students see the relevance of the material and apply it to more intricate situations.

- Encourage Creative Problem-Solving: Open-ended questions that allow for multiple solutions push students to think outside the box and develop innovative approaches.

Implementation:

- Progressive Challenges: Gradually increase the complexity of the problem to stretch students' thinking and problem-solving abilities.

- Real-World Applications: Present problems grounded in real-life situations to engage students with complex, multi-layered scenarios that require deeper thinking.

Benefits:

- New Perspectives: Tackling more complex problems enables students to break free from rigid thought patterns and approach challenges with fresh insights.

- Enhanced Problem-Solving Skills: Engaging with advanced problems fosters critical thinking and improves students' overall problem-solving capabilities.

- Increased Motivation: Successfully solving more complex problems boosts confidence, motivating students to tackle challenges with greater resilience.

Deliberate vulnerability

The concept of deliberate vulnerability in teaching is a nuanced approach that involves intentionally allowing students to perceive the teacher as fallible, approachable, and open to mutual growth. This pedagogical strategy embraces the idea that the teacher-student dynamic is not solely about the dissemination of knowledge but also about fostering a collaborative and empowering learning environment. Deliberate vulnerability, in this context, encourages a shift from traditional power dynamics to a more egalitarian relationship, ultimately contributing to a more positive and effective learning experience.

At the heart of deliberate vulnerability in teaching is the willingness of the instructor to acknowledge and share their own learning journey, including moments of struggle, uncertainty, and even mistakes. This transparency breaks down the traditional teacher-student hierarchy, creating a space where students feel comfortable expressing their own challenges and uncertainties without fear of judgment.

One way to manifest deliberate vulnerability is through sharing personal anecdotes or stories of academic struggles. By recounting instances where they faced academic challenges, made errors, or experienced setbacks, the teacher becomes relatable and humanizes the learning process. This transparency serves as a powerful tool to destigmatize mistakes, creating a culture where errors are seen as opportunities for growth rather than as failures.

Moreover, deliberate vulnerability involves being open to learning from students. Teachers can explicitly communicate that they value the unique perspectives and experiences each student brings to the classroom. This acknowledgment fosters an environment where students feel empowered to share their insights and take an active role in the learning process. In doing so, the teacher models humility and a genuine appreciation for the diverse talents and knowledge that exist within the classroom.

Another facet of deliberate vulnerability is creating space for student-led discussions or projects where their input significantly influences the direction of the lesson. By relinquishing some control and allowing students to take ownership of their learning, the teacher demonstrates trust in their abilities and fosters a sense of responsibility. This approach not only enhances student engagement but also reinforces the idea that learning is a collaborative endeavor where both teacher and students contribute to the collective understanding.

Deliberate vulnerability can also be expressed through the acknowledgment of the ever-evolving nature of knowledge. By demonstrating a willingness to learn alongside students, the teacher communicates that education is a dynamic process, not a static body of information. This attitude cultivates a growth mindset within the classroom, encouraging students to embrace challenges, persist through difficulties, and view learning as a continuous journey.

In summary, deliberate vulnerability in teaching is a powerful approach that transforms the traditional teacher-student relationship into a collaborative and empowering dynamic. By openly sharing personal challenges, acknowledging the value of student input, and embracing a continuous learning mindset, the teacher creates an environment where students feel seen, heard, and inspired. This intentional vulnerability not only fosters a positive and supportive learning atmosphere but also equips students with essential skills such as resilience, critical thinking, and a lifelong love for learning. Ultimately, the deliberate vulnerability of the teacher becomes a catalyst for student success, empowering them to overcome obstacles and emerge as confident, independent learners.

Opportunities to praise the students

Who doesn't like praise? Everyone knows the wonders praise can do to people. Praising students at the right moments can significantly boost their motivation, confidence, and engagement in learning. Give clear, specific, and authentic verbal praise to the student. Here are 20 opportunities to praise students:

1. Completing a Difficult Assignment: When a student successfully completes a challenging task, acknowledge their hard work and perseverance.

2. Consistent Participation in Class: Praise students who regularly contribute to class discussions, showing their engagement and understanding.

3. Improvement Over Time: Recognize students who have shown noticeable improvement in their work or behavior, even if they aren't at the top yet.

4. Helping Peers: Praise students who assist their classmates, fostering a collaborative and supportive classroom environment.

5. Creativity in Problem-Solving: When a student comes up with an innovative solution to a problem, acknowledge their creativity.

6. Completing Tasks on Time: Recognize students who consistently meet deadlines, reinforcing the value of time management.

7. Showing Initiative: Praise students who take the initiative to start projects, ask questions, or seek extra help.

8. Positive Attitude: Highlight students who maintain a positive outlook, especially in challenging situations.

9. Active Listening: Recognize students who actively listen and engage with the material and their peers.

10. Excellent Group Work: Praise students who effectively collaborate with their peers during group activities or projects.

11. Perfect Attendance: Acknowledge students who attend class regularly, reinforcing the importance of consistency.

12. Academic Excellence: Celebrate students who achieve high scores or grades on exams, assignments, or projects.

13. Overcoming Obstacles: Praise students who manage to overcome personal or academic challenges, showing resilience.

14. Respectful Behavior: Recognize students who consistently demonstrate respect towards their peers, teachers, and the learning environment.

15. Effective Communication: Praise students who clearly and effectively communicate their ideas during discussions or presentations.

16. Curiosity and Inquiry: Acknowledge students who ask insightful questions, demonstrating a deep interest in the subject matter.

17. Leadership: Praise students who step up as leaders, guiding their peers in group activities or class discussions.

18. Exemplary Homework: Recognize students who consistently submit well-done homework, reflecting diligence and understanding.

19. Outstanding Projects: Celebrate students who produce exceptional work in projects, showing dedication and effort.

20. Positive Peer Influence: Acknowledge students who positively influence their classmates, helping to create a supportive and encouraging classroom atmosphere.

Chapter 10: The Pivotal Role of Kindness in Teaching

Teachers are prone to frustration, and students are prone to boredom, which can create an atmosphere of stress that permeates the classroom. When frustration and disengagement take root, the process of teaching and learning can become laborious and draining for both parties. Teachers may struggle to maintain enthusiasm and focus, while students find it difficult to stay engaged and motivated. At least occasionally, it is a reality for either party or both. As this cycle intensifies, the classroom dynamic can shift from one of curiosity and growth to one of tension and stagnation. Breaking this cycle requires conscious effort from both teachers and students to foster a positive, supportive, and engaging learning environment.

Students are diverse, and there are many; teachers are diverse, and there are many. No single technique is universally applicable at all times. However, if there is one approach that students, teachers, and everyone alike can accept and expect, it is kindness. Kindness transcends differences and acts as a universal language that resonates in all spaces and across all times. It fosters respect, understanding, and connection, creating a positive environment for both teaching and learning. Whether in the classroom or beyond, kindness remains an enduring and effective tool for building meaningful relationships and fostering growth. Kindness always works.

In the realm of education, where the primary goal is to facilitate learning and personal growth, the significance of kindness cannot be overstated. Kindness transcends mere professional competence; it is the cornerstone of effective teaching and profoundly influences both students and the educational environment. This essay explores why kindness is the most crucial attribute in the teaching profession, illustrating its impact on student development, classroom dynamics, and overall educational success.

The Foundation of Trust and Respect

Kindness establishes a foundation of trust and respect between teachers and students. When teachers approach their students with genuine empathy and understanding, they create an environment where students feel valued and supported. This trust is essential for fostering a positive learning atmosphere. Students are more likely to engage actively in their education, seek help when needed, and strive for academic success when they know their teachers are kind and approachable. Research supports this notion, indicating that positive teacher-student relationships enhance student motivation and academic performance.

Enhancing Emotional Well-being

The emotional well-being of students is intricately linked to their academic success. Kindness from teachers can significantly affect students' mental health, reducing stress and anxiety related to their educational experiences. Teachers who show kindness are better equipped to identify and address students' emotional needs, creating a supportive space where students can thrive both academically and personally. This supportive environment is crucial for students facing challenges, as it helps them develop resilience and a positive outlook on their educational journey.

Promoting a Collaborative Learning Environment

Kindness fosters a collaborative and inclusive classroom environment. When teachers model kindness, they set a standard for how students should interact with one another. This modeling helps to cultivate a classroom culture where collaboration, mutual respect, and constructive feedback are valued. Students are more likely to engage in cooperative learning activities, respect diverse perspectives, and contribute positively to group work when kindness is at the core of their classroom interactions. This approach not only enhances the learning experience but also prepares students for future collaborative endeavors in their professional and personal lives.

Building Long-term Impact

The impact of kindness extends beyond the immediate classroom environment. Teachers who demonstrate kindness leave a lasting impression on their students, influencing their attitudes towards learning and their personal development long after they leave school. Former students often recall teachers who showed them kindness as having been pivotal figures in their lives, shaping their values and approach to both their careers and personal relationships. This enduring influence underscores the profound effect that kindness can have on individuals and their future success.

Practical Implementation of Kindness in Teaching

To effectively integrate kindness into teaching practices, educators can adopt several strategies:

1. Active Listening: Engage in active listening to understand students' concerns and perspectives, demonstrating empathy and respect.

2. Positive Reinforcement: Use positive reinforcement to acknowledge and encourage students' efforts and achievements, fostering a supportive learning environment.

3. Personal Connections: Build personal connections with students by showing genuine interest in their well-being and academic progress.

4. Constructive Feedback: Provide feedback in a constructive and supportive manner, focusing on students' strengths and areas for improvement without diminishing their confidence.

5. Inclusive Practices: Implement inclusive practices that ensure all students feel valued and included, promoting a sense of belonging and acceptance.

In the teaching profession, kindness is not merely an ancillary attribute but a fundamental quality that underpins effective teaching and fosters a positive learning environment. By prioritizing kindness, educators can build trusting relationships with students, enhance their emotional well-being, promote collaborative learning, and leave a lasting impact on their lives. Kindness, therefore, stands as the single most important asset for any teacher, transcending other professional skills and contributing profoundly to both student success and personal fulfillment in the educational field.

Kindness and Smile: The Universal Language of Love and Respect

In our interconnected world, where language often serves as a barrier, kindness and a smile emerge as universal languages that transcend cultural differences. These simple gestures communicate love, respect, and warmth, fostering connections that words alone may fail to achieve. Kindness embodies empathy and compassion. Acts of kindness—whether offering help, listening, or showing understanding—affirm our shared humanity and meet the innate human need for connection and belonging. In classrooms and communities, kindness cultivates trust, diffuses tension, and promotes cooperation, allowing for harmonious interactions. A smile is a powerful non-verbal communication tool that conveys warmth and friendliness. Its contagious nature fosters positive atmospheres in professional and educational settings, encouraging openness and reducing anxiety among students.

Be approachable

Approachability is a critical trait for teachers, as it fosters a positive learning environment, builds trust, and encourages student engagement. An approachable teacher creates a safe space where students feel comfortable seeking help, asking questions, and expressing themselves. Here are several effective ways to enhance approachability:

Creating an approachable atmosphere in the classroom is vital for fostering a supportive and engaging learning environment. A warm and friendly demeanor is foundational; a genuine smile and positive body language make you appear welcoming and approachable. Maintaining eye contact and nodding while students speak signals engagement and receptiveness. Furthermore, expressing enthusiasm for teaching and interactions encourages a lively classroom atmosphere, enhancing student motivation.

Open communication is another critical component. By encouraging questions and fostering an environment where students feel comfortable seeking clarification, you promote a culture of inquiry. Being accessible for one-on-one conversations and providing clear contact information reinforces your approachability. Active listening further strengthens this connection; giving full attention to students and acknowledging their concerns validates their feelings and builds trust.

To create a supportive atmosphere, demonstrate empathy toward students' challenges and successes. Offering constructive feedback that highlights strengths while gently addressing areas for improvement shows that you care about their growth. Additionally, using clear, simple language and being flexible in your teaching methods cater to diverse learning styles.

Fostering relationships by learning about students' lives outside academics and promoting peer interactions enhances rapport. By maintaining professionalism, respecting diversity, and promoting inclusivity, you create a safe space where students feel valued and motivated to engage actively in their education.

Teacher Vs. Friend

Have you seen a meme that says, "A friend teaches better than a teacher?" The notion that "a friend teaches better than a teacher" taps into fundamental psychological and philosophical principles about learning, authority, and human interaction. Learning, at its core, is a deeply relational process. It flourishes in environments that foster trust, emotional security, and openness. Psychologically, this aligns with the idea that the emotional and cognitive dimensions of learning are inseparable. When a teacher takes on qualities associated with friendship—such as warmth, patience, and a non-judgmental attitude—it helps reduce the emotional barriers that can impede learning, such as fear, anxiety, and insecurity.

From a psychological perspective, social learning theory emphasizes that individuals learn best through observation, imitation, and social interaction. A friend, being on equal footing and familiar with the learner's experiences, is often perceived as less of an authority figure and more of a peer. This peer dynamic creates an environment in which learners feel comfortable experimenting, making mistakes, and learning through trial and error. The absence of formal judgment frees the learner to take cognitive risks, a process known as "playful learning," which fosters creativity and deeper engagement.

Additionally, in the absence of the pressure to "perform" for a grade or external validation, students in peer-like interactions often engage in more intrinsic motivation. Intrinsic motivation—the desire to learn for the sake of curiosity and personal growth—can be stifled in more traditional, hierarchical teacher-student settings, where extrinsic motivators like grades and evaluations dominate. A friend's lack of formal authority means that the learning is driven by mutual interest, exploration, and support rather than by external validation. This connects deeply to self-determination theory, which highlights the importance of autonomy, competence, and relatedness in fostering optimal motivation. When teachers emulate this dynamic, they promote an environment conducive to self-directed, meaningful learning.

Philosophically, this idea traces back to the Socratic method, where dialogue and shared inquiry are central. The ancient Greek notion of learning through "dialectic" conversations—where ideas are exchanged freely, and the learning process is a shared journey—mirrors the dynamic often found between friends. A friend-teacher relationship aligns with this dialogical process, in which both teacher and student engage in a mutual exploration of knowledge rather than a one-directional transmission of information. This reflects the concept of "philosophical friendship," where growth occurs not through rigid hierarchy but through shared pursuit of truth.

However, while adopting a friendly approach is beneficial, it must be balanced with the teacher's role as a guide and authority figure. Philosophically, the teacher as a "philosopher-king," as Plato described, is still necessary. They have a responsibility to maintain intellectual rigor and to lead students through complex material. The challenge lies in creating a balance between friendship and authority. Teachers must provide structure and expertise, but they can do so in a way that fosters mutual respect and openness.

The key is finding the equilibrium where the authority of the teacher doesn't stifle the student's intellectual curiosity but instead nurtures it. This balance of authority and relatability can foster what philosopher Paulo Freire called "co-intentional education," where both teacher and student are active participants in the learning process. The goal is not to relinquish authority but to humanize it—recognizing that the role of a teacher is to facilitate, rather than dictate, the learning journey.

By integrating psychological insights and philosophical approaches, teachers can create an environment that combines the best elements of friendship—support, trust, and openness—while maintaining the necessary authority to guide students through their intellectual development. This dual approach can unlock deeper levels of student engagement and learning, ultimately leading to a more profound and transformative educational experience. "To be a good teacher, one must become one with the students."

Using "please," "sorry," and "thank you."

In the realm of teaching, the use of powerful words such as "please," "sorry," and "thank you" significantly enhances the dynamics of the classroom environment. The word "please" is not merely a formality but an essential component of respectful communication. When a teacher uses "please" while making requests, it conveys respect for the students' autonomy and fosters a collaborative atmosphere. For instance, asking, "Please hand in your assignments by Friday," rather than giving a command, helps in establishing a culture of mutual respect. This simple word demonstrates that the teacher values the students' cooperation and acknowledges their role in the learning process.

Apologizing with the word "sorry" is equally crucial in maintaining a positive learning environment. When a teacher admits mistakes or acknowledges misunderstandings by saying, "I'm sorry for any confusion I caused," it humanizes the teacher and fosters trust. Apologies can diffuse tension, correct errors, and show that the teacher is open to feedback and committed to improving the learning experience. Such humility not only repairs relationships but also models emotional intelligence and responsibility for students, encouraging them to approach their own errors with a constructive mindset. I make an effort to address any friction in the classroom promptly. I arrange a meeting to resolve the issue as soon as possible and actively work to diffuse the situation. Even if the fault is not mine, I apologize to the student. Although it can be difficult and challenging for my ego, I believe it is necessary to reduce tension and foster a peaceful and progressive environment. Apologizing, despite being a difficult task, is a crucial step towards maintaining harmony and facilitating growth.

Expressing gratitude through the word "thank you" reinforces positive behaviors and contributions within the classroom. When a teacher says, "Thank you for your participation today," or "I appreciate your effort on this project," it acknowledges and values the students' hard work. This recognition boosts students' motivation and morale, creating an encouraging environment where they feel valued and understood. Regularly incorporating "thank you" into interactions helps build a supportive classroom culture where students are more likely to engage, contribute, and develop a sense of belonging. By effectively using these powerful words, teachers can cultivate a respectful, empathetic, and appreciative learning environment that enhances both teaching and learning.

Here are a few sentences.

1. "Please make sure to submit your assignments on time; it helps me stay organized and ensures that your work is graded promptly."

2. "I'm sorry for any confusion caused by the instructions earlier; let's clarify them to ensure everyone understands."

3. "Thank you for your patience while I address your questions; your understanding is greatly appreciated."

4. "Please remember to respect each other's opinions during discussions; it creates a more inclusive learning environment."

5. "Sorry for the inconvenience caused by the schedule change; we'll make sure to adjust it to better suit everyone's needs."

6. "Thank you for participating actively in today's class; your contributions greatly enhance our discussions."

7. "Please let me know if you need any additional help with the material; I'm here to support your learning."

8. "I'm sorry if I seemed rushed during the lecture; I'll make sure to allocate more time for questions in the future."

9. "Thank you for being so diligent with your homework; your commitment to your studies is commendable."

10. "Please feel free to reach out if you're struggling with any concepts; together, we can work through any difficulties you're facing."

Finding Mistakes Graciously: Confront and Comfort

As a new professor, I used to find a certain satisfaction in identifying mistakes in my students' answers. There was a sense of pleasure in pointing out these errors, especially during viva voce or when reviewing student project presentations. The process felt like a demonstration of my expertise and authority in the subject matter. I noticed this satisfaction was particularly strong when I could pinpoint gaps in their knowledge or misunderstanding. But over time, something shifted. I began to notice the impact it had on the students. Some were misinformed, and others struggled with nerves. I even witnessed a few students tear up, overwhelmed by the experience. I am sure that I have attracted a lot of hatred and a negative reputation, which I suspect still lingers around.

This realization softened me. I didn't stop finding mistakes—it's a core part of the teaching process—but I changed the way I approached it. Instead of bluntly pointing out errors, I started giving hints and guiding students toward self-correction. It became more about helping them discover the right answers for themselves than showing where they had gone wrong.

I adopted the principle of "confront but comfort." Confrontation is necessary because pointing out errors is part of growth, but it's equally important to cushion that with empathy. I've seen some teachers avoid confrontation altogether, which I believe does a disservice to the students. If we fail to address mistakes, we fail to fulfill our role as educators. But if we address them without compassion, we harm the student's confidence. Balancing these two elements is what I've learned is essential to the integrity of teaching.

Sharing humorous mistakes from both a student and teacher perspective can serve as a powerful reminder that learning is a continuous, shared journey and that errors are an inevitable part of growth. There will be some mistakes in the book, too! As a student, many of the mistakes I made were both humbling and hilarious in hindsight, from mixing up basic biological terms during exams to overcomplicating simple concepts. These experiences, though embarrassing at the time, provided valuable lessons that stuck with me throughout my academic career.

When I became a teacher, the tables turned, and I found myself on the other side of the desk, observing similar blunders from my own students. Yet, I wasn't immune to making mistakes myself. From accidentally giving students conflicting information to realizing mid-lecture that I had been explaining a concept incorrectly, I've had my fair share of "teachable" moments. I remember one time during a viva voce, I confidently asked a student a question about a biological process, only to realize later that I had framed the question completely wrong! We laughed it off, and it reminded me how human we all are in the classroom.

I am sure I will make more mistakes, just that I acknowledge that I might make mistakes and that I am tolerant of others' mistakes in my professional sphere. What these experiences taught me is that mistakes, whether from students or teachers, can be approached with humor and understanding. They are opportunities to lighten the atmosphere, build connections, and encourage a more resilient attitude toward learning. When students see that even their teachers are fallible, it fosters a more open and positive environment where mistakes aren't feared but embraced as part of the educational journey. After all, it's these moments that make the classroom more relatable, more human, and, quite often, more fun.

In any educational system, it is the teacher's duty to identify and correct students' mistakes, encompassing gaps in knowledge, misconceptions, or performance errors. While this process is vital for learning, it can be problematic if the act of pinpointing mistakes begins to inflate the teacher's sense of pride or superiority. The temptation to view error identification as a sign of expertise can lead to an unchecked ego, negatively impacting the teacher both professionally and personally. A teacher's primary role should focus on guiding students toward growth and understanding rather than asserting dominance.

Psychologically, students often experience embarrassment when their mistakes are highlighted, particularly in front of peers. This emotional pain is exacerbated by social context; the larger the audience witnessing the error, the greater the potential for shame. Public correction can damage a student's self-esteem, leading to long-term effects on motivation and emotional well-being.

Teachers, having once been students, should remain attuned to these emotions and avoid deriving satisfaction from exposing mistakes. Instead, they must remember that the focus should always be on the student's development. By adopting an empathetic approach that softens the impact of mistakes and provides constructive feedback, teachers can foster a safe environment where students feel comfortable making errors and learning from them, ultimately cultivating resilience and confidence. Sensitivity to individual emotional needs is crucial in this feedback process, as students' reactions can vary widely, from defensiveness to withdrawal or frustration. A compassionate educator not only supports student growth but also enhances their own professional development.

Confronting softly

1. "I noticed a small mistake here, but that's okay—we can work through it together."

2. "This part needs a bit more clarity; I know you can fix it with just a little adjustment."

3. "You're almost there; just a few tweaks are needed to make this perfect."

4. "Let's take a closer look at this section; I think you might have misunderstood something, but it's an easy fix."

5. "There's a slight error here, but don't worry, it's all part of the learning process."

6. "I see where you went off track here, but I'm confident you'll get it with a little more focus."

7. "This answer isn't quite right, but you're really close—let's refine it."

8. "I can tell you put effort into this, but there's a small gap that we can fill together."

9. "This could use a bit more detail or explanation, but you've got a great foundation."

10. "There's a mistake here, but don't let it discourage you—we all learn from these moments."

Comforting

1. "Mistakes are just stepping stones to improvement, and you're already on the right path."

2. "Everyone makes mistakes; what matters is that you're learning and growing from it."

3. "Don't be too hard on yourself—this is just part of the process, and you're doing great."

4. "I've seen so much progress in your work, and this small mistake doesn't change that."

5. "The fact that you're here, learning and trying, is what truly counts."

6. "This is just a bump in the road; you'll be back on track in no time."

7. "You've got the potential, and this mistake is just one of many learning opportunities."

8. "I've made similar mistakes myself—it's how we all get better."

9. "Remember, mistakes don't define you, but how you respond to them does."

10. "You've handled this well—let's move forward and focus on what you're going to achieve next."

<u>Building a reputation</u>

Reputation in an academic setting is the perceived image a student or teacher holds, shaped by their actions, achievements, and interactions within the community. It is a powerful psychological force, influencing how others engage with and judge them. A strong reputation can lead to increased respect, trust, and opportunities, while a negative reputation can isolate and limit a person's potential. Students often work harder to preserve a positive image, driven by a need for recognition and acceptance. For teachers, maintaining a good reputation impacts their influence, authority, and ability to motivate and inspire students effectively.

Reputation holds immense importance because it precedes and shapes first impressions, serving as a foundation for how individuals are initially perceived. Before any direct interaction, reputation informs others about a person's reliability, competence, and character. In academic settings, a strong reputation can open doors for trust, collaboration, and respect even before a formal introduction, giving an individual a head start in social and professional dynamics. Conversely, a poor reputation may prejudice others, making it harder to form positive connections. Essentially, reputation sets the stage for first impressions, influencing relationships and opportunities before they even begin.

Building a reputation begins the moment one steps onto campus, or even earlier, as the impressions formed at first sight are powerful and enduring. The social media signature also accounts for the reputation in the modern world. Psychological research supports the idea that people make snap judgments within seconds of meeting someone, often based on non-verbal cues such as appearance, body language, and overall demeanor. These initial perceptions, which are heavily influenced by grooming, posture, and the subtle "air" one carries, can set the tone for how others view a person's competence, confidence, and social standing. The halo effect, a cognitive bias where positive impressions in one area influence perceptions in other areas, underscores the importance of making a strong first impression through careful attention to one's outward appearance and behavior.

Following the initial visual assessment, language becomes the next critical component in building a reputation. The way one speaks—encompassing vocabulary, tone, and delivery—serves as a reflection of intellectual capacity, emotional intelligence, and social acumen. Psycholinguistic studies reveal that language not only conveys information but also signals social status, educational background, and personality traits. A refined use of language, characterized by clarity, sophistication, and appropriateness to the context, can elevate one's perceived authority and likability. In contrast, poor language use can undermine an otherwise positive impression, highlighting the interconnectedness of appearance and speech in reputation formation.

The saying "*vesham bhasha*," from Telugu culture, succinctly captures the psychological progression of impression formation: appearance first, followed by language. This reflects a deep understanding of human psychology, recognizing that while initial judgments are often based on what we see, lasting reputations are built on what we hear and how we communicate. The combination of visual presentation and verbal articulation forms a comprehensive image of an individual, influencing how they are perceived and remembered by others. Therefore, those entering a new environment, such as a campus, must be mindful of both their physical presence and their linguistic expression to build a positive and lasting reputation.

Building a reputation as a quality teacher extends far beyond the confines of the classroom and significantly influences the broader educational environment. Such a reputation is not only a reflection of a teacher's effectiveness but also a crucial factor in shaping the attitudes and behaviors of students, their families, and colleagues.

Beyond appearance and language, a person's reputation is also shaped by deeper attributes such as knowledge, intelligence, integrity, and humor. These qualities, which emerge over time through interactions and observations, form the bedrock of how others perceive an individual's character and capabilities. Knowledge and intelligence demonstrate competence and the ability to contribute meaningfully to conversations and tasks, while integrity reflects a steadfast commitment to ethical principles, earning trust and respect. Humor, when appropriately applied, can make one more relatable and likable, fostering positive connections with others. Together, these traits contribute to a well-rounded reputation that balances intellectual prowess with moral and emotional depth.

The dynamics of how one navigates authority and relationships—such as how stern or forgiving one is, or how approachable and open one appears—also significantly impact reputation. A stern demeanor may convey decisiveness and strength, yet if balanced with forgiveness and understanding, it can also demonstrate fairness and compassion. Approachability signals openness to others' ideas and concerns, which fosters trust and collaboration, while openness itself—both in thought and action—invites diversity of perspectives and encourages meaningful dialogue. These interpersonal dynamics require a delicate balance; too much of one trait without its counterbalance can lead to perceptions of rigidity or leniency, detachment or over-familiarity. Thus, reputation is not only about what one knows or says but also about how one interacts with others and adapts to varying social contexts.

For example, once a person earns a reputation for being humorous, the work of making people laugh becomes effortless. The audience, already primed by the person's reputation, anticipates humor in everything they do or say. Even the simplest gesture, like a sneeze, can provoke laughter. The psychology behind this lies in expectation—when people expect humor, their minds are more receptive to finding it, even in ordinary actions. The humorist, then, doesn't need to constantly strive for comedic brilliance; their established reputation does half the job, setting the stage for even subtle moments to be perceived as amusing. The same goes with a serious person or a profound person.

Reputation is a complex construct shaped by personal interactions and social dynamics. It evolves through impressions based on appearance and communication, solidified by knowledge, integrity, and humor. By maintaining professionalism and integrity, educators can cultivate a reputation that reflects their true qualities, positively influencing student engagement and learning outcomes.

Here are some tips to help establish and maintain such a reputation:

- Demonstrate Expertise: Consistently display deep knowledge of the subject and keep explanations clear and engaging. Share insights that go beyond textbooks to inspire curiosity.

- Effective Communication: Articulate thoughts with clarity and precision, fostering an open, respectful dialogue with students. Encourage questions and discussions.

- Consistency and Fairness: Be consistent in grading and evaluations. Treat all students fairly, building trust in your impartiality.

- Supportive Feedback: Provide constructive feedback that helps students grow. Acknowledge improvements and guide them through challenges.

- Approachable Personality: Maintain a warm, approachable demeanor, making students feel comfortable seeking help. Show empathy and patience.

- Sportive Spirit: Encourage healthy competition and participation in extracurricular activities, promoting balance between academics and sports.

- Humor and Positivity: Integrate humor into teaching to create a light, positive classroom environment. This fosters enjoyment and engagement.

- Professionalism: Exhibit punctuality, preparedness, and a strong work ethic, modeling professional behavior for students to emulate.

Liberal and stringent teacher

The role of a teacher is a delicate balancing act. Being a teacher requires not only the delivery of knowledge but also the cultivation of personality, confidence, discipline, and motivation in students. This dual role, especially in environments where motivation and productivity are low, necessitates both softness and harshness. While empathy, kindness, and understanding are essential traits, an overly soft approach can backfire, creating a lack of respect, discipline, and engagement from students. On the other hand, controlled harshness, when applied thoughtfully, can challenge students to push beyond their limits and meet expectations. The key lies in balancing these two extremes, ensuring that both compassion and firmness are wielded for the sole purpose of student learning and upliftment.

Risks of Being Too Soft as a Teacher

When a teacher is perceived as overly soft, there is a tendency for students to become complacent. In classrooms where productivity and motivation are already low, the absence of firm boundaries and consequences can lead to several adverse outcomes:

1. Erosion of Authority: Students may begin to test the limits of a teacher's patience, pushing boundaries further because they feel no real consequences exist. In such cases, the teacher's authority becomes eroded, and students start viewing the teacher as more of a peer than an instructor. The danger here is not just a lack of discipline but a breakdown of the very structure that is necessary for learning to occur. Without respect, teaching becomes infinitely harder.

2. Lack of Motivation: In an environment where expectations are not clearly enforced, students lose the drive to excel. The absence of challenges means that students will often settle for mediocrity. Being soft too often can communicate to students that their teacher has low expectations of them, which diminishes their own self-expectations. With no sense of challenge, there is little reason for them to exert themselves.

3. Undermined Accountability: A soft teacher may avoid enforcing consequences for missed assignments, disruptive behavior, or underperformance. While this may seem empathetic in the short term, it ultimately deprives students of learning essential life skills, such as responsibility and accountability. Without these, students are not prepared for the demands of the real world, where consequences for inaction and failure are inevitable.

4. Lack of Preparedness: Finally, a teacher's primary duty is to prepare students not just academically but for life beyond the classroom. If a teacher shields students from the natural consequences of their actions by being too lenient, they may unintentionally leave students ill-equipped to face the challenges and setbacks of adulthood.

In my experiences as a soft person, the lack or loss of motivation has been the biggest issue. Productivity declined significantly, and the attitude towards learning almost disappeared. While classes proceeded smoothly, any take-home assignments or outside classwork were often left unfinished and sometimes not even started. The entire purpose of teaching and learning, as well as my role as a teacher, was compromised.

Why Controlled Harshness is Necessary

Controlled harshness, when applied thoughtfully and with the right intention, becomes an essential tool for motivating students, especially in scenarios where general motivation and productivity are lower than average. It is important to understand that harshness does not mean cruelty or humiliation. Rather, it refers to setting firm expectations, providing clear consequences, and, when necessary, delivering constructive criticism in a manner that demands attention and improvement.

1. Establishing Boundaries: Students, especially those who lack intrinsic motivation, need structure. They need to understand that there are rules in place and that failure to meet these expectations will have consequences. A firm approach ensures that boundaries are clear, and this consistency creates a learning environment where students feel secure. Within this structure, students are often more motivated to meet the standards set before them.

2. Building Resilience: Failure is an inevitable part of life, and students need to be exposed to this reality in a controlled environment where they can learn from their mistakes. Harshness in the form of constructive feedback and strict expectations teaches students to deal with adversity, manage disappointment, and develop resilience. These traits are crucial not only for academic success but for life.

3. Driving Improvement: Students sometimes need an external push to recognize their potential. Controlled harshness can act as that catalyst, challenging students to rise above their comfort zones and strive for excellence. When students understand that there are consequences for complacency, they are more likely to make an effort to avoid failure and seek success.

4. Encouraging Self-Discipline: Consistent, firm expectations teach students self-discipline. When a teacher holds students accountable for their behavior and their academic performance, students gradually internalize the importance of meeting expectations, even

when external pressures are absent. This self-discipline is key to their long-term success, far beyond the classroom walls.

Transitioning from being soft to harsh is both challenging and stressful, particularly when it involves concerns about one's image or reputation as a teacher. The shift often causes discomfort, as students may struggle to adjust to the new expectations and perceive the change in demeanor negatively. However, it became clear that establishing authority and enforcing deadlines was essential to fostering responsibility and discipline. Without setting firm boundaries, work remained unfinished, and the learning process stagnated. I realized that I had to prioritize the students' progress and development over my own concerns about how I was perceived. In doing so, I demonstrated that while empathy and understanding are important, structure and consequences are equally necessary to guide students towards their own growth and success. Balancing firmness with care ultimately served their best interests, even if it initially affected my reputation.

Balancing Softness and Harshness for Student Upliftment

The real challenge lies in finding the delicate balance between being too soft and too harsh, ensuring that both approaches serve the ultimate goal of student learning and personal growth. Striking this balance requires self-awareness on the part of the teacher, as well as a deep understanding of the individual needs and personalities of each student. Here's how this balance can be maintained:

1. Set Clear Expectations with Flexibility: The teacher must establish firm rules but also be open to bending them when the situation demands it. Being rigidly harsh in every scenario will alienate students while being too lenient undermines authority. A teacher can achieve balance by setting clear expectations and showing understanding when exceptional circumstances arise.

2. Compassionate Consequences: It is possible to be firm and still express compassion. When consequences are enforced, the teacher can explain the rationale behind them and offer support for improvement. For instance, if a student misses a deadline, they should face consequences, but the teacher should also guide them on how to manage their time better in the future.

3. Recognize and Reward Progress: Alongside strictness, there should always be acknowledgment of progress. Random acts of praise can encourage students to continue striving. A student who struggles but makes an effort should receive recognition, balancing out the times when they face constructive criticism.

4. Mix Criticism with Encouragement: Constructive feedback is vital, but it must be paired with words of encouragement. A teacher can be harsh in critiquing a poorly done assignment but should follow it up with clear steps for improvement and a statement of belief in the student's ability to do better. This mix ensures that students do not feel demoralized.

5. Keep Students Accountable, But Offer Help: While it is essential to hold students accountable for their actions, it is equally important to be approachable. When students know that the teacher will not tolerate slacking but is also willing to help them when they struggle, they are more likely to remain engaged.

6. Model Respectful Authority: A teacher must embody the balance of authority and empathy. Students respect teachers who are firm but fair, and this respect encourages better behavior and engagement in the long run. Harshness must never be equated with belittling or humiliating students.

7. Encourage Open Dialogue: Communication is key in maintaining this balance. Teachers should encourage students to express their concerns or struggles and be willing to listen. This

openness fosters a deeper connection, where students feel valued but still understand the importance of meeting expectations.

Teaching is not a profession of extremes. It is a nuanced art where the soft and harsh elements must work in harmony for the benefit of the student. While kindness, empathy, and understanding are central to building rapport and trust, controlled harshness is equally essential to instill discipline, accountability, and resilience. In environments where motivation and productivity are already low, the need for both softness and firmness becomes even more pronounced. The goal of a teacher should always be to uplift students, to help them realize their potential, and to prepare them for the challenges of life. This balance is not easy to maintain, but when done well, it can have a profound and lasting impact on the students, helping them grow not only academically but also as individuals.

The Ideal Teacher: A Balance of Encouragement and Challenge

In my view, the ideal teacher embodies two essential facets: the ability and energy to continuously encourage and motivate students and the skill, knowledge, and intelligence to challenge them. These two dimensions, when harmonized, create a teaching environment that not only nurtures students' growth but also pushes them to achieve their highest potential. This balance is necessary for effective education, fostering both emotional resilience and intellectual rigor. Let us explore the logical arguments for each facet and why their combination is vital.

The Ability and Energy to Encourage and Motivate Students

1.1. Emotional and Psychological Support: Students encounter various personal and academic challenges that can hinder their learning. An ideal teacher recognizes these struggles and provides essential emotional support and encouragement. By fostering a positive and safe learning environment, the teacher helps students feel valued, thereby boosting their confidence. This motivation is crucial for overcoming feelings of inadequacy or fear of failure, enabling students to engage more fully in the learning process.

1.2. Sustained Engagement and Participation: Motivation directly influences student engagement. An energizing teacher maintains students' interest in the subject matter, leading to active participation. When students feel supported, they are more inclined to ask questions and take intellectual risks. This encouragement builds resilience, allowing them to persevere through challenges.

1.3. Developing Intrinsic Motivation: Beyond external rewards, the ideal teacher nurtures intrinsic motivation by fostering curiosity and a love for learning. When students derive satisfaction from the learning process itself, they develop lifelong educational habits that promote independence and intellectual fulfillment.

The Skill, Knowledge, and Intelligence to Challenge Students

Cognitive Development: While encouragement is vital for emotional well-being, intellectual challenges are essential for cognitive development. The ideal teacher possesses the knowledge to push students beyond their comfort zones, fostering deeper thinking and critical analysis. This intellectual challenge prepares students for real-world complexities.

Avoiding Intellectual Stagnation: Solely encouraging students risks intellectual complacency. The ideal teacher presents problems and tasks that stretch cognitive abilities, ensuring students remain intellectually active and engaged.

Preparing for Future Complexities: Education's role is to equip students for the complexities of life. The ideal teacher presents real-world problems, developing critical thinking and decision-making skills necessary for navigating ambiguity and complexity.

The Importance of Balancing Encouragement and Challenge

Nurturing Growth Through Balance: The ideal teacher maintains a balance between encouragement and challenge. Excessive encouragement without rigor can hinder intellectual advancement, while too much challenge can overwhelm students. The key lies in providing achievable challenges paired with encouragement to foster perseverance.

Creating a Growth Mindset: Balancing encouragement and challenge fosters a growth mindset—an understanding that abilities can be developed through effort. Teachers who support and challenge students help them view difficulties as opportunities for growth, reinforcing the idea that failure is part of the learning process.

Cultivating Resilience and Intellectual Curiosity: The ideal teacher promotes resilience and nurtures curiosity. Encouragement fosters belief in students' abilities, while challenges stimulate their exploration of new ideas. This combination cultivates active learners who are emotionally secure and intellectually ambitious, empowering them to pursue knowledge independently and face future challenges with confidence.

The Illusion of the Perfect Teacher

The concept of a "perfect teacher" represents an unattainable standard, suggesting an educator with flawless attributes and skills. However, this ideal is unrealistic, as effective teaching is a continuous process of adaptation and improvement, acknowledging that no teacher can embody perfection in all facets of their role. The effectiveness of teaching is subjective and varies among different contexts and students; strategies that benefit one group may not suit another due to diverse learning styles and individual needs. Additionally, a teacher's ability to facilitate learning is significantly influenced by student attributes, such as prior knowledge and motivation. Classroom diversity further complicates the teaching landscape, as teachers must adapt their methods to meet the varied needs of students. This reality underscores that teaching effectiveness is a dynamic interplay of factors. Rather than striving for an unattainable ideal, teachers should focus on refining their practices, fostering engagement, and nurturing a genuine enthusiasm for learning, as their impact is best observed over time through consistent efforts and visible student growth.

With changing times and technology, society evolves, needs shift, and the type of learners change, requiring teaching methods to change as well. There is no teaching approach that will remain valid forever. However, if something holds eternal significance in the realm of teaching and learning, it is kindness, encouragement, and evaluation. In my view, the most successful teacher is one who has motivated the greatest number of students and empowered them to surpass the teacher, ultimately becoming their own guides and educators. This idea is grounded in the belief that the ultimate goal of education is not simply the transfer of knowledge but the cultivation of autonomous, critical thinkers who can continue learning beyond the classroom and even after formal education. A teacher who facilitates this transformation ensures that education serves as a foundation for lifelong learning.

The challenge of teaching and fostering growth in average or underperforming students is a significant aspect of educational practice. While it is natural to take pride in students who excel academically, it is equally, if not more, important to focus on those who struggle. The achievements of bright students often reflect prior support and encouragement from various sources, including family and previous educators. In contrast, the true measure of a teacher's impact can often be seen in their ability to elevate the performance and engagement of students who face challenges.

To all educators and prospective teachers, your role is invaluable, and your influence is far-reaching. The work you do, often behind the scenes, is crucial in fostering a love for learning and building self-confidence in your students. Each day you dedicate to your craft is a step towards creating a brighter future for those you teach. Embrace the challenges and celebrate the victories, however small, knowing that your dedication to uplifting your students makes you an extraordinary teacher. Your passion and commitment are the driving forces behind the success and well-being of your students, and for that, you deserve profound appreciation and admiration. You are the perfect teacher.

Concluding a Course

In my teaching practice, I use rewards to recognize and celebrate student achievements, which is an integral part of my approach to fostering motivation and creating a positive learning environment. I invest my own resources in providing various rewards such as chocolates, ice cream, pens, keychains, books, and wristwatches. These rewards are not merely tokens of appreciation but are carefully selected to symbolize the significance of the students' efforts and achievements.

The process begins with calculating the cumulative scores from all internal assessments at the end of the course. I reward the top three students with the highest cumulative scores (consistent performance), as well as three students who have made the most significant improvement in their internal assessments throughout the course. Over the years, I have given chocolates and additional tokens that are long-lasting, such as keychains, pens, cards, books, and watches. The award ceremony is a very fulfilling experience.

My preferred recognition is for the "Best Improvement" made by a student, which is determined by comparing their initial and final assessment scores. This approach not only highlights the value of progress and personal growth but also encourages a focus on continuous improvement rather than merely achieving high scores. Presenting these rewards personally, with direct eye contact and a smile, aims to reinforce a sense of accomplishment and build a personal connection with each student. This method seeks to leave a deep and lasting impression, providing sincere encouragement and fostering a strong bond between the teacher and the students. The act of giving, coupled with positive reinforcement, helps to motivate students, validate their hard work, and inspire them to strive for further excellence.

Reward systems significantly influence both students' and teachers' psychological well-being. For students, rewards like chocolates or books enhance intrinsic and extrinsic motivation by satisfying their needs for competence and autonomy, resulting in greater academic engagement. Recognizing personal growth boosts self-efficacy and fosters resilience, while rewards enhance emotional well-being and self-esteem. Additionally, personalized rewards strengthen teacher-student relationships, promoting trust and creating a supportive learning environment. For teachers, implementing reward systems enhances job satisfaction and fulfillment, aligning with Herzberg's Two-Factor Theory. This practice fosters positive teacher-student dynamics and increases perceived effectiveness, deepening teachers' connections to their students and commitment to teaching.

Sentences that a teacher can use while rewarding students

1. "Your dedication and hard work throughout this course have been truly remarkable; I am confident that the skills and knowledge you've acquired will propel you to achieve great things in your future endeavors."

2. "Every challenge you faced and every obstacle you overcame has not only strengthened your abilities but also paved the way for future successes. Keep believing in yourself, and you will continue to rise to new heights."

3. "Your progress has been nothing short of inspiring. The effort you put into this course has not gone unnoticed, and I am excited to see how you will apply your newfound skills to make a difference in the world."

4. "Remember that greatness is not defined by perfection but by the courage to keep pushing forward and learning. Your journey through this course has showcased your resilience and potential for excellence."

5. "As we wrap up this course, take pride in how far you've come. Your commitment to learning and growing has set a solid foundation for all the incredible achievements yet to come."

6. "I am incredibly proud of your achievements in this course. You have shown exceptional growth and determination, and I have no doubt that you will continue to excel and make a significant impact."

7. "Your enthusiasm and persistence have made a lasting impression. Embrace the knowledge you've gained and use it to fuel your passions and aspirations—great things are within your reach."

8. "Every step you took in this course was a step towards greatness. Your dedication has been inspiring, and I am optimistic about the bright future that awaits you as you continue on your path to success."

9. "The hard work you've demonstrated is a testament to your character and capabilities. Trust in your abilities, and remember that each challenge is an opportunity for growth and learning."

10. "As you conclude this course, remember that this is just the beginning of an exciting journey. Your potential is limitless, and I am excited to see how you will harness your talents to achieve extraordinary things."

11. "As you move forward from here, I hope you continue to find joy in your journey and remember that staying connected with your peers and mentors can be a powerful source of support and inspiration."

12. "Your personal and professional growth is a testament to your hard work and dedication. Stay in touch and share your successes—seeing how far you've come will not only bring you happiness but also inspire those around you."

13. "Keep celebrating your achievements and milestones, no matter how small they may seem. Staying connected will allow us to cheer you on and be a part of your ongoing journey to greatness."

14. "Your happiness and success are incredibly important. Maintain those connections you've built during this course, as they will be valuable resources for encouragement and guidance throughout your career and life."

15. "As you pursue your dreams, remember that happiness often comes from sharing your experiences with others. Stay engaged and keep us updated—we're excited to see where your journey takes you next."

16. "Your potential is limitless, and staying connected with those who have supported you can provide a network of encouragement

and insight. We look forward to hearing about your continued success and growth."

17. "Embrace every opportunity to stay connected and share your progress. Knowing that we are cheering you on will help you stay motivated and remind you of the great strides you are making in your personal and professional life."

18. "Cherish the relationships and networks you've built here, as they will be invaluable throughout your journey. Keeping in touch will allow us to celebrate your achievements together and provide support whenever needed."

19. "Finding joy in your accomplishments and sharing them with others can be incredibly fulfilling. Stay in touch, so we can celebrate your continued success and support you as you navigate your future endeavors."

20. "Your happiness and success are important to us. As you advance in your career and personal life, remember that staying connected not only enriches your journey but also keeps the bonds we've formed alive and strong."

21. "I want all of you to surpass me in knowledge, intelligence, accomplishment, happiness, and fulfillment. Strive to operate at your full potential and achieve your grandest goals in both your personal and professional lives. Keep learning and stay happy!"

Chapter 11: The Institution

School systems worlds apart.

In the developed world, such as Denmark where I studied masters, students often have the freedom to choose courses and programs aligned with their interests and passions. This autonomy fosters a sense of ownership over their education, encouraging deeper engagement and intrinsic motivation. Educational systems in these contexts emphasize creativity, critical thinking, and collaboration, allowing students to explore various subjects before specializing. Such an approach not only promotes a more fulfilling academic experience but also equips students with a diverse skill set that can be beneficial in a rapidly changing job market. The facilities are better, the student to teacher ratio is less and the infrastructure is excellent.

In stark contrast, students in the developing world frequently select programs based on their potential for professional success, driven by economic realities and societal expectations. The focus often shifts toward vocational and practical training, as many students prioritize fields that promise greater job security and financial stability. This pragmatic approach is rooted in the necessity to secure stable employment in competitive job markets, leading to a curriculum that may prioritize immediate economic returns over personal interests and passions. Consequently, while this strategy can lead to job security, it may stifle individual creativity and long-term satisfaction in one's career.

The educational landscape in developing countries presents unique challenges that complicate the teaching process. Teachers often face limited resources, large class sizes, and varying levels of student preparedness, which can hinder their ability to engage students effectively. In these environments, the act of teaching becomes an arduous and complex task, requiring educators to navigate obstacles that are not as prevalent in more resource-rich contexts.

To address these challenges, educators in the developing world must employ innovative strategies that motivate students and create meaningful learning experiences. Understanding the socio-economic realities that influence education in these regions is crucial. Many students come from backgrounds where educational opportunities are limited, and they often bear the weight of familial expectations regarding their career paths. As a result, teachers play a vital role in not only imparting knowledge but also in fostering resilience and a growth mindset among their students.

Moreover, while the challenges are significant, there is immense potential within these educational settings. Teachers who adapt their methods to meet the diverse needs of their students can create a dynamic classroom environment that encourages exploration and critical thinking. This book aims to shed light on the complexities of teaching in the developing world, providing insights and practical approaches that can enhance teaching effectiveness and improve educational outcomes. By examining both the struggles and successes of educators and students in these contexts, the goal is to offer a comprehensive understanding of the intricacies between teaching, learning, and societal influence.

This exploration highlights the importance of balancing personal interests with professional viability in education. By advocating for an educational framework that recognizes individual passions while also preparing students for the realities of the job market, we can foster a more holistic approach to learning that benefits both students and society at large. Through this lens, we aim to inspire educators to embrace their vital role in shaping the future, even in the face of adversity.

Art–filled campus as an educational tool

An institution should be a vibrant place where mental, creative, and physical work converge, creating an atmosphere of constant activity and growth. Every corner of an educational system should be alive with energy—be it intense intellectual discussions, creative pursuits, or sports and physical activities. The infrastructure should never be idle; every space must foster interaction, excitement, and productivity. Such an environment naturally generates happiness and motivation, making the institution a hub of enthusiasm.

Psychologically, this vibrant setting stimulates both the mind and body, ensuring that students are fully engaged. Mental work challenges cognitive faculties, fostering critical thinking and problem-solving. Creative endeavors tap into imagination, allowing for the development of innovative and flexible thinking. Physical work through sports or activities not only promotes health but also releases endorphins, lifting mood and combating stress. Together, these elements form a holistic approach to education, where happiness and productivity feed into each other, creating a cycle of motivation and achievement.

A university's primary role is to prepare and orient young minds and bodies, sharpening their faculties so they are recognized and respected in the world. An institution that embraces such diversity of activity ultimately nurtures students who are well-rounded, energetic, and ready to excel in all areas of life.

A student, before going to bed, should be filled with thoughts of the myriad of activities awaiting them the next day—classes, discussions, creative projects, and physical pursuits. The excitement of possibilities should keep the student's heart in motion, creating a strong emotional attachment to the campus. This anticipation is what draws students back to the institution each day, eager to immerse themselves in the vibrant energy that defines their academic environment.

A campus without this pulse of enthusiasm, where people gather yet lack the spirit of activity, becomes a dull and uninspiring place. The energy of a campus is not just in its physical presence but in the meaningful engagements it offers—whether through mental challenges, social interactions, or athletic endeavors. When students are drawn to these activities, the campus transforms into a lively ecosystem where each individual contributes to the collective buzz of excitement.

In such an institution, no day is wasted, no corner of the campus remains stagnant, and no student feels disengaged. It is this energy that makes the campus not merely a place of study but a community that fosters growth, motivation, and a lifelong connection to learning.

Recently, I revisited the school where I spent my formative years, from first to tenth grade. Completing a decade of schooling there thirty years ago, the visit evoked a poignant blend of nostalgia and sorrow. The emotional weight stemmed from seeing how much has changed; the familiar elements of my childhood were absent. Now, my life revolves around my responsibilities as a teacher, a parent, and a member of society. During my visit, only my former principal, Dr. Suresh Kumar, remained from that time. Yet, the school's spaces—its words, statues, gateways, pillars, stairs, boards, trees, swings, and paintings—brought back vivid memories. I realized that spaces themselves have intrinsic value, shaping and preserving memories in ways that people alone cannot.

I share this experience to highlight the importance of creating environments that foster lasting memories. An institution should be designed to be memorable, encouraging deep connections akin to those formed with individuals. Art, such as paintings and sculptures throughout the campus, can evoke positive emotions and attachment, enhancing the educational experience. By integrating artistic elements, schools can stimulate happiness and ensure that students build enduring bonds with their learning environment. The most effect that I had was from the University of Southern Denmark where I pursued Masters program. The universities floor and walls were filled with modern art. There were sculptures at multiple places, all of modern arts. That is how I ended up liking more of modern minimalist and abstraction art.

The significance of art in educational institutions extends beyond aesthetic appeal; it plays a crucial role in shaping students' psychological experiences and fostering a conducive learning environment. As I revisited my former school, the familiar elements evoked powerful memories. This underscores the intrinsic value of spaces in preserving and shaping memories, a concept supported by psychological theories of environmental influence on emotional and cognitive processes.

Psychologically, art in educational settings contributes to creating a stimulating environment that enhances emotional well-being and cognitive engagement. Art can significantly impact mood, motivation, and overall mental health. For instance, studies indicate that exposure to aesthetically pleasing environments, including art, can reduce stress and anxiety, promoting a sense of calm and focus. Art also stimulates cognitive development by encouraging creativity, critical thinking, and problem-solving skills. The presence of art in schools can foster an atmosphere that is not only visually engaging but also intellectually and emotionally enriching.

Integrating artistic elements such as paintings and sculptures throughout a school campus can evoke positive emotions and foster a sense of attachment to the environment. This connection enhances students' engagement and satisfaction, making the educational experience more memorable and impactful. Creating spaces that students find meaningful and emotionally resonant can encourage them to form lasting bonds with their learning environment, leading to improved academic performance and personal development.

By deliberately designing educational spaces to be both visually and emotionally stimulating, schools can support students' overall well-being, creativity, and academic success. Art, thus, becomes an integral component in shaping a nurturing and effective learning environment. Art's influence on students extends well beyond their school years, shaping their emotional, cognitive, and social development in meaningful ways. By fostering emotional well-being, creativity, and cultural awareness, art contributes to the formation of well-rounded individuals who carry these attributes into their adult lives, enriching their personal and professional experiences.

Incorporating art into a campus environment can significantly enhance its aesthetic appeal and foster a sense of community and pride. To achieve a powerful visual impact while remaining cost-effective, consider the following approaches to include paintings and large-scale sculptures in open spaces:

1. Murals and Large-Scale Paintings

Murals: Large murals painted on the sides of buildings, fences, or prominent walls can become focal points on campus. These murals can be created through collaborations with students, local artists, or community groups. The expansive surface allows for vibrant, detailed artwork that can convey school values, cultural themes, or abstract designs.

Canvas Paintings: For areas with less wall space, large canvas paintings can be used. These can be hung in open hallways, atriums, or lobbies where they can be easily viewed. Choosing weather-resistant frames or protective coatings ensures durability, particularly if displayed in semi-exposed areas.

2. Large-Scale Sculptures

Outdoor Sculptures: Install large sculptures in prominent outdoor areas such as courtyards, gardens, or entranceways. These sculptures can be made from durable materials like metal, stone, or concrete, ensuring they withstand the elements. Abstract forms, symbolic representations, or nature-inspired designs can make a strong visual impact.

Interactive Sculptures: Consider interactive or kinetic sculptures that engage students. These can include moving parts or elements that react to touch or environmental conditions. Interactive art not only beautifies the space but also encourages engagement and exploration.

3. Installation Art

Public Art Installations: Temporary or semi-permanent installations can be used to transform open spaces. These can include large-scale art pieces, such as geometric shapes, artistic arches, or innovative structures. Installation art can be a dynamic way to refresh the campus environment periodically.

Land Art: Incorporate land art or earthworks into gardens or open areas. Sculptures made from natural materials, such as wood or stone, can blend with the landscape and create a harmonious visual experience.

4. Collaborative Projects

Community Involvement: Engage the local community, including students, parents, and local artists, in creating large-scale art projects. Collaborative efforts can lead to unique and meaningful installations that reflect the collective identity of the campus.

Art Competitions: Organize art competitions for students to design large-scale paintings or sculptures. Winning designs can be produced and displayed on campus, fostering a sense of accomplishment and ownership among the students.

5. Thematic Sculptures

Symbolic Sculptures: Create sculptures that symbolize the values or history of the institution. These can be designed to reflect themes such as unity, knowledge, or innovation. Placing these sculptures in key areas can serve as constant reminders of the school's ethos.

Historical and Cultural Art: Integrate art that reflects the local culture or history of the region. Sculptures or murals that depict significant local events or figures can help students connect with their community and understand their heritage.

6. Maintenance and Preservation

Protective Measures: Ensure that both paintings and sculptures are protected from weather and vandalism. Use weather-resistant materials and coatings for outdoor artworks and establish a regular maintenance schedule to keep the art in good condition.

Community Stewardship: Encourage students and staff to take part in the care and preservation of the art. This can include organizing cleaning days, repair workshops, or educational sessions about the importance of maintaining public art.

Art is not just an aesthetic enhancement but a powerful tool that enriches the teaching-learning experience. By stimulating creativity, evoking wonder, uplifting mood, and improving the overall ambience, art contributes significantly to more effective and enjoyable educational outcomes. Give an opportunity for the students to make memories of their prime time with place and their people. That will enrich their lives but standards and tastes of living.

An iconic sculpture or building provides an institution with a strong visual identity, fosters pride, enhances appeal, and serves as a lasting symbol of its values and achievements. By investing in such landmarks, institutions can create a meaningful and memorable impact that extends well beyond the campus boundaries. The attachment that students develop with their school buildings and their art plays a significant role in fostering long-term loyalty and contribution from alumni. This connection is not merely sentimental; it can have practical implications for both the individuals and the institution.

Emotional Attachment and Nostalgia: Students often form deep emotional bonds with their school environment, including the buildings, spaces, and art that populate the campus. These elements become intertwined with their formative experiences, creating a sense of nostalgia that persists long after graduation. This emotional connection can drive alumni to maintain a positive relationship with their alma mater. When alumni reflect on their time at school, they are more likely to recall the nurturing environment and the personal growth they experienced, leading to a desire to give back to the institution that played a pivotal role in their development.

Identity and Belonging: The school's physical environment becomes a part of the students' identity and sense of belonging. Iconic buildings, well-maintained spaces, and artistic elements contribute to a collective memory that enhances the school's role in the alumni's personal history. This sense of belonging can encourage alumni to support the school through donations, volunteering, or participating in alumni events. They may feel a sense of responsibility to contribute to maintaining and improving the environment that shaped their educational journey.

Legacy and Contribution: A strong attachment to the school's buildings and grounds often translates into a commitment to preserving and enhancing these spaces for future generations. Alumni who cherish their school experiences are more inclined to contribute financially or through other means to projects that benefit the institution. This can include funding renovations, supporting new construction, or endowing programs that align with their positive memories of their time at the school. By investing in their alma mater, alumni help ensure that current and future students can enjoy a similarly enriching environment.

Community and Networking: The attachment to school buildings can also foster a sense of community among alumni. Reunions, school events, and alumni gatherings often take place in familiar settings that evoke shared memories and reinforce the bond among former students. This sense of community can lead to increased engagement with the school, creating opportunities for networking, mentorship, and collaborative initiatives that benefit both the institution and its graduates.

The emotional attachment that students develop with their school buildings is crucial for fostering a lasting relationship between alumni and their alma mater. This bond enhances their sense of identity, belonging, and responsibility, driving them to contribute positively to the institution and support its continued growth and success. There should be no space in the institution that doesn't speak to the students. Art enlivens the institution.

Prochange or Antichange

In the constantly evolving landscape of education, the question of whether to embrace or resist change becomes a significant topic of discussion. This dichotomy between "prochange" and "antichange" reflects the varied attitudes of institutions, educators, and students. These attitudes shape not only the future of education but also the growth, adaptability, and success of the system as a whole.

Institutional Attitudes: Navigating Tradition and Innovation

Institutions, by their very nature, often find themselves balancing between tradition and innovation. Established educational systems tend to rely heavily on long-standing practices that ensure stability, consistency, and predictability. The adherence to historical practices can make many institutions inherently "antichange." The bureaucratic structure, often slow-moving, results in hesitation towards rapid reform, which can be seen as a threat to institutional identity, values, and traditions.

However, modern institutions increasingly recognize the need for "prochange" attitudes to adapt to shifting societal needs, technological advancements, and the global economy's demands. Institutions that adopt a forward-thinking mindset are more likely to innovate curricula, incorporate technology, and support progressive policies such as inclusive education and interdisciplinary learning. This openness to change can lead to transformative educational experiences, but it requires overcoming institutional inertia, addressing resource limitations, and reconciling different stakeholders' interests.

Educators: The Gatekeepers of Change

Educators hold a pivotal role in determining the prochange or antichange direction within education. Their professional development, personal philosophies, and experiences influence their approach. Many educators who have long relied on traditional methods may lean towards "antichange," viewing innovations with skepticism. They might feel that new approaches undermine proven methodologies or demand an overwhelming learning curve. The rapid integration of digital tools, for instance, has sparked debates on whether technology enhances or dilutes the depth of teaching.

Conversely, educators who are "prochange" see value in continuous improvement, adaptability, and innovation. They embrace new teaching techniques, technologies, and methodologies, understanding that the future requires educators who can prepare students for uncertain and rapidly changing environments. The key challenge for these educators lies in finding the balance between modern teaching strategies and maintaining the depth of critical thinking, creativity, and inquiry in students. Moreover, prochange educators often serve as role models, demonstrating to students the importance of growth, resilience, and adaptability.

Students: The Learners' Perspective on Change

Students, who are the direct beneficiaries of education, often embody a spectrum of attitudes towards change, shaped by their personal experiences, backgrounds, and motivations. Some students, particularly those who thrive in traditional educational settings, may resist change. These "antichange" students may feel more comfortable with familiar structures, well-established assessment methods, and conventional learning environments. They may struggle with, or even fear, the uncertainty and challenges that come with evolving pedagogies and flexible learning models.

On the other hand, many students in the modern world are more "prochange" in their attitudes, largely because they are digital natives. They are used to the rapid pace of technological advancements, personalized learning platforms, and flexible study patterns. This cohort often advocates for more interdisciplinary approaches, global perspectives, and skills-based learning rather than the rote memorization often associated with traditional education systems. However, the speed at which changes are introduced can overwhelm some students, especially if they are not provided with sufficient guidance or resources to adapt.

A Synthesis of Attitudes: The Paradox of Change

The challenge within educational settings is that change is both necessary and contested. Institutions, educators, and students all play a role in determining whether change is accepted, resisted, or transformed into something practical and sustainable. The paradox of change is that while many argue for it, its implementation can destabilize existing systems, create discomfort, and challenge established norms.

To navigate this paradox, educational systems must find a middle path that acknowledges the need for stability while promoting change where it is most effective. Institutions should foster a culture of continuous improvement, where change is not feared but embraced in a manner that aligns with the institution's core mission. Educators must be empowered to engage with new teaching methods while respecting traditional values where necessary, and students must be supported in their learning journeys to become adaptable, creative, and resourceful individuals.

The debate between prochange and antichange within education reflects the tension between maintaining tradition and adapting to the future. While change is inevitable, the attitude with which it is approached will determine whether it becomes a source of growth or contention. Successful educational systems are those that can strike a balance, fostering an environment where change is meaningful, purposeful, and ultimately beneficial for all stakeholders involved.

Prochange or antichange can be analyzed through several psychological underpinnings that explain the behaviors, motivations, and attitudes towards change. These psychological mechanisms—rooted in cognitive, social, and developmental psychology—help to understand why different educational stakeholders (institutions, educators, and students) adopt either a "prochange" or "antichange" stance.

1. Cognitive Dissonance and Resistance to Change

One of the most prominent psychological concepts explaining the "antichange" attitude is cognitive dissonance. Cognitive dissonance occurs when individuals experience discomfort due to a discrepancy between their long-held beliefs or behaviors and new, contradicting information or practices. Institutions and educators who have adhered to traditional educational systems for years may find themselves uncomfortable when confronted with the need for change, as it challenges their established worldview. To reduce this dissonance, they may resist change and cling to familiar methodologies that have provided stability and predictability in the past. In cognitive terms, resisting change minimizes the psychological discomfort caused by uncertainty.

Conversely, those who are "prochange" often have a more fluid cognitive schema. These individuals are open to modifying their mental frameworks and integrating new information. This flexibility is aligned with the psychological principle of cognitive flexibility, which refers to the brain's ability to switch between different concepts or adapt to new rules. Prochange individuals see change not as a threat but as an opportunity to learn and grow, thereby reducing cognitive dissonance by adapting to the new reality.

2. Social Identity and Institutional Resistance

Social identity theory suggests that people derive part of their self-concept from their membership in social groups, such as institutions. Many institutions possess a strong cultural and historical identity, which shapes the behaviors and attitudes of individuals within the institution. An institution's resistance to change, therefore, can be seen as a collective attempt to preserve its social identity. The psychological desire for group cohesion and stability drives the institution to maintain traditions, even if those traditions no longer serve the evolving needs of education.

For educators, their professional identity is closely tied to their expertise and established methodologies. Changing the curriculum, pedagogical methods, or institutional structure can feel like a direct challenge to their sense of competence and self-worth, triggering status quo bias. This bias leads individuals to prefer things as they are, believing that the current system is better simply because it has existed for a long time.

On the other hand, institutions and educators who embrace change often have a forward-looking social identity that aligns with future-oriented goals. These institutions view themselves as progressive and adaptable, which enhances their collective identity as innovative leaders in education. This alignment between institutional identity and prochange attitudes fosters a culture of adaptability and continuous improvement.

3. Motivation: Intrinsic vs. Extrinsic Drivers of Change

The psychological distinction between intrinsic and extrinsic motivation helps explain why certain stakeholders are more likely to embrace change. Intrinsic motivation refers to engaging in a task for its own sake, driven by personal satisfaction and interest, while extrinsic motivation is driven by external rewards or pressures. Prochange educators and students are often intrinsically motivated—they find personal fulfillment in learning new methods, experimenting with innovative teaching practices, and adapting to changing educational needs.

In contrast, antichange attitudes are often driven by extrinsic motivation, where the focus is on maintaining the status quo to avoid negative consequences, such as loss of control, job security, or reputation. These individuals may resist change because they perceive it as a threat to their external rewards or social status within the institution.

4. Developmental Psychology: Adaptation and Growth Mindset

Developmental psychology offers insight into how individuals adapt to change based on their developmental stage and psychological readiness. The concept of a growth mindset, developed by Carol Dweck, is critical here. A growth mindset involves the belief that abilities and intelligence can be developed through effort, learning, and perseverance. Educators and students with a growth mindset are more likely to adopt a prochange attitude, seeing challenges and changes as opportunities for growth.

On the other hand, those with a fixed mindset believe that abilities are static, and as a result, they may resist change out of fear of failure or the belief that they cannot improve beyond their current capacity. This fixed mindset contributes to the antichange attitude, as individuals feel safer maintaining established routines that do not challenge their perceived limitations.

5. Uncertainty and Anxiety

Change inevitably brings uncertainty, and the psychological response to uncertainty often manifests as anxiety. The concept of uncertainty avoidance explains how individuals respond to ambiguous situations. Institutions and individuals who are high in uncertainty avoidance prefer clear, structured environments where the future is predictable. These stakeholders are more likely to resist change, as it introduces variables they cannot control, triggering anxiety and a desire to return to familiar patterns.

Prochange individuals, however, are more likely to tolerate or even embrace uncertainty. They may possess higher levels of resilience and self-efficacy, which enable them to approach change with confidence, knowing they can manage the challenges that come with it. Their positive coping mechanisms reduce anxiety and allow them to navigate the unknown with a sense of purpose and curiosity.

A Psychological Paradox of Change

The psychological underpinnings of prochange and antichange attitudes reveal the deep-seated cognitive, social, and emotional processes that govern human responses to educational innovation. While institutions, educators, and students may differ in their capacity to adapt, these differences are rooted in fundamental psychological principles that influence how they perceive, process, and react to change. Ultimately, fostering a culture that balances stability with adaptability, and addressing the psychological barriers to change, is crucial for creating a dynamic and forward-thinking educational system.

<u>System-level strategies to chaperone the freshers</u>

Chaperoning incoming high school students as they transition into college as freshmen is a crucial role that requires both guidance and empathy. This period marks a significant shift in their lives as they move from a structured school environment to the more self-directed and challenging world of higher education. Here's a comprehensive approach to effectively support these young adults during this transition:

1. Understanding Their Concerns and Anxieties

- Approach: Acknowledge that the transition from high school to college can be overwhelming. Common concerns include academic expectations, social integration, independence, and future career paths.

- Action: Hold orientation sessions that specifically address these concerns, allowing students to voice their anxieties and receive reassurance. Share personal experiences or those of senior students to normalize these feelings.

2. Fostering Independence and Responsibility

- Approach: High school students are used to a more controlled environment. College demands greater self-discipline and time management.

- Action: Provide workshops or resources on effective time management, study skills, and balancing academic and social life. Encourage them to take ownership of their schedules and responsibilities from the outset.

3. Building a Supportive Community

- Approach: The social aspect of college is critical. New students need to feel a sense of belonging and support.

- Action: Organize icebreaker events, peer mentoring programs, and group activities that encourage interaction and friendship-building. Create opportunities for students to connect with peers who share similar interests or academic goals.

4. Guiding Academic Expectations

- Approach: College academics are more rigorous and require different study strategies than high school.

- Action: Introduce students to the academic resources available, such as tutoring centers, libraries, and writing workshops. Offer guidance on understanding syllabi, managing coursework, and seeking help when needed.

5. Encouraging Curiosity and Exploration

- Approach: College is a time for intellectual exploration and personal growth.

- Action: Encourage students to explore different fields of study, join clubs, and participate in extracurricular activities. Highlight the value of curiosity in both academic and personal development.

6. Providing Emotional and Mental Health Support

- Approach: The transition can be emotionally taxing, and mental health is a critical aspect of overall well-being.

- Action: Ensure that students are aware of counseling services, mental health resources, and support groups available on campus. Promote a culture where seeking help is seen as a strength, not a weakness.

7. Navigating Campus Life

- Approach: College campuses can be vast and complex, and navigating them can be daunting for newcomers.

- Action: Offer campus tours, map out key locations, and provide information on campus resources such as dining halls, health services, and student centers. Ensure they know where to find help and who to contact for various needs.

8. Instilling Confidence and Self-Belief

- Approach: This new phase requires confidence in their abilities and decisions.

- Action: Reinforce their strengths and accomplishments, reminding them of why they were admitted to college in the first place. Encourage them to embrace challenges as opportunities for growth.

9. Balancing Freedom with Responsibility

- Approach: College offers more freedom, which can be both exciting and risky.

- Action: Discuss the importance of making responsible choices, whether in academics, social life, or personal health. Provide scenarios or case studies that illustrate the consequences of poor decisions and the benefits of responsible behavior.

10. Continuous Support and Check-Ins

- Approach: The transition is ongoing, and students may need continued support as they adapt.

- Action: Establish regular check-ins, either through formal advising sessions or informal meetings. Be approachable and available for guidance throughout their first year.

Chaperoning high school students as they enter college is more than just providing orientation; it is about equipping them with the tools, confidence, and mindset needed to thrive in this new environment. By offering support in academic, social, and personal aspects, educators and mentors can help these young adults navigate the challenges and opportunities of college life, setting them on a path to success.

Enhancing Institutional Success Through Student Partnership

Our students are our most vital partners in the success of this institution. However, a significant challenge we face is the issue of classroom heterogeneity, which undermines many of our initiatives.

Challenge:

The current challenge lies in the wide-ranging heterogeneity among students, particularly in terms of focus, productivity, personality, communication skills, and enthusiasm. This diversity makes it difficult for class teachers to effectively implement strategies and initiatives. On average, students tend to exhibit lower productivity levels, whether in academics, extracurricular activities, or co-curricular engagements.

Target Group:

Our primary focus is on first-year students, as they generally display higher levels of enthusiasm and compliance. To cultivate a culture of productivity on campus, we propose several measures, detailed below with their respective rationales.

Proposed Measures:

1. Professional Uniform (First-Year Students Only):

- Objective: Introduce a professional uniform to foster a sense of unity, discipline, and professionalism among first-year students.

- Rationale: A uniform can minimize distractions, enhance focus, and promote a professional atmosphere. Students will wear the uniform, including appropriate footwear, on all working days except Wednesdays and Saturdays.

2. Enhancement of Individual Performance:

- Objective: Incorporate touch typing and poster presentation into the curriculum to improve students' productivity and communication in the digital age.

- Rationale: A touch-typing competition for first-year students, along with workshops and public speaking sessions, will boost self-confidence, communication skills, and overall sophistication. More opportunities for poster/model presentations will further solidify a culture of productivity on campus.

3. Separate Sports and Cultural Festivals:

- Objective: Organize distinct sports and cultural festivals exclusively for first-year students.

- Rationale: These events provide platforms for students to showcase their talents, fostering greater participation and engagement in campus life.

4. National Cadet Corps (NCC) and Similar Clubs Expansion:

- Objective: Expand the National Cadet Corps (NCC) to include navy and air force wings.

- Rationale: This expansion will enhance leadership development opportunities and discipline, adding prestige and structure to campus activities.

5. Training Camps:

 - Objective: Conduct training camps in sports, arts, and gardening, offering students the opportunity to learn new skills.

 - Rationale: All available campus spaces and infrastructure should be fully utilized, ensuring that students interested in any craft or skill have the means to pursue their passions.

6. Productivity Coaches:

 - Objective: Assign mentors to act as productivity coaches, guiding students to maximize their potential.

 - Rationale: These coaches will play a crucial role in fostering individual productivity helping students set and achieve personal goals.

7. Induction Program:

 - Objective: Launch or conclude the first year with an induction program that includes academic recognition, cultural performances, and guest speakers.

 - Rationale: This program will celebrate students' achievements and instill a sense of mission for their remaining years in the engineering program, reinforcing a sense of belonging and purpose.

Creating habits of productivity, efficiency, and motivation in freshers requires a strategic and supportive approach, combining consistent monitoring, encouragement, appreciation, and incentivization. At the outset, it is essential to establish clear expectations regarding work ethic and goals, ensuring that students understand the importance of developing these habits early on.

Constant and consistent monitoring plays a crucial role, as it enables the teacher to track each student's progress, identify potential areas of improvement, and provide timely feedback. This creates an environment of accountability, where students feel responsible for their performance but supported in their growth.

Encouragement, through positive reinforcement, helps foster a growth mindset. By regularly appreciating students' efforts, even in small tasks, teachers can instill a sense of achievement and self-worth, motivating them to continue striving for better results.

Incentivization, whether through tangible rewards or personal recognition, reinforces good behavior and achievement. When students see their hard work acknowledged, it boosts their confidence and inspires them to pursue greater efficiency. Over time, these practices cultivate an intrinsic motivation for productivity, allowing freshers to build sustainable habits that carry forward into their academic and professional lives.

If these measures are implemented, we anticipate a significant transformation within four years, resulting in a more vibrant campus culture characterized by increased productivity, enthusiasm, and engagement. These initiatives will undoubtedly yield positive outcomes, enhancing both the academic and social environment of our institution.

Improving campus culture to foster productivity, personality development, and academic excellence requires a multifaceted approach that integrates various elements of student life. Here are some strategies to create a vibrant, productive, and enriching campus environment:

1. Holistic Curriculum Development

- Integrated Learning: Develop a curriculum that balances academics with opportunities for personal growth. Incorporate courses that emphasize critical thinking, creativity, leadership, and communication skills alongside traditional academic subjects.

- Interdisciplinary Projects: Encourage interdisciplinary projects that require students to collaborate across different fields of study. This not only enhances academic learning but also promotes teamwork, problem-solving, and adaptability.

2. Extracurricular Activities and Clubs

- Diverse Clubs and Societies: Establish and support a wide range of student clubs and societies that cater to various interests, from arts and culture to technology and entrepreneurship. Participation in these groups allows students to explore their passions, develop new skills, and build a well-rounded personality.

- Leadership Opportunities: Provide opportunities for students to take on leadership roles within these clubs, fostering responsibility, decision-making, and organizational skills.

3. Workshops and Seminars

- Skill Development Workshops: Regularly conduct workshops on essential skills such as public speaking, time management, emotional intelligence, and financial literacy. These sessions can equip students with practical skills that complement their academic knowledge.

- Guest Lectures and Seminars: Invite industry experts, successful alumni, and thought leaders to deliver lectures and seminars. These events expose students to real-world experiences and inspire them to pursue excellence in their personal and professional lives.

4. Mentorship and Counseling

- Mentorship Programs: Implement mentorship programs where senior students or faculty members guide juniors in both academic and personal development. This helps new students navigate campus life and encourages a culture of mutual support.

- Counseling Services: Ensure that students have access to professional counseling services for academic advice, career planning, and mental health support. A focus on well-being is essential for sustained productivity and personal growth.

5. Encouraging Innovation and Creativity

- Innovation Labs and Hackathons: Create spaces where students can experiment with new ideas, such as innovation labs or maker spaces. Organize hackathons and competitions that challenge students to develop creative solutions to real-world problems.

- Creative Arts and Expression: Support initiatives that promote the arts, including theater, music, writing, and visual arts. Creative expression can be a powerful tool for personal development and can enhance the cultural vibrancy of the campus.

6. Community Engagement and Social Responsibility

- Service Learning: Integrate community service and social responsibility into the curriculum. Encourage students to participate in service projects that benefit the local community, teaching them the value of empathy, civic engagement, and ethical responsibility.

- Sustainability Initiatives: Promote sustainability on campus through student-led projects focused on environmental conservation, waste management, and energy efficiency. This not only contributes to a better world but also instills a sense of responsibility and purpose.

7. Recognition and Reward Systems

- Awards and Recognition: Establish awards and recognition programs that celebrate academic achievements, leadership, creativity, and community service. Public recognition motivates students to excel and fosters a culture of appreciation and pride.

- Incentivized Participation: Offer incentives such as scholarships, internships, or academic credits for active participation in extracurricular activities, leadership roles, and innovative projects.

8. Physical and Mental Wellness Programs

- Wellness Initiatives: Promote a healthy lifestyle through campus-wide wellness programs, including fitness challenges, yoga sessions, and mindfulness workshops. Physical well-being is closely linked to productivity and mental clarity.

- Stress Management Resources: Provide resources and workshops on stress management, coping strategies, and work-life balance. Ensuring students can manage stress effectively is crucial for maintaining a positive and productive campus culture.

9. Fostering a Collaborative Environment

- Collaborative Spaces: Design campus spaces that encourage collaboration, such as common areas for group study, discussion rooms, and interactive lounges. A collaborative environment encourages peer learning, knowledge sharing, and collective problem-solving.

- Cross-Departmental Initiatives: Promote cross-departmental initiatives and projects that bring together students and faculty from different disciplines. This encourages a broader perspective and enhances the academic and social integration of the campus community.

10. Feedback and Continuous Improvement

- Student Feedback Mechanisms: Establish regular feedback mechanisms where students can voice their opinions on campus culture, academic programs, and extracurricular activities. This feedback is invaluable for continuous improvement and ensuring that the campus environment evolves to meet student needs.

- Actionable Changes: Act on the feedback by implementing changes that address student concerns and suggestions. Demonstrating responsiveness fosters trust and shows a commitment to creating an optimal learning environment.

By implementing these strategies, institutions can create a campus culture that not only prioritizes academic excellence but also nurtures personal growth, creativity, and social responsibility. Such a balanced approach ensures that students are well-equipped to thrive in their future careers and contribute positively to society.

Integrating psychological approaches can significantly enhance the pursuit of excellence in extracurricular activities and skill development. These approaches focus on understanding and influencing student behavior, motivation, and mindset, creating an environment that encourages active participation and continuous improvement. Here are some strategies:

1. Growth Mindset Cultivation

- Mindset Education: Teach students the concept of a growth mindset, where they understand that abilities and talents can be developed through dedication and hard work. Highlight the importance of effort, resilience, and learning from failure as key components of success in extracurricular activities.

- Celebrate Progress: Focus on incremental progress rather than just outcomes. Recognizing and celebrating small achievements helps reinforce the belief that improvement is possible and motivates students to keep pushing their limits.

2. Self-Determination Theory (SDT)

- Autonomy Support: Encourage students to choose extracurricular activities that genuinely interest them. When students have a sense of autonomy—feeling that they are in control of their choices—they are more likely to be intrinsically motivated and committed to pursuing excellence.

- Competence Building: Provide opportunities for students to develop and demonstrate competence in their chosen activities. This can be achieved through structured skill-building sessions, regular feedback, and challenges that are appropriately matched to their skill levels.

- Relatedness and Connection: Foster a sense of community and belonging within extracurricular groups. When students feel connected to their peers and mentors, they are more likely to engage deeply and strive for excellence.

3. Positive Reinforcement

- Recognition and Rewards: Use positive reinforcement to encourage continued effort and achievement. This can include formal recognition through awards, praise from peers and mentors, or tangible rewards such as certificates or privileges. The key is to make the reinforcement timely and meaningful.

- Public Acknowledgment: Acknowledge student achievements in front of their peers, such as during assemblies, newsletters, or social media platforms. Public recognition enhances self-esteem and motivates others to strive for similar accomplishments.

4. Goal-Setting Techniques

- SMART Goals: Teach students to set SMART (Specific, Measurable, Achievable, Relevant, Time-bound) goals for their extracurricular activities. Clear and realistic goals help students focus their efforts, monitor their progress, and experience a sense of achievement as they reach their milestones.

- Goal Laddering: Encourage students to break down their long-term goals into smaller, manageable steps. This "laddering" approach helps reduce overwhelm and provides a clear roadmap to achieving excellence.

5. Motivational Interviewing (MI)

- One-on-One Coaching: Use motivational interviewing techniques in one-on-one sessions with students to explore their interests, identify their motivations, and set personalized goals. This approach helps students clarify their reasons for pursuing certain activities and builds intrinsic motivation.

- Ambivalence Resolution: Address any ambivalence or uncertainty students may have about participating in extracurricular activities. By guiding them through their thought processes and helping them resolve conflicting feelings, you can empower them to commit fully to their chosen pursuits.

6. Flow Theory

- Encouraging Flow States: Create conditions that allow students to enter a state of "flow," where they are fully immersed and focused on their activities. This can be achieved by ensuring the challenges of the activity match the students' skill levels and providing immediate feedback.

- Designing Optimal Challenges: Structure activities in a way that they are challenging but achievable. When students experience flow, they are more likely to enjoy the process and pursue excellence naturally.

7. Visualization and Mental Imagery

- Mental Rehearsal: Teach students to use visualization techniques to mentally rehearse their performance in extracurricular activities. This psychological practice can enhance their confidence, reduce anxiety, and improve actual performance.

- Positive Imagery: Encourage students to visualize successful outcomes and the steps required to achieve them. Positive mental imagery can reinforce a proactive mindset and increase the likelihood of success.

8. Resilience Training

- Coping Strategies: Provide training on coping strategies for dealing with setbacks and failures in extracurricular activities. This includes teaching students how to reframe negative experiences as learning opportunities and how to bounce back from disappointments.

- Stress Management: Equip students with tools for managing stress, such as mindfulness, relaxation techniques, and time management skills. Managing stress effectively allows students to maintain focus and motivation, even under pressure.

9. Peer Influence and Role Models

- Positive Peer Pressure: Create an environment where excellence in extracurricular activities is celebrated and valued by peers. Peer influence can be a powerful motivator, encouraging students to aspire to higher standards.

- Role Models and Mentors: Connect students with role models or mentors who have excelled in similar activities. Seeing the success of others who have walked the same path can inspire students to pursue excellence with greater determination.

10. Emotional Intelligence Development

- Self-Awareness and Regulation: Teach students to be aware of their emotions and how these affect their motivation and performance. Helping students develop emotional regulation skills can enhance their ability to stay focused and driven.

- Empathy and Social Skills: Foster a culture of empathy and strong social connections within extracurricular groups. Students who feel emotionally supported are more likely to take risks, try new things, and strive for excellence.

When chaperoning new students for productivity, it is critical that the entire campus ecosystem—comprising infrastructure, management, and faculty—works in harmony to provide continuous and consistent reinforcement. This holistic approach ensures that students receive a uniform message from all fronts, creating an environment that normalizes productive behavior. Psychologically, consistent reinforcement taps into the principles of operant conditioning, where repeated positive reinforcement for productive behaviors solidifies these actions into habits.

Relying on one faculty member alone is insufficient for sustainable change. When all faculty members, through their courses, personal interactions, and involvement in extracurricular activities, encourage students to engage fully in their tasks, it sends a collective signal about the value of effort. This creates a sense of belonging and shared goals, key elements in social learning theory. Over time, students internalize these norms, viewing work not as a burden but as an opportunity for achievement and growth.

As students' minds become occupied with meaningful work, the cognitive load of productivity shifts from stress to intrinsic motivation. What initially might have been viewed as stressful transforms into a positive challenge, creating a sense of competition and pride. This shift aligns with the theory of flow, where sustained engagement in activities leads to both skill development and personal satisfaction. The end result is an ideal educational environment where students are constantly honing skills like reading, writing, and creative thinking.

An ideal educational institution should be a sanctuary for intellectual and personal growth, fostering an *ambience of a growth mindset*. Here, students and staff alike would view challenges as opportunities to learn and improve. Mistakes would be celebrated as essential steps in the learning process, with everyone encouraged to persist through difficulties. This mindset, embedded in the institution's culture, would empower learners to continually seek improvement and embrace change.

Moreover, such an institution would cultivate an *atmosphere of enthusiasm*. The enthusiasm of teachers, administrators, and students would be palpable in every classroom and interaction. Passion for learning, discovery, and collaboration would drive the institution forward, inspiring both students and staff to engage deeply with their work. This positive energy creates an environment where curiosity thrives and where every individual is motivated to contribute to the collective success.

Finally, a *culture of productivity* would permeate the institution. This would not be about relentless busyness but about meaningful, focused work that leads to tangible progress. Time and resources would be used efficiently, with clear goals and accountability, fostering an environment where creativity and discipline co-exist. In such an institution, students would develop the habits and mindsets that prepare them for sustained success in their personal and professional lives.

Alumni anchoring

Anchoring outgoing graduates to maintain strong ties with their educational institution is an essential part of building a lasting connection between the alumni and the university. To achieve this, educational institutions must foster a sense of belonging and identity that graduates carry with them, transforming them into lifelong ambassadors of the university. This sense of connection can be strengthened through several psychological mechanisms rooted in theories of identity, memory, and social belonging.

Fostering a Sense of Identity

One of the key elements to ensure that graduates remain attached to their institution is to foster a strong sense of identity during their time on campus. The Social Identity Theory posits that individuals derive a sense of self from the groups to which they belong. By building an institutional culture where students feel they are part of something larger than themselves—be it through the values, traditions, or unique academic community of the university—the students develop a strong affiliation with their alma mater. Graduates who perceive their university experience as a core part of their identity are more likely to maintain emotional ties and return as alumni.

The emotional connection students form with their campus is essential for building lasting alumni relationships. This attachment strengthens their sense of identity and belonging, encouraging continued support for the institution. Every space should resonate with students, as vibrant environments, including art, foster this enduring bond and institutional loyalty.

Creating strong student-alumni interactions during a student's time on campus is a powerful way to build this identity. Hosting events, lectures, and mentorship programs that include alumni allows students to envision themselves as part of the alumni community. As they move toward graduation, they begin to see themselves as future members of this distinguished group, reinforcing the idea that their journey with the institution does not end with graduation.

Memory and Emotional Anchoring

The power of memory, particularly emotional memory, plays a significant role in keeping graduates connected to their university. Institutions that create emotionally charged experiences, such as memorable graduation ceremonies, cultural events, or unique student traditions, anchor the university in the emotional memories of the students. According to the Emotional Memory Theory, people are more likely to remember experiences that are tied to strong emotions, whether joy, pride or even nostalgia. By ensuring that the last moments on campus are particularly meaningful, the university increases the likelihood that graduates will look back fondly and feel compelled to return.

Graduation ceremonies, farewell events, and personalized tokens of appreciation can create lasting emotional memories. A letter from a favorite professor, a class photo, or symbolic gifts tied to campus traditions may evoke nostalgia and remind the graduates of the value of their experiences, encouraging them to return and stay connected. In addition, maintaining personalized communication post-graduation, such as anniversary messages or alumni newsletters, helps to sustain these emotional connections.

Building Social Bonds and Network Opportunities

Maintaining social bonds among graduates and with their professors or peers can play a significant role in ensuring alumni engagement. Social belonging is a fundamental psychological need, as noted in Maslow's hierarchy of needs. When graduates feel they belong to a social group that is respected, appreciated, and connected to their university, they are more likely to maintain ties with the institution.

To capitalize on this, educational institutions can offer networking opportunities, workshops, or reunions that facilitate continued social interaction among alumni. Creating alumni networks, both in-person and digital, enables former students to maintain professional and personal relationships. These networks not only help alumni but also reinforce their loyalty to the university. An active and dynamic alumni community provides an outlet for shared experiences and memories, keeping the bond with the institution alive.

Encouraging Brand Ambassadorship

For a university, alumni who remain engaged and stay in touch are natural brand ambassadors. Educational institutions can foster this by emphasizing the value of the alumni in promoting the university's reputation and ensuring that graduates see themselves as key players in the institution's continued success. By celebrating alumni achievements, the institution enhances the graduates' status and pride in their university, motivating them to represent the institution positively.

Psychologically, this taps into self-determination theory, where people are motivated to act by a sense of competence, autonomy, and relatedness. Highlighting the graduates' achievements through social media, newsletters, and alumni spotlights gives alumni a sense of validation and pride. When they feel their successes are tied to the institution, they are more likely to advocate for the university in their professional circles.

Moreover, alumni can be actively encouraged to participate in university events, whether as speakers, mentors, or contributors. Offering alumni the opportunity to give back through volunteer work, donations, or advisory roles strengthens the reciprocal relationship. This involvement is not only beneficial for the institution but also for the alumni, as it reinforces their importance and belonging.

Creating an Alumni-Friendly Environment

Lastly, universities must create an environment that makes it easy and appealing for alumni to return to campus. Regular events, reunions, and career development opportunities can act as magnets for alumni, providing them with reasons to stay connected. Institutions can also provide incentives, such as discounts on further education, access to university resources, or invitations to exclusive events to keep alumni engaged.

The use of digital platforms to maintain communication is essential in today's world. Social media groups, online events, and interactive newsletters can keep alumni informed and connected, even when they are far from campus. Personalized invitations and updates reinforce the personal connection that graduates feel to their institution, making them more likely to return or contribute in the future.

To ensure that outgoing graduates remain in touch and act as brand ambassadors, educational institutions must leverage the psychological principles of identity, memory, social belonging, and self-determination. By creating a strong sense of identity, fostering emotional memories, promoting social bonds, encouraging alumni achievements, and creating an alumni-friendly environment, institutions can maintain a lasting connection with their alumni. This relationship not only benefits the university but also enriches the lives of the alumni, providing them with continued opportunities for growth, networking, and personal fulfillment.

Chapter 12: You are a great teacher

There are institutions where teaching takes place under almost ideal conditions—where infrastructure is top-notch, resources are abundant, and students arrive already highly motivated and eager to learn. In such places, the "science" of teaching thrives, rooted in well-planned curriculums, technological advancements, and a sense of order that makes every step of the teaching-learning process systematic and predictable. The teachers in these environments can focus purely on the mechanisms of education, applying proven methods, assessments, and instructional designs. While this scientific approach is invaluable, I believe the true art of teaching reveals itself in far less ideal circumstances.

Where the chips are down—where teachers face the daunting challenges of limited resources, low student motivation, or cultural and socioeconomic barriers—that is where the art of teaching is born anew every single day. In these places, the role of a teacher transcends imparting knowledge. Here, the teacher's task is far more profound: to awaken minds that may be clouded by apathy, to inspire curiosity in hearts weighed down by external pressures, and to instill confidence in students who may feel invisible or incapable.

The Art of Teaching in Adversity

To teach in such circumstances requires more than a command of the subject matter. It requires creativity, empathy, perseverance, and, above all, a deep understanding of human nature. When faced with students who seem indifferent or unmotivated, the teacher must find ways to spark a light within them. This is not achieved through mere instruction but through the ability to connect deeply with students as individuals. The art of teaching in these challenging environments involves recognizing the unique struggles of each student, understanding their strengths and weaknesses, and tailoring approaches that address their specific needs.

The science of teaching might tell you how to structure a lesson, but it is the art of teaching that helps you adapt that structure when half the class hasn't completed the readings or when a student feels alienated due to shyness or personal issues. Science might provide methods for classroom management, but the art is in knowing when to push a student to excel and when to offer a word of encouragement instead. In the most difficult teaching environments, this is a daily balancing act.

The art of teaching is born in struggle. It emerges when the teacher confronts the very real and persistent challenges of trying to nurture unmotivated or shy students with limited resources, often working without the recognition or encouragement that would sustain others. Yet, it is precisely in these circumstances that the teacher's craft is sharpened, where they learn to innovate, to make do with less, and to turn the seemingly impossible into something achievable.

Teaching as the Training of Minds

At its heart, teaching is the training of one mind by another. However, true teaching is more than just passing along information—it is about nurturing the potential within the student to surpass even the teacher's own abilities. It is about guiding students to think critically, to question assumptions, and to push the boundaries of their own knowledge. To do this requires more than a structured curriculum or a well-designed lesson plan. It requires a teacher to engage with students on an emotional and psychological level, understanding not just what they need to learn but how they need to learn it.

The real artistry in teaching is in knowing how to motivate a mind to think for itself. When students are passive, or when they are shy or unsure of their own capabilities, the art of teaching involves gently drawing them out of their shells, providing them with just enough support to build their confidence while at the same time encouraging them to take ownership of their learning. The teacher's goal is not just to impart knowledge but to instill the drive and determination to seek out knowledge independently, to go beyond the material taught in class and to develop a genuine love for learning.

To train a mind with minimal stress is an essential part of this process. Many students already face significant pressures, whether academic, social, or personal. The art of teaching, particularly in less-than-ideal circumstances, is to recognize this and create a learning environment that is nurturing rather than overwhelming, challenging, yet supportive. When teachers push their students to greater heights, it is not through intimidation or fear but through an understanding of what each student needs in order to flourish. This requires patience, empathy, and a willingness to adapt to the needs of each student, even when resources are scarce and time is limited.

Instilling Motivation and Confidence

At its core, the art of teaching is about instilling motivation. Motivation is not something that can be forced upon a student; it must be carefully cultivated. In the most challenging classrooms, where students might feel overwhelmed by external circumstances, it is the teacher's responsibility to find ways to make learning relevant and exciting. This might mean relating the material to the students' own lives or showing them how the skills they are learning can be used to achieve their goals. It means demonstrating, in both words and actions, that learning is not a chore but a powerful tool that can open doors and change lives.

Equally important is the role of the teacher in building confidence. Many students—particularly those who are shy or who have struggled academically—lack the self-belief necessary to take risks and push themselves. The art of teaching involves providing these students with opportunities to succeed, even in small ways, and then celebrating those successes. When a student accomplishes something, no matter how small, it is essential that the teacher recognizes that achievement and helps the student to see the progress they have made. Over time, these small successes build up, and the student begins to develop a sense of their own capabilities.

Confidence is not just about feeling good in the moment; it is about developing the resilience to face future challenges with determination and self-belief. When teachers instill this kind of confidence, they are not just preparing students for the next test or assignment—they are helping to shape them into people who will face life's challenges with courage and conviction.

Personality Building: The Ultimate Goal

Perhaps the most important aspect of the art of teaching is the role it plays in personality building. While the science of teaching focuses on imparting knowledge and skills, the art of teaching recognizes that education is also about shaping the person behind the student. This means helping students to develop qualities like grit, curiosity, empathy, teamwork, and integrity. It means encouraging them to push beyond their comfort zones, to take risks, to fail, and to try again.

Personality building requires interactions that go beyond the formal classroom setting. It involves the teacher taking an active role in the student's overall development, encouraging them to explore their interests, engage with the world around them, and develop a sense of responsibility for their own growth. This kind of teaching cannot be measured by test scores or grades, but it is perhaps the most important and lasting impact a teacher can have.

Accept positive and negative feedback with grace.

Being open to feedback and encouraging students to provide it is essential for a teacher's professional growth and for cultivating a responsive learning environment. This begins by establishing a classroom culture where students feel safe sharing their thoughts, which can be achieved through explicit invitations for feedback. Regularly asking questions such as, "How did today's lesson go for you?" fosters a sense of respect and consideration. Structured opportunities for students to share their insights—through anonymous surveys or reflection forms—can also facilitate honest communication.

Furthermore, modeling constructive feedback practices reinforces the idea that feedback is a tool for growth rather than criticism. This dynamic enhances the educational experience for both teachers and students. For teachers, feedback provides valuable insights into their teaching effectiveness and helps identify areas for improvement. For students, engaging in the feedback process encourages a sense of agency, enhances critical thinking skills, and reinforces the value of their opinions. When students see their feedback leads to tangible changes, it boosts their motivation and engagement. By fostering this mutually beneficial feedback culture, teachers and students alike can thrive, creating a more enriching educational experience.

Educating students on your style of teaching and being.

Educating students about a teacher's style, along with the psychology behind classroom activities, strategies, and methods, is an essential aspect of creating an environment conducive to deeper learning and self-regulation. As educators, we are not simply passing on information; we are facilitating the development of the mind, fostering critical thinking, and nurturing character. By making students aware of the underlying reasons for our approach, we invite them to be partners in the learning process rather than mere recipients of instruction. This transparency serves several key purposes that ultimately enhance both the effectiveness of the teaching and the engagement of the students.

Establishing Trust and Understanding

When students understand the rationale behind their teacher's approach, a sense of trust is built. They are more likely to view the classroom as a space of intentionality rather than one governed by arbitrary rules. For example, if a teacher employs randomness in questioning or assessment, explaining that this method helps maintain constant readiness and active participation allows students to see that the unpredictability is not about catching them off guard but rather about fostering attentiveness and consistent effort. Without this explanation, students may misinterpret randomness as unfair or erratic, which can breed resentment or disengagement. Educating them on the psychology behind these methods assures them that every action serves a specific pedagogical purpose, ultimately benefiting their intellectual and personal growth.

Encouraging Active Participation and Responsibility

A critical advantage of explaining one's teaching style and strategies is that it encourages students to take more responsibility for their own learning. When students understand that certain activities or approaches are designed to build specific skills—whether it's critical thinking, problem-solving, or emotional resilience—they are more likely to participate actively and invest in the process. For instance, when students are aware that random testing cultivates regular study habits and deeper engagement with the material, they are more likely to take ownership of their preparation rather than relying on short-term strategies like cramming. This shifts their mindset from passive learning to an active, involved pursuit of knowledge.

Reducing Anxiety and Stress

Many students experience anxiety when faced with uncertainty or unpredictability in the classroom. Whether it's a pop quiz, random questioning, or an unannounced reward or consequence, students can feel undue pressure if they don't understand the reason behind these strategies. By explaining the psychological foundations of these methods—such as how unpredictability encourages consistent effort or that occasional challenges help them build resilience—teachers can alleviate some of this anxiety. Students will understand that the goal isn't to induce stress but to help them grow. This reframing can transform their experience of these activities from stressful disruptions into valuable learning opportunities.

Cultivating Critical Thinking and Meta-Learning

One of the most important skills a student can develop is meta-cognition: the ability to think about how they think and learn. When teachers explain their methods, they provide students with insights into the learning process itself. For example, discussing why certain group activities are used to foster collaboration and communication skills or why failure is sometimes accepted as part of the learning process encourages students to think critically about how they approach their own education. They begin to see the classroom not as a place of rigid instruction but as a dynamic environment where they can experiment, reflect, and refine their thinking. Understanding the reasoning behind the methods makes them more reflective learners and helps them apply these skills beyond the classroom.

Building Resilience and Adaptability

Explaining the use of strategies like randomness in rewards, testing, or classroom management helps students develop adaptability—an essential trait not just for academic success but for life. By understanding that the teacher is intentionally introducing unpredictability to build their resilience, students learn to approach challenges with a positive mindset. They recognize that they won't always have control over when or how their knowledge is tested or when rewards are given, but they can control their readiness and attitude. This lesson in adaptability is invaluable, as it prepares students to navigate a world that often operates in unpredictable ways.

Enhancing Motivation through Transparency

When students are made aware of the reasons behind classroom strategies, they become more intrinsically motivated. Transparency cultivates a sense of purpose; they know that every task, question, or activity is tied to their long-term development. For example, if students know that random rewards are given to encourage consistent good behavior rather than rewarding only the highest achievers, they are more likely to see the value in maintaining those behaviors over time. This knowledge transforms their motivation from simply trying to meet a teacher's expectations to understanding how their own actions contribute to their success and growth.

Fostering a Collaborative Classroom Environment

Educating students on teaching styles and strategies also shifts the classroom dynamic from teacher-centered to more collaborative. When students understand the "why" behind what is being done, they feel more like partners in the learning process. This invites dialogue, questions, and a deeper engagement with the material. It encourages students to ask not just "What are we doing?" but "Why are we doing this?" and "How does this help me grow?" This collaborative spirit builds a stronger connection between teacher and students, creating an environment where learning is a shared endeavor.

Preventing Misunderstandings and Conflict

Misunderstandings can easily arise when students don't understand why certain methods are employed. For example, without an explanation, random questioning could be seen as punitive, or selective rewards could be perceived as favoritism. However, when students are educated on the psychological reasoning behind these strategies, it reduces the potential for conflict. They see that these actions are not arbitrary or personal but carefully thought-out tools to help them develop important life skills such as accountability, adaptability, and perseverance. By making students aware of these intentions, teachers can maintain a positive and supportive classroom atmosphere.

Reinforcing Ethical and Philosophical Principles

When teachers articulate the ethical and philosophical foundations of their teaching strategies, they reinforce important life values such as fairness, integrity, and respect for the learning process. For instance, a teacher might explain that doubting student answers or requiring justification for certain statements encourages intellectual honesty and humility. By grounding classroom practices in larger philosophical principles, students learn that education is not just about acquiring knowledge but also about developing ethical reasoning and character.

Educating students on a teacher's style of teaching and the psychology behind it transforms the classroom experience. It builds trust, reduces stress, and fosters a more engaged, reflective, and motivated group of learners. It turns the classroom into a collaborative environment where students understand their role in the learning process and take greater responsibility for their growth. In doing so, the teacher not only imparts knowledge but also equips students with the skills, mindset, and character they need to thrive both inside and outside the classroom.

Some sentences that a teacher can utter to the class.

1. "Each activity we do is designed not only to help you learn the material but also to challenge your thinking and problem-solving skills."

2. "I use different teaching methods to engage all kinds of learners, so if one approach doesn't resonate with you, the next one might."

3. "When I ask you to work in groups, it's because collaboration helps you see different perspectives and prepares you for real-world teamwork."

4. "I may question your answers sometimes, not because I doubt you, but to encourage deeper thinking and make sure you're confident in your reasoning."

5. "The random quizzes are meant to keep you sharp and ensure that you're consistently engaged with the material—learning is a continuous process."

6. "When I don't give immediate feedback, it's so you can reflect on your own understanding before relying on my answers—self-assessment is key to growth."

7. "I ask you to present your work because explaining your thoughts to others helps solidify your understanding and builds your confidence."

8. "By switching between discussions, lectures, and hands-on activities, I aim to develop both your knowledge and your ability to apply it in different contexts."

9. "The unpredictability in my teaching methods is there to help you develop adaptability—a skill you'll need throughout your life, not just in class."

10. "Remember, everything we do here is meant to build not only your academic knowledge but also your character and confidence, so keep participating and stay open to learning in new ways."

The Art of Teaching as a Daily Creation

The art of teaching is not something that can be perfected or mastered in a single lesson or even in a single career. It is something that must be created and recreated every day, in every interaction with students, especially in environments where resources are limited and challenges are abundant. It is in these environments that the true artistry of teaching shines—where teachers must rely on their creativity, empathy, and passion to inspire their students and help them to become more than they ever thought possible.

For those who teach under ideal conditions, the science of teaching may be enough. But for those who face the daily struggles of limited resources, unmotivated students, and systemic challenges, the art of teaching is essential. And it is this art—this ability to connect with, inspire, and uplift students—that defines the true power of education. In the end, the most important thing a teacher can do is not just teach but also help their students become better people equipped with the confidence, curiosity, and resilience they will need to navigate the world.

The reality in most schools and classrooms often falls far short of the ideal. Teachers face obstacles that extend far beyond the lesson plan—challenges related to infrastructure, attitudes of fellow educators, students, and administrators, and complex cultural and socioeconomic dynamics. These factors make teaching not just a task but a genuine test of resilience and creativity. Yet, it is precisely in these challenges that the seeds of transformation are sown.

As you, a teacher, reflect on your own journey while reading this book, it is impossible not to appreciate the immense dedication and adaptability you have shown. Many of you work in environments that are far from perfect, where resources are limited and expectations are high. And yet, despite all of this, you continue to show up, day after day, with a commitment to inspire, to teach, and to nurture. Whether you have the freedom to experiment with new methods or are bound by rigid constraints, your perseverance and passion are what truly make a difference.

For those working in institutions with limited infrastructure or where even basic resources are scarce, your efforts are nothing short of heroic. You are the lifeblood of change. It is through your hands, your words, and your unwavering dedication that future generations will be shaped. You may not always receive the recognition you deserve, but your impact is profound.

As you reflect on your teaching, it is important to recognize the depth of your achievements. Think of the students you have nurtured, the minds you have shaped, and the confidence you have instilled. When you look back, you will see that your journey as a teacher has been filled with triumphs—some big, some small, but all significant. You will realize that your commitment to constantly improving your knowledge, your ability to connect with students, and your drive to make the learning experience more meaningful have made you a beacon of hope in their lives.

In this reflection, you will undoubtedly feel a sense of pride. You will see how far you've come and how much you've grown, not just as a teacher but as a mentor and a guide. And as you continue to evolve, adapting to new challenges and embracing new opportunities for growth, your students will feel it too. They will admire you for your strength, your wisdom, and your willingness to go beyond the basics of teaching.

Through your efforts, you will earn the respect and admiration of your students, not because you've always had the perfect classroom but because you've shown them what it means to rise above challenges. Your influence goes beyond the subject matter—you've taught them resilience, kindness, and the value of continuous growth. In the end, they will remember you not just as a teacher but as someone who inspired them to become better, more thoughtful human beings.

And in that, your greatest achievement lies. You will not only feel the pride of being a great teacher but you will also be recognized by your students as someone who made a lasting difference in their lives. That is the true measure of success in teaching—knowing that you have touched lives in ways that go beyond the classroom, leaving behind a legacy of knowledge, empathy, and inspiration.

The great teacher you are

I never wanted to be a teacher because I am shy and introverted. I am also an anxious and highly emotional person with low self-esteem. During my postgraduate studies, I declared to my friends that I would become a researcher, working in quality control, production, or management. I emphasized that I would never take up teaching. Look where I am now! I ventured into teaching because I was desperate to obtain a PhD, which I could pursue while being in academia as a teacher.

Now, with 15 years of experience teaching diverse students and managing heterogeneous classes, I have found that this profession has profoundly impacted my life. Teaching has transformed my life—or perhaps revitalized it. Despite its challenges, I would not trade my job for any other. The teaching profession provides me with an environment rich in knowledge and immense opportunities for learning and growth. The days are vibrant, and the years are purposeful. I have built a great network of student friends spread across the globe, among many other rewards.

Teaching has changed my personality and persona, for which I am grateful. Bear in mind that I am far from a perfect teacher, and I have many more decades to grow. I believe that there is no such thing as a perfect teacher. In terms of teaching effectiveness, a teacher is only as good as the students are and will become. The type of students, along with their diversity, discipline, motivation, and the overall academic atmosphere, all play significant roles in a teacher's abilities. Therefore, a good teacher is one who can encourage students to learn and acquire knowledge.

There is no option for you but to know that you are a great teacher every moment. Teaching is not a profession where doubt or hesitation can linger long. The very nature of the job demands confidence, not for its own sake, but for the sake of the students you are shaping. Every day you walk into the classroom, you are a figure of authority, guidance, and inspiration, whether you realize it or not. Students look to you for direction—not just in their studies but in how they see themselves and their potential. You may face obstacles, misunderstandings, and moments of frustration, but remember, these are the inevitable bumps on the road to greatness. They don't define you; rather, they refine you. With every challenge, you grow stronger, more adaptable, and more capable of doing what you do best—teaching.

You must also remember that every interaction you have—whether with students, colleagues, or administrators—offers you a window into the minds and hearts of others. Teaching is not just about imparting knowledge; it is about understanding the people around you. The shy student who struggles to speak up, the colleague who appears indifferent, the administrator who seems more focused on policies than people—these are all minds you've had the opportunity to study. You are an expert in this field, even if you don't always feel like it. You have spent years reading not just books but people, and you know how to use that understanding to create positive change. The very fact that you are still here, still teaching, and still giving your best every day is proof of your resilience and commitment.

What a great profession teaching is! Few other jobs allow you to witness the growth of another human being in such a direct and impactful way. The fulfillment that comes when a student who once struggled or doubted themselves finally spreads their wings and flies is incomparable. This is the true joy of teaching— knowing that you played a part in their journey, even if they may never acknowledge it directly. We, as teachers, don't expect praise or gratitude. We do it because we believe in the power of education, in the potential of each student, and in the idea that what we do matters, even if we never see the full results.

And yet, there is a bittersweetness to this profession as well. Just as the students begin to fly, we are left behind, watching from the nest. The empty nest syndrome is something every teacher knows, even if we don't often talk about it. We pour our hearts and souls into our students, and then they leave off to pursue their dreams, leaving us to begin the process all over again with a new group. It can feel lonely at times, especially when we wonder whether they remember us or whether they ever think of the lessons we taught them, both academic and personal. But we don't let that stop us. We move on to the next batch of students with the same passion and energy, knowing that this is the cycle of teaching. Each year brings new challenges, new opportunities, and new chances to make a difference.

There is no room for cynicism in teaching. You may never know whether your students look back at you or whether they remember your words or actions, but you keep watching just in case. You keep an eye on their progress and are ready to offer help if they ever reach out, but do not expect it. This quiet, unwavering support is what makes teaching so unique and, at times, so emotionally exhausting. It is a profession of the mind, yes, but it is also a profession of the heart. We give, and we give, and we give some more, often with little in return. But that's all right because we know that the impact we have made is out there, living on in the minds and lives of our students, whether or not they acknowledge it.

What a great teacher you are! It takes a special kind of person to continue in this profession year after year, facing all the ups and downs, the frustrations and the triumphs, and still come back with the same enthusiasm and dedication. You have done this, and you will continue to do this because it is who you are. Teaching is not just something you do; it is something you embody. It is in every conversation you have with a student, every lesson plan you create, and every challenge you help a student overcome. You are shaping not just minds but futures. And that is no small feat.

I salute you. Teaching is often called a "thankless" job, but that's not true. The thanks may not always come in the form of words or recognition, but it is there—in the success of your students, in their growth, in the knowledge that you helped them get to where they are. The tiredness you feel at the end of the day is not just fatigue; it is the result of a job well done. You have given your all, and it shows. Every moment you spend teaching is a moment spent contributing to something far bigger than yourself. It is a moment spent making the world a better place, one student at a time. I shamelessly tell my students, "I want to be a part of your success because each time you succeed, I succeed with you. This way, I keep winning, not just once, but many times every year. Your victories become my own, and that's the greatest reward of teaching."

So, keep going. Keep believing that you are a great teacher because you are. Keep pushing through the obstacles because every one of them is shaping you into an even better educator. Keep watching your students fly, knowing that you played a part in their journey. Most of all, keep finding joy in the process because there is joy to be found, even in the most difficult moments. Teaching is not easy, but it is worth it.

In the end, the respect and admiration of your students will come, whether you see it or not. You will leave a lasting legacy, not in plaques or awards, but in the lives of the students you have touched.

Happy and Healthy Teaching!